Alexander Trocchi:

The Making of the Monster

Your Positive work
that you put into
man hill ment so
much to so many
People who have
came and gone
But the saddest
loss was you

Jim Brontt

A true Brother
and yours in
truth

Jim Brontt

X

*Alex Trocchi painting a 'futique', London, 1963
(Courtesy: Sally Child)*

Alexander Trocchi:
The Making of the Monster

Second, revised and extended edition

Andrew Murray Scott

Kennedy & Boyd

Kennedy & Boyd
an imprint of
Zeticula Ltd
The Roan
Kilkerran
KA19 8LS
Scotland

http://www.kennedyandboyd.co.uk
admin@kennedyandboyd.co.uk

First published in 1991 by Polygon, Edinburgh.
This revised and extended edition first published 2012

ISBN 978-1-84921-072-0

British Library Cataloguing-in-publication Data
A catalogue record for this book is available on request from the
British Library

Sources and Acknowledgements

THE first edition of this book had its origins in a biographical essay I wrote in winter 1982 for the Scottish magazine *Cencrastus*. Alex read several drafts of that and made amendments in various places. I had first met him in 1981 when he agreed to an interview as part of an article I was writing for the *Glasgow Herald*. Shortly afterwards, I took off for Venice and three weeks hitch-hiking around Italy and on my return received a grandiloquent note from him; he wanted to see me urgently. He had conceived a notion that I might move in as a paying lodger with an associate, the Hon George Rodney (son of the 17th Baron Rodney, of the family of England's second-greatest Admiral) in Hornton Street, just around the corner from Observatory Gardens. Alex considered that I would be a stabilizing influence on George, (several years my senior but then a patient on the methadone programme). Being good-looking in a Byronic sort of a way and a habitué of the Chelsea Arts Club, George always seemed to have a young model on his arm and his set of friends included artist Melissa Scott-Miller, Adrian (later A.A.) and Cressida Gill (daughter of Cyril Connolly), the Hon John Opie and Eliza Bonham-Carter (whom I went out with for a while), Eric Clapton and many more. Once, Marianne Faithfull arrived, desperate to see Alex who wasn't in, so she slept on the sofa at George's. Alex seemed to be at the centre of a social scene which regarded him as a pater-familias. As a tenant of George's flat in Hornton Street, I saw Alex on an almost daily basis from then until six months before his death when I moved to Harlesden and although I turned down several times the offer of a 'job' as his personal assistant, often discussed projects and literary matters with him. 'To Andy, with love and appreciating his infinite patience' he wrote, perhaps sarcastically, on the flyleaf of my copy of *Cain's*

Book. I was always cajoling and badgering him about the need to write and trying to convince him how easily a new book could be created using the copious amounts of unpublished material lying around. He sometimes went along with it, made vague promises but there were always other more distracting opportunities. There was always the brightness of great things in the offing. And I was writing obsessively too, even if I could get little published. He agreed to read the manuscript of a novel although our conversations never got beyond the first half dozen pages of which he was highly (and rightly) critical. I cannot now remember anything about that typescript of mine which later perished in the fire along with much of Alex's own material. But there were many pleasant afternoons in the Lindsay Club, the Cherry Pie or any of the pubs in the vicinity, particularly the Elephant & Castle and sociable evenings in restaurants or the apartment in Observatory Gardens. I cherished his company and felt honoured to have it.

Some time after his death, I sounded out his publisher, John Calder, on the idea of editing a collection of biographical reminiscences by the talented and famous who had known him much better than I, but gradually found myself being drawn into a full-scale biography. However, Calder, despite initial enthusiasm, became uncontactable and since I had to obtain funds to conduct research for the book, I was fortunate to have an offer of support from Peter Kravitz at Polygon, which allowed me to obtain a Travel & Research Grant from the Scottish Arts Council. Hearing of this, Calder became antagonistic and attempted to extort unreasonable sums from Polygon for use of material which he claimed to have under contract. This was, and remains, spurious and I have seen documentation which proves this. Calder then had a meeting with Sally Child and produced what he claimed to be 'accountings' (along with a paltry cheque) for Trocchi works for a period of nearly 20 years, in an attempt to deny that these had long since been out of print. He had obviously forgotten that I have a letter from him dated 1985 in which he explains that he has been unable to find a single copy of Alex' works (other than *Young Adam* and *Cain's Book* to aid me in my research!) Calder then attempted – and largely failed - to influence reviewers against the book when it finally appeared. The *Scotsman* review was so biased and nasty that it provoked several letters to the paper by writers whom I did not then have any connection with, particularly Paul Henderson Scott (no relation). This ferocious onslaught was ostensibly penned by a person who was at the time employed by the Scottish Arts Council Literature Department! He attacked the book, the publisher and me on all fronts and essentially suggested that I was the 'monster'. And opposite this full page denunciation, was a full page article by Calder about Trocchi! The inference was obvious. Sadly, Mr Calder's article seemed to be composed entirely from his own memory of events over several decades without recourse to research or documentation and perpetuated some basic errors of fact. But the book has survived such an obvious assassination attempt and without exception all other reviews found the book valuable and well-researched. One well-known and influential literary agent, in a private letter to me, referred to my title, *The Making of the Monster*, and suggested that I should write a biography of Calder and that he was 'sure I would have no trouble in coming up with a title.' In the years since publication of the first edition, I acted as key source on Trocchi and assisted publishers and others to contact the Estate executors regarding reprinting. I also compiled a detailed Annotation of all his surviving papers and assisted many journalists and radio and TV reporters to compile features and reports on Trocchi's life and works.

In this second edition I have had the benefit of greater distance from the subject and because of the interest which the first edition generated - resulting in reprinting of almost all of his books - less need to proselytise on his behalf and therefore more space for objectivity. 'If you can't read my writing, Andy, perhaps it's because you ain't interested in what I have to say ...' Alex had jotted in the margin of my essay, when I complained of his elliptical script and that sentence burned in my mind during the initial work on the first edition.

Writing a work of this kind would have been even harder than it has been without the willing assistance of a great many individuals and I must record my particular thanks to Sally Child, Jack

Robertson, Elizabeth Creevey and Jane Lougee Bryant, without whose co-operation it would have been impossible. I am grateful also to the Scottish Arts Council, whose Travel & Research Grant initially enabled me to conduct important research in the USA and interview the late William Burroughs, the late Terry Southern, Lawrence Ferlinghetti, Austryn Wainhouse, Richard Seaver, George Plimpton, John Marquand Jr and Jane Lougee. I am grateful to all of them for their patience and hospitality.

I also gratefully acknowledge assistance from other interviewees and those who patiently answered my interminable questions, including: Paul Ahearne, John Calder (see above), Iain Cameron, Robert Creeley, Don Cumming, Diane Di Prima, Ed Dorn, Pete Faulkner, Gail Gerber, Maurice Girodias, James Grauerholtz, Mrs Nan Harnson, Jim Haynes, Marion Holloway, Gordon S. Kinloch, Naomi Klein, Professor Jim Knowlson, R.D. Laing, Timothy Leary, Tom Lisanti, Christopher Logue, Robert MacDonald, Norman Mailer, Tom Maschler, Tom McGrath, John McHale, Mrs Bessie McLaren, Mrs Margaret McLaren, Professor Edwin Morgan, Robert Nedelkoff, Harry Nilsson, Jeff Nuttall, Lesley Richmond, Jack Rillie, Mary B. Rodger, Anthony Sheil, Frank Smith (E-1), Martin Seymour-Smith, Roy Smith, Victor and Gladys Trocchi, Margot Trocchi, John A. Walker, Larry Wallrich, Bernie Waverman, and Les Wilson.

The published works of Alexander Trocchi, in numerous editions, remain a pivotal source. The main source of information apart from the direct testimony, is the large collection of papers presently held by the Estate and my thanks are due to Sally Child for allowing me virtually unlimited access to this source. The Trocchi Collection (a total of 22 boxes), held in the archive of the Olin Library at Washington University, St Louis, Missouri, includes many of the early notebooks, diaries and manuscripts. My thanks are due to Mr Kevin Ray, the Curator there, for his enthusiasm and patient assistance with my queries. I also acknowledge the assistance of Mr Carl Spadoni, Research Collections Librarian of the William Ready Division of Archives of McMaster University Library, Hamilton, Ontario, for making available materials (Box 1, file 22) of their Samuel Beckett Collection, which includes correspondence to and from Trocchi. Collections of private letters are kept by Jane Lougee Bryant, Jack Robertson and Elizabeth Creevey, who have kindly allowed me access to these invaluable sources.

I am grateful to Peter Kravitz, Editor, and the individual authors, (Chris Logue, Tom McGrath, John Calder and Edwin Morgan) of the reminiscences which appeared in issue 70 of the *Edinburgh Review* in 1985, from which I have been allowed to 'borrow' anecdotes, and, similarly, George Plimpton, Editor of *The Paris Review*, who allowed me to 'borrow' material from the 25th aniversary issue (no 79) of that journal. I must also acknowledge a debt to the work of Mr Patrick Kearney, whose books *The Secret Record* and *Paris Olympia Press* are crucial to an understanding of Trocchi's Paris period.

Reviews of the First Edition

"Andrew Murray Scott has to be commended for the forthright way in which he has recorded Trocchi's life, without evasion and with a minimum of judgement ... it is gratifying that he should reopen the case for a writer who occasionally reminds us that the battleground between Eros and Thanatos also includes Scotland."

Archie Hind - *The Herald*

"*The Making of the Monster* is a strange and saddening book, and I read it with a mixture of nostalgia and gloom... I began to get an insistent feeling that I had read something like it before. Then it came to me: John Symond's *The Great Beast*, the life of Aleister Crowley. Trocchi was not a 'magician,' but he had Crowley's enthusiasm for experimenting with drugs and sex, and he left behind the same trail of wrecked lives behind him. At least he has been lucky in this excellent biography... which conveys something of his charm and charisma."

Colin Wilson - *Literary Review*

"*The Making of the Monster* is a far above average biography... recalls Symond's *The Quest For Corvo*. The subject is a potentially considerable but impossible to integrate idealist, whose career can be reconstructed only in retrospect by a sympathetic but not contemporary biographer. His account of Trocchi's private life is as objective as possible."

John Gray - *Books in Scotland*

"Andrew Murray Scott's biography traces the facts with some diligence and there are some good stories... interesting and helpful."

Edwin Morgan - *Times Literary Supplement*

"... will introduce a rare and tragically unfulfilled talent to a new generation."

W. Gordon Smith - *Scotland on Sunday*

"Details of the writer's early background help piece out with interest the pattern of his later life, and it's possible a reader new to his work might be persuaded that the man who started out 'Toke' or 'Wee Tochle' in Bank Street, Hillhead and later became a notorious parcel of incongruities, was also a writer of skill and power."

Alexander Hutchison - *Scotland on Sunday*

"Trocchi deserves attention as a unique figure in post-war literature... if he had been American, there is no doubt he would have been canonised by now, like William Burroughs... his overdue critical reappraisal is gathering momentum."

Sean O'Hagan - *Esquire*

Trocchi is not sufficiently appreciated or known... and it's good that Andrew Murray Scott has brought out this biography, some of which gives a peculiarly convincing feel of a character and his intensity of purpose."

Hugh MacPherson - *Scottish Book Collector*

Contents

Illustrations

Preface:

... It is as though I have been writing hesitantly, against the tide, with the growing suspicion that what I have written is in some criminal sense against history, that in the end it can only lead me to the hangman ... Notes towards the making of the monster ... that was one title I considered ... it is, I suppose my last will and testament ...

This is a story of heartbreak and pain, the minutiae of squalor, tragedy, obsession, of chemical addictions, sexual experimentations, promiscuity and desertion, suicide – and literary genius.

There is a smell of flames about this subject. An author cremated, whose books were burned by order of the courts, whose manuscripts were ravaged by mysterious fires. It is perhaps an Icarus-like warning about extremes.

Trocchi is often referred to as Britain's best-known 'beat writer' although he was never a beat and detested that kind of lazy reductive labelling. He was one of the true originators of the post-war avant-garde and paid a high personal price for it. All around him he left considerable wreckage. His is a life-story of damage and contradiction and paradox. It is fragmentary, dramatic, often shocking. Just when you feel you can chart his direction, he sets off on an incredible tangent. His direction *was* a tangent. He was sixteen when his mother died. He loved her intensely and wrote 'her death was my direction'. It was a perceptive remark and might explain much of his reckless lifestyle and his relationships with women but not his huge lust for living. He was after all, an immensely positive person, who embraced every possibility open to him. But after twenty years of living on the edge, he was physically and mentally exhausted. He had committed 'spiritual hari-kari' he said, the only direction possible to him, although he had fourteen years left to live.

The best of his writing is effortlessly original but the sporadic re-appearance of his novels and the vaguely underground tag with which he is still associated mean that some critics rate his work very highly while others regard him as a footnote to the reputations of Ginsberg, Burroughs and Beckett. Trocchi was a mass of contradictions, inspired an equal measure of fear, tolerance and awe but it is his bizarre lifestyle which has sustained and renewed interest in him. That he should care to go so 'far out' must mean his writing is worth reconsidering even if just as some kind of awe-inspiring warning.

It was necessary to include a prefatory note in the first edition of this biography to indicate exactly who Trocchi was and why a biography should be written of him. It is no longer necessary to do that. Renewed interest has led to the reprinting of many of his works and a successful film of *Young Adam*, (GB, Dir: David Mackenzie, 2003), starring Ewan McGregor – an irony given the number of abortive attempts to film his works during his lifetime involving underground tyros, Hollywood directors and even the Mafia!

Although I got to know him well in the last few years of his life, I did not get a comprehensive overview of his literary importance until I started to research the biography.

He was particularly well-known in America. Allen Ginsberg, who wrote most of 'Kaddish' in Trocchi's apartment in Venice West, thought him 'the most brilliant man I've met... another Neal Cassady.' Leonard Cohen, who assisted him to make his desperate escape from the clutches of the FBI thought he had 'a noble presence' and later suggested he was 'the contemporary Christ.' To Terry Southern everything he did was 'heroic, Wagnerian... he was Great!' Norman Mailer thought him 'a fascinating personality and a very fine writer' and penned the jacket quote 'It is true, it has art, it is brave' for *Cain's Book*. Diane De Prima regarded him as 'a fierce adventurer of the spirit.' Robert Creeley presented a fine fictional portrait of him in his novel, *The Island* and forged a strong bond with him. William Burroughs, to whom he was perhaps the closest in the early 1960s regarded him as 'an unique and pivotal figure.'

Many other figures whom I came into contact with during the research such as the late Harry Nilsson and the late Dr Timothy Leary responded with 'Trocchi? Wow!' exclamations. Patti Smith and Tom Verlaine had been into Trocchi, also Jim Morrison, John Lennon – the list was apparently endless. And most had been personal friends. There were many Trocchi stories, often contradictory or dubious; he was an icon of the underground, almost a testament of faith but there was little real information on the details of his existence. After the First edition came out, I received letters from as far afield as Turkey, Italy, Mexico and Alaska from people who thought he was still alive (and would I pass on the enclosed to him?) or those who had assumed his death in 1961. Key-in his name to an internet search engine and you will find there are many thousands of pages about him. And an even-stranger thing has happened. Trocchi has been restored to the mainstream of Scottish writing and now invariably features in the 'top ten' of best Scottish writers. *Young Adam* recently featured in the 'Best 100 Scottish Books of All Time' chart devised by The Scottish Book Trust and the 'List' magazine.

It is a great privilege to be allowed to revisit the original text and correct errors of interpretation where these had occurred and to be able to take into account the thoughts and reminiscences of the many readers who have contacted me since 1991. In particular, I am delighted to have been able to restore a chapter on Trocchi's 'Paris Novels' which had been removed by Polygon prior to publication on the grounds that it disrupted the narrative flow. The absence of this was rightly criticised by Edwin Morgan in a review. I'm glad to restore it and would also like to record my regret at Professor Morgan's recent demise, a considerable loss to Scottish cultural life.

Revised and re-organised throughout and slightly expanded, this edition also now has an index and will I hope stimulate new interest in the extraordinary story and endeavour of Alexander Trocchi.

AMS
2012

Chapter 1: Young Alex

Alexander Whitelaw Robertson Trocchi was born in Glasgow on 30 July 1925. The 'second city of the empire' was, to most people who did not live there, a sprawling, slum-ridden city of razor gangs, sectarianism, revolutionary socialism, bad unemployment and a particularly narrow sense of moral rectitude. But like all cliches it is only one side of the story. The Trocchi family lived in Abbotsford Place in a comfortable part of the South Side, having moved from Smith Street in genteel Hillhead the year before. Alexander was the third son of Alfredo Luigi Trocchi, in a family which on both sides, was reasonably well-off and securely middle class. His mother's parents had been even better-off; had employed a house maid in their imposing house but since the depression life even for them had become a struggle to keep up the facade of doing well. On Alex's father's side, the history had typically been a struggle of integration to establish themselves in Scotland since their arrival in the early 1870s.

Alexander's grandfather, Ferdinand Trocchi had left Italy and his father, Filippo, (who was a Captain in the Italian army) and mother Anna, to travel to Scotland. He obtained a job in Edinburgh as a hotel waiter and, in November 1879 at the age of twenty-six, married Mary Mackenzie Dow, a book-keeper, four years older, the daughter of a Tax Inspector. The couple had three sons; Phillip and Alfredo, both born in Edinburgh and a daughter, Elvira and the third boy Julius, born in Dennistoun after the family moved to Glasgow. Ferdinand, who subsequently became a celebrated and highly respected chef, died in 1913 in a train near Crosshill Station - it was presumed from 'cardiac disease'. The family was then living in Cathcart, an area of rising prosperity. Ferdinand's brother back in

Italy was now a Cardinal, a very senior official in the Vatican and a cousin, albeit several times removed, was Avocato Trocchi, a lawyer in Rome and legal adviser to the Papacy. His daughter, Cecilia Trocchi, was Professor of Humanities at Rome University. On his mother's side, the Robertsons were successful in business and the professions. A Grandfather, an accountant, had been a Provost of Paisley and two uncles had been involved in the cinema industry.

Alfredo Luigi Trocchi, brought up in Glasgow, was therefore half Italian and developed an early aptitude for music. He had a career in various Music Hall acts, appearing in the summer shows at seaside resorts. There is an early photograph of him dressed as a white-faced clown, taken at the Gaiety Theatre, Ayr. When called-up during the First World War, he played piano in the Officers' Mess but also participated in the heavy fighting against the Turks in Palestine and Mesopotamia, where he was wounded in the head by a piece of shrapnel which found its way through his helmet. When he was discharged from service, he married Annie Robertson at Dennistoun Parish Church on 4 June 1919. He was then thirty-two.

Alfredo resumed his career as a musician, playing piano in restaurants and hotel lounges, and then managed orchestras and bands for hotels and restaurants. At one time, he was managing five bands and orchestras simultaneously. But there was a change in the public's taste in music and Alfredo was unable to adapt to it and his bands disintegrated as bookings dried up. The development of arthritis, and later of angina, led to the premature end of his own playing career. He managed to get a job as the Scottish representative for the Performing Rights Society, a post which involved extensive travelling but Alfredo eventually lost the job because of his excessive travel expenses claims. This was a blow from which Alfredo never really recovered and he remained unemployed thereafter. Consequently, the family struggled to make ends meet. In a certificate, five months after Alexander's birth - and the official registration of the birth itself was not completed until 10th September - the name 'Robertson' was added as a third Christian name. Later, his brothers were to drop their surname entirely in favour of their mother's surname, mainly for business reasons but partly because of the lingering prejudice in Glasgow against 'Eye-ties'. Alfredo became a tidy, meticulous, but rather pompous idler, living in grandiose dreams; a fragile world created of his own self-importance and in which all his time was spent in shoring up the cracks in his self-esteem. Or at least this is the picture presented of him to the world in the fiction of his son, and it accords with the memories of other members of the family.

Annie Jack Langley Robertson came from a stable middle-class background and her family felt that she had married beneath her. 'She was too humble ... quiet, unobtrusive, polite, utterly Christian. I often thought as a child she was the only Christian I ever met,' her son later wrote. 'I am horrified to discover that I have no really coherent notion of what she was like. My relationship to her seems to have been entirely intuitive, emotional and inarticulate. But I can remember that in spite of her usual dowdiness, which at the beginning sometimes embarrassed me in front of my richer friends, she seemed to command the respect of whoever was near her. Other children fled to my mother for a kind of reassurance they were unable to get from their own. Other parents, when they spoke of my mother, seemed to speak more gently, almost in awe.' Alex's love of his mother was a complicated and intense emotional reservoir, which he was to ponder over at various times throughout his life.

While Alfredo Trocchi was in employment, the entire family went off every year for two month's summer holiday and all three boys were dressed in white '... not like your cousins ... with bonnets to match. Your mother wouldn't have you in anything but white and neither would I. Always out of a bandbox, you children...' their father later reminded them. The family holidays were spent in Leven, Blackpool or Southport. The children were immaculately turned-out on all occasions, Alf and Jack in kilts with green jackets with silver buttons and tartan stockings, always neat, a testament to the pretensions of the father and the craving for convention of the mother. In the pages of *Cain's Book*, Alex lampooned his father's obsessions with regularity, cleanliness and ritual orderliness, although he was, in later life, to admit to considerable regret over the treatment he accorded his father in print.

When Alfredo finally became unemployable, the family was forced to move again, this time to 26 Bank Street near Kelvingrove Park, where Annie had found a flat that she could run as a boarding house. If Alfredo was unable to support the family - she could. Consequently, since he neither participated in the running of the boarding house nor earned significant income of his own, Alfredo became, finally, a figure of ridicule, a clown performing for a family audience.

At the age of four, Alex fell from a swing and broke an arm. After it was set in plaster he took to living in a wooden box beside the fire in the kitchen, which had a lid he could shut on the world. He lay for hours in the dark, listening to the sounds of his mother moving about, of others coming and going from the kitchen, sensing the heat of his own presence. Eventually his father angrily demanded the removal of the box and ordered Alex out into the fresh air. It would seem that even at an early age, Alex liked to have an 'inner space' of his own, where he could be in the world but not of it. A contemplative distance between himself and reality. The reality outside his door was 'a street of bank-clerks, insurance agents, shopkeepers. The women of the street, tired, genteel, dignified, poor.' He later wrote of 'the ruin of women's faces in a street of surprised, indignant men ... plagued by the curse of respectability on a small income.'

Their new house was a 'main door house'. They could enter through their own garden - 'a small plot of wiry grass that was never green, hedged in by a sparse privet hedge' - or by the back entrance in the close. His father was very proud of this social status. One of a great list of Alfredo Trocchi's petty regulations restricted the rights of access by this front door, which only the adults were allowed to use. Children, including those of the lodgers or 'paying guests' as they were euphemistically called, and tradesmen, were required to use the entrance from the close.

At the age of five years and one month, Alexander joined his elder brothers at Hillhead Primary School. Founded in 1885, and one of five Glasgow High Schools, Hillhead was originally Hillhead Public School, and retains its French motto: *Je Maintiendrai*, from

*Alex and Jack in the cubs/Scouts, c.1936 (Alex is third from right, Jack
extreme left)*
(Courtesy: Jack Robertson)

the arms of the House of Orange, and many other traditions which it guards proudly. The three Trocchi brothers and their younger cousin Victor did well academically and athletically, throughout their school careers, and the middle brother, Jack, was the most notable, being in most years winner of a certificate in his class and, at fourteen, a winner of the school's General Excellence Prize. The eldest, Alfred left school in 1936 at the age of fifteen when Alex was only ten years old, to work in a shipping office.

'Brother Alf, my mother's son, had wavy red hair, of the same sort as she. My mother's hair I used to brush at night, making it shine gold. I didn't brush Alf's hair. By the time he was sixteen he was seldom at home. He was our man of the world and more often than not I had to wait for a day or two before I had an opportunity to talk with him. Alf was out, and it was bedtime. How good Jack and I felt when some time during the night our bedroom door opened and Alf's voice whispered: 'you two asleep?' Pavlov's dogs? Jack and I were awake with our tongues out. Two voices: Alf!' Despite the fact that he had had rheumatic fever as a kid and that this left him with 'a weak heart', my brother Alf was strong and quick as an Apache; no-one bullied Jack or myself and got away with it. Had it not been for Alf we would have had a bad time. As it was, the local boys thought twice before they interfered with us. 'Yure Alfie's brither? Aw awright then...' Alf, more so than Jack and myself, was a child of the Depression. And he was hard as nails ... that big, red-haired hero of mine.'

Alexander was a small and rather undernourished boy, known as 'Toke' by his classmates, a nickname whose origin is from 'wee Tochle', or he was often simply just 'Eck.' After school and at weekends young Alex would play with his toy soldiers with his best friend 'Dozy,' (Cecil Strachan), and Jack and Victor. They collected fragments of gaily-coloured china, beads and artificial jewellery, glass marbles and foreign stamps, especially those of Egypt, Persia and Zanzibar. At Halloween, they dressed up as pirates, carried daggers, cutlasses and turnip lanterns and went begging for ha'pennies from door to door. Young Alex was acutely conscious of girls and his own shyness and embarrassment in their presence. He later described the 'agony of singing in well-lighted rooms in front of girls of our own age. Blushing beneath our grease-paint.'

Alex went up to the 'Big School' in 1937 and began to study the formal subjects. Although his results throughout secondary school in English, History, Geography, Maths, Latin, French and Science continued to be well above average, he scored barely pass marks in Art, (though in adult life he was to become Visiting Lecturer in Sculpture at St Martin's College of Art, and sell his own paintings to London dealers). In his secondary school years he played rugby, tennis and cricket and was good in all these sports, developing into a strong boy, though rather small. His family background of the cinema and show business had given him a definite tendency towards showing off. He loved an audience.

Despite his good academic record, Alex was also a rebel. It was, after all, a good way to ensure an audience. He once boasted that he had provoked a teacher into giving him 'six of the best' twenty-nine times in one day, ('at being belted I was, year after year class champion') and also that he had urinated in his school cap - though in relating this story the point of the anecdote was not the act itself but the qualification that it was 'an old school cap. One that my mother had said could be thrown out.' It was therefore a studied, careful act of moderate rebellion. Then there was the performance of the toilet roll affair, where toilet rolls from a second floor toilet were thrown or dropped and ended up strewn across the playground and out of the school into Oakfield Avenue almost as far as Bank Street, a distance of some hundred yards. At this point, Authority, in the bulky shape of Dr Merry, the headmaster, the antithesis, the young Alex quipped, of the popular conception of a merry Doctor, intervened. Alex, in the vicinity, he claimed, by sheer coincidence, was collecting the roll since it had landed at his feet. Dr Merry did not agree. A blow was struck from the epicentre of an angry physical force. Explanations then began and accusations were made. Dr Merry claimed that he had seen Trocchi kick the rolls. Alex confessed that he had 'kicked it into my hands like a rugby ball, played it over my head like a complex bolus twice, and begun to gather it in.' For he was a tidy boy. Explanations became oratory and anger subsided; Trocchi walked free.

With Jack and Victor he went on petty pilfering raids on the local shops and hid their spoils in the cellar at the end of the back green. On one occasion they were chased, caught and reported. They were duly ashamed and such expeditions were never repeated. He spent more time sitting alone in this cellar pondering his future: 'to my horror I discovered that I was not interested in doing anything. Didn't want to be a farmer or an engineer or a lawyer or a doctor. Sometimes I pretended. But even then I had no ambition unless it was to be Prime Minister or God almighty or something of that nature ... Later, when I decided that that career was probably less suited to my nature than any other ... only the autocracy of God remained undefiled by the limiting contagion of the mass. Unfortunately, this ambition did not provide me with an answer to the kindly enquiries of my relatives. To the question: What do you want to be when you grow up? I could hardly have replied, Oh, I'm going to be God - they wouldn't have understood...'

When the Spanish Civil War broke out, the playground at Oakfield Avenue became a mini-battlefield for the twelve-year-olds. Alex and four friends were 'the rebels', a role that he was to play throughout his life in varying guises. Two years later, at the outbreak of the Second World War, Hillhead High School prepared for evacuation. The classes re-assembled for the winter term on Saturday 26th August, and for the next few days, pupils attended the School daily, with labels fixed to themselves and their luggage. There was a rehearsal march to Kelvinbridge Station and then, on Sunday 3rd September, the entire school boarded the Dumfries train. Unfortunately, in Dumfries there was no accommodation and the pupils had to be dispersed. Alex and three others ended up in a small house with no sanitation or water in Kirkpatrick Durham, sleeping two to a bed. When the old woman who owned the house became ill, the boys were re-assigned. Alex and Roy

Alex in 1st Fifteen at Cally House, c.1941 (Alex is extreme left, back row)
(Courtesy: Les Wilson, STV)

Betty Whyte in tennis team at Cally House, c.1941 (extreme right, front row)
(Courtesy: Les Wilson, STV)

Smith found themselves in the Church of Scotland manse in the village. Strangely, while they were ate with the maid in the kitchen when Alex was there, when Alex went home to Glasgow for the weekend, Roy found himself summoned upstairs to eat with the Minister. Perhaps the Minister had overheard Alex boast that his great-uncle, Cardinal Trocchi, was on the short leet for the vacant position of Pope! As indeed, he was.

Not long afterwards, the boys were transferred to Cally House School at Gatehouse of Fleet - now the Cally Palace Hotel - a former 18th Century mansion. Here were pupils of no less than nine different Glasgow Schools and these were exciting times for teenagers. The school was co-educational, a wartime measure, and the 100 acres of garden, loch and woodlands encouraged many secretive - though innocent - dalliances. Alex was an out-going and extrovert student, fond of pranks and all sorts of high jinks. He wrote a parody of the Canterbury Tales in Middle English about the Cally staff, which proved popular among his fellow-pupils. He came early to maturity and was the leader of a set of boys - Roy Smith, Iain MacKenzie, Gus Murray, and Ross McConnell - who gathered every night for long earnest discussions on politics, religion, art and other topics, the so-called 'Hen's Convention'. Since two of the boys had deserted the Boy Scouts, and widespread disaffection was feared, the 'Convention' was discouraged, but finally ended when older, bigger boys threatened them with violence. Alex also exhibited interest at this time in the subject of U.F.O.s that had featured in newspaper articles after alleged sightings in the area. Being an extra-terrestrial obviously appealed to him more than being a dull politician, for, when mock-elections were held, and a classmate, Tommy Lowther, was giving a serious political speech as the Labour Candidate, he was interrupted by Alex Trocchi and friends, dressed in tinfoil and tinsel as 'Martians' who emerged from behind a bush in mid speech to hijack the voters. The 'Martian Party' subsequently won the election by a large majority! It might be reading too much into such youthful high jinks to propose this as evidence of his 'otherness', his opposition to the mundane, which was to form such a large part of his career as a writer.

In any event, Alex conformed in other ways. Sports played a large part in the curriculum and Alex was selected for the Cally 1st Fifteen - essential to any boy with pretensions to leadership - and played scrum-half alongside Iain, Donald and Angus Cameron, the latter two of whom were to play for the Scottish national side. Iain Cameron's girlfriend at that time was Elizabeth Nan Whyte, a very pretty girl, whom Alex idolised: 'From the age of twelve on she was the princess of my immediate experience, first evidence that beautiful girls existed beyond the shadowy, teasing images of the cinema. Her beauty, I felt, would serve to put a frame round my own which, sad to say, had up till that time attracted the attention of few connoisseurs. I most desperately needed evidence that in spite of the obvious deficiencies of my birth I was, after all, a prince, and I treasured intimations of things or imaginings to come as jealously as a protector his bag of samples. Daydreams anyway, drained of all assurance each time I was confronted by Betty in the flesh, too struck and captivated by her brilliant presence to have ulterior thoughts; indeed, I had no more freedom than a yo-yo, Every dangerous act of rebellion - in time I attained a relative mastery - was consecrated to her, a classroom infested by six hundred and forty-two bees, a fallen ceiling in the north wing, endless acts of sabotage to break the monotony of the long school day. She was flattered by the grandeur of some of these love tokens but remained out of reach. My thoughts of her well beyond puberty were of a ghastly purity. Softs and damps were taboo. If she had dropped her pants I might have hanged myself.' Interesting that the young Trocchi should connect his romantic aspirations with 'acts of sabotage'. His leadership aspirations seemed to be clearly anti-establishment; the 'rebel leader', though whether the specific 'dangerous acts' he refers to are actual or imagined is dubious.

Later in the year in October 1941, his older brother Jack left Hillhead High School, signed on as a Junior Clerk in a shipping office and began to take evening classes for a Certificate in Book-keeping. Their eldest brother, Alf, exempted from war service by reason of his weak heart, had gone into the confectionery business, had worked something of a miracle, and was soon in a position to put their father in charge of one of his two sweetie shops, in Byres Road, (the other being in Shawlands). Alf was to make a great success of the business and soon bought a large, turreted house in Hyndland.

Just before the Christmas holidays in 1941, the Cally Headmaster informed Alex that his mother was seriously ill. He was sent back to Glasgow on the train. Annie Trocchi died a few days later, on 4th January 1942. The cause of death was given as acute bacillary dysentery. Although it was felt by some that she had simply worn herself out through overwork, the source of the infection was discovered to have been a tin of pilchards. The family was later to blame the doctor for a bad diagnosis and a post-mortem was conducted at their request. After three weeks of investigations, the diagnosis was upheld. The Procurator Fiscal decided there were no grounds for criminal proceedings and the funeral was finally held. Alex was deeply affected and later wrote 'the last vital link with existence (was) cut. Lowered into a grave that was my extinction. Men and women in black. Brothers. Aunts. Uncles. Lingered on the green slope like quavers on a musical score. Sixteen at the time. And my father said to me; "You will never see your mother again," like a drain running out. But she continued to exist. Her death was my direction.'

He would suffer bad nightmares for some time after her death and became for a time innately insecure, almost claustrophobic - the fear of confinement. Perhaps in his teenage mind, her death was construed as desertion, for there is no doubt it was to colour the pattern of his unsatisfactory adult relationships. Alfredo Trocchi's morale never really recovered from his bereavement, although he was to marry again. Jack had been rejected by the Royal Navy on account of peritonitis, (he had almost died several years earlier), he left his employment and managed, with 'inside help' in May 1942, to join the Merchant Navy. He was posted, as Writer, to a rather battered cargo ship, the *Gloucester Castle* bound from Liverpool to Cape Town. The cargo included war materials and crates containing 'knocked-down', or part-assembled fighter aircraft, the ship being part of a vast convoy escorted by navy destroyers, which set off from homeport in June.

Alex won the class prize for history in 4th and 5th year, yet the prize for English continued to elude him. He expressed little interest in the subject of art.

In the last few days of Summer term, Alex and some other boys, inspired by the approaching freedom which they anticipated, stayed up all night and made themselves tea in the Staff Room after a late night walk in the grounds. This was regarded as a heinous sin by the Headmaster and the boys' leaving certificates, without which entrance to University or employment would be impossible, were denied them and finally presented only at the very last moment through the windows of the bus by Mr Burt, as the bus left Cally for Glasgow.

Certificate in hand, Alex promptly presented himself at Glasgow University and enrolled in the MA degree class in English, Political Economy and Logic. He knew that he was merely marking time. He had declared himself a pacifist but, in a conversation around the hall fireplace at Cally, he had agreed with Roy Smith that if they had to join-up, they would join the Fleet Air Arm. Above all, he remembered Elizabeth saying that she would marry a pilot. He attended classes for barely six months, for, on 5th February 1943, his call-up papers finally came through and he travelled to Torquay to commence pilot training for the Fleet Air Arm.

Chapter 2: Initiations

Alexander Trocchi completed the latter part of his pilot training in Canada. There is a story that he and a colleague went on a training flight during which - for a prank - they bombed the airbase with toilet rolls. Perhaps he had imagined the buildings beneath were Hillhead High School, and possibly that one of the angry figures gesticulating at him looked extraordinarily like Dr Merry for the free movement of toilet rolls, whether thrown, or dropped from a great height, remained, for Trocchi, a symbol of rebellion and anarchy. The episode reputedly led to an investigation and disciplinary action; both trainee pilots were ignominiously transferred back to Britain. Whether this is true or not is a matter for debate - although it is much in keeping with Trocchi's arrogantly grand manner. Other sources relate that his training was simply curtailed due to the proximity of the end of the war. In fact, he was only three weeks away from qualifying as a pilot when - one way or another - his training came to an end. He was given the choice of being demobbed or transferring into the Royal Navy as a seaman. Surprisingly, Alex chose the latter. After completing his basic seaman's training at Chatham in 1944, he found himself on HMS Campbeltown escorting the arctic convoys to Murmansk. This was a dangerous war zone and, with the Arctic conditions, quite an initiation for a young man. Despite his later assertions that he had spent most of his time below decks leaning on a broom in a quiet corner reading, he was rapidly promoted - to Acting Leading Seaman - to Leading Seaman, so that at the end of the war, he was to be offered a commissioned warrant as an officer. He was never to forget the savagery of the arctic winters where his icy breath froze on his face, where touching bare metal with an ungloved hand led to ice burns. He was to receive initiation of another sort entirely during shore leave in Edinburgh:

'I made love for the first time with a prostitute. Princes Street, Edinburgh. Ten shillings for a short time in an air raid shelter. I had never seen such ugly thighs nor ever imagined it like that, exposed for me in matchlight, the flaccid buttocks like pale meat on the stone stairs, the baggy skirt raised as far as her navel and with spread knees making a cave of her crotch, the match flickering and this first sex shadowy and hanging colourless like a clot of spiderweb from the blunt butt of her mound. She rubbed spittle on it brusquely, as my mother with a handkerchief rubbed spittle against my cheek when we were visiting. She rubbed spittle on it and it was like someone scratching his head. It bristled then and bared its pretty pink fangs. She told me to hurry up. The stone steps were cold. Above in the street there was a fine rain and I could hear the swish of tyres on the wet macadam. At my naked thighs I felt the night wind. The match was out. In the almost total obscurity of the shelter I lay on top of her and felt her belly sink cool and soft and clammy under my own. I was a seaman in the Royal Navy at the time. I remember walking alone back to the YMCA where I was staying. I went over it again and again in my mind, and by the time I reached the YM little feeling of guilt remained. I was even in a vague way proud, callow possibly, but I experienced an authentic feeling of relief. I savoured it with a cup of milky coffee in the tearoom of the YM.'

He had started to write down his thoughts and feelings, and several poems from this period survive, some dated from Chatham in 1944, mainly short love poems, with titles such as 'Two Thoughts', although 'The Dirge Of Life', dedicated to Mollie, is seven pages long, Mollie was 'a passing infatuation ... met in a teashop in Canterbury ...(who) had passed out of reality into myth.' There exists a short piece of prose describing his revulsion at the bullying and taunting that went on in the navy. One particular victim was a Catholic of Irish descent, with a big shapeless body and sad grey eyes, mentally retarded. Alex took his side but was unable to prevent the persecution of this helpless, grinning simple soul, which made him 'boil inside ... Wipe yer nose, Paddy! Wipe yer bloody beak...' The previous Christmas, docked at Portsmouth, he had spent some time with four friends, attending a dance at Southend, taking home some girls, kissing them goodnight and then walking back, with his comrades in the cold night, to the ship. On Christmas 1945, he found himself lonely, on watch duty. Earlier, he had gone into the town on his own and attended a dance in a canteen, at which older ladies of the town were officiating. There was holly and mistletoe and streamers and tinsel string. The ladies were pouring tea from huge brown teapots, glad to be doing something for the boys and girls on leave, some of whom were dancing in a small cleared space, to music from a gramophone. But there were too many men. Alex walked back to the ship. He 'planned to explore Christmas with a noggin of rum and a book of poetry.' He had never felt lonelier. He hated the ship, 'the constrictions, the metal everywhere, the paint, the hawsers, the chains, the studded plates of the deck, the nightmare of iron and steel which ran his mind to limits all about him. And the cold air which lay along the ship forcing the mind to an intense consciousness of its isolation ... With a book of poetry instinct with one's own extended pain. Christ! To get away from those false shambling shadows and into the sun! To get away from words that followed him like footstep down his own mind! To escape from thoughts and ideals and words.'

He dropped the book into the water. He watched the pages slacken and bend wetly downwards, half-sunk ... he could create, he could also destroy.

In July 1942 his father received an Admiralty telegram informing him that Jack was missing, presumed drowned. What actually happened to Jack was not revealed until much later. He was alive, but only just, in a Japanese Prisoner of War camp in Osaka. The convoy had begun to disperse off Freetown and, unescorted, in the relatively safe waters of the South Atlantic, the ship fell prey to a German surface raider that had opened fire believing, in the early evening gloom, that the steamer was a British Q ship. Amid the confusion, noise and panic, Jack was swept into the sea and was eventually picked up, with two young children whom he had rescued, by the raider itself and was to spend the rest of the war in Japan. The arrival of the telegram however, bringing news of Jack's apparent demise within a month of leaving home for the first time, was a further blow to the family's spirit.

The information that Jack was alive was not received until 11th November the following year - received with great relief, although Alex' duty on the convoy routes in the Arctic waters, one of the most dangerous war zones, was a source of constant anxiety. The war came to an end with no further disasters for the Trocchi family and Alex was released in Class A on 16th November 1946. He declined the commissioned warrant and instead accepted an ex-servicemen's grant to re-enter Glasgow University as a student of English and Philosophy. He had spent a lot of his off-duty time below decks voraciously reading anything he could get his hands on and had written a number of short stories and poems. He had passed from the innocence and bashfulness of youth to the confidence of adulthood in three exciting and dangerous years; an initiation accelerated by the war. Indeed, he had undergone a complete transformation. From the small, undernourished boy of the school photographs he had become a man, fully six foot tall, broad and well-muscled and, above all, he had gained a great deal of self-confidence. He was old beyond his years.

Chapter 3: 'The Bright Young God'

A taller, stronger, altogether more confident and worldly Alexander Trocchi attended classes and tutorials in English literature, British History, Logic and Mental Philosophy at Glasgow University in 1947. On the staff of the English Department were Sean Purser and Edwin Morgan, who had joined the faculty that same year. The Senior Lecturer was Jack Rillie, who recalls Trocchi as a student 'manifestly of genius.'

Some marked University essays survive, on subjects such as 'The Development Of Ideas In Keats' Poetry', Dryden's Satire, John Donne, Pope's 'Eloise and Abelard' ('a very good essay, suffers from a reluctance to define...') Marlowe, Jonson, Milton, 'The Nature And Validity of Allegory In Spenser's Faerie Queen'. 'Notes for an Essay on Imagination' was marked by Rillie as 'sound, provocative and interesting...' and 'a good, perceptive essay' was his judgement on a piece of work on *The Canterbury Tales*. Alex brought a great deal of enthusiasm to his studies and gained a thorough grounding too in Philosophy, studying Deductive and Inductive Logic, Metaphysics, Morality, Ancient and Modern Philosophy and Theory of Knowledge: He read Plato, Descartes, Locke, Hume, Aristotle and Kant. F.N. Bradley's *Principles of Logic* and *Appearance and Reality* were cornerstones of the course. Trocchi was confident enough at this time to launch an attack on F.N. Bradley in an essay titled 'Bradley's View of the Relation Between Thought and Reality.' As Professor Campbell, the head of the Philosophy school was the leading authority on Bradley; this necessitated an attack on the Professor's views. Professor Campbell conceded that some of Trocchi's criticisms were fair, and noted on the essay; 'Extremely good ... you have a view here, which is in

*Alex and Betty (seated) with Cecil Strachan at Garronhead, c.1948
(Courtesy: Jack Robertson)*

course of development, and is not quite ripe for formal statement. I shall be glad to hear more of it ...' Trocchi had decided that he was a 'positivist', a follower of the ideas expounded by A.J. Ayer, the well-known English philosopher and author of *Language, Truth and Logic*. Many friends considered that the attraction of Ayer was the lack of a body of ethics associated with the creed - so that Trocchi could manufacture his own, and thereby justify his own by now rather extravagant behaviour ...

While his lecturers regarded him as a highly intelligent and original student and considered his work to be of excellent quality, he was at times unreliable and his essays appeared erratically. One of the reasons for this was that Alex, after initially living at home with his father, was now living with Betty Whyte in a tiny cottage at Garronhead in the Campsie Fells, about ten miles out of town. This extraordinary circumstance had followed upon their chance meeting in the Kelvin Art Gallery near the University. Trocchi was still in the navy at the time, waiting for demob and working in teaching and intelligence. Betty was a 4th year student at the Royal Veterinary College. Despite her previous lack of interest in him at School, she could sense a change in him, a new confidence, an intellectual authority. 'He was impregnable, like a bright young god.' She felt that he was her equal, that he was no longer the boy whom she had pitied for his devotion; an intense love affair developed. At first, they had lived together in a rather awkward menage with Alex's father in the boarding house, then on a whim they had taken the cottage. They both faced considerable difficulties in getting to their classes. Alex would frequently turn up late at tutorials in tatty pullovers, a battered tweed hat and muddy wellington boots, having tramped across fields to get to Balfron Station. Some of his university essays were typed on the back of Betty's lecture notes, which also caused confusion on occasions. Of course, their living together was very much contrary to her parents' wishes. The Whytes' family home was in Lothian Gardens, a very well to do area of North Kelvinside, and her father, Ernest, a Stores Inspector for the Air Ministry, was rather old-fashioned - even eccentric - in his views. Those who remember the interior of the Whytes' house recall that it was a 'museum' to the career of Squadron-Leader

Whyte RAF, DFC and Croix de Guerre. The living room of the house displayed the full-sized propeller of a fighter aircraft, and there were items of war memorabilia on every wall and in every room. On Alex' first visit he was chased out of the house by Betty's father: 'get out! Get out! I've shot better men than you!'

By contrast, life at Garronhead was spartan. Alex and Betty were completely isolated in the tiny, former shepherd's cottage, which stood in the middle of a muddy field. The walls were bare. There was virtually no furniture. They had taken the cottage on a whim of Alex's to be a pig breeder. He had heard of the money that could be made by this means but the outbuildings were tumbledown and so they decided to build their own pigsty. They bought a horse and cart at an auction and were feeling pleased with themselves at having got a cheap bargain. Now they could carry the bricks to their cottage using the horse and cart. The farmer, George McLaren, stood quietly watching this operation, leaning on the fence, and smoking. When Alex and Betty had loaded about a dozen bricks, he permitted himself to remark: 'That's about all she'll take!' They had better luck with hens and also cultivated vegetables. There was a large iron stove in the cottage, which visitors remember Alex and Betty feeding with logs and even with paraffin. The couple were remembered by Mrs Bessie MacLaren, and her parents, who describe them as 'both very likeable young students, sometimes affluent, sometimes hard up. They were very happy.' In the summer they went to the Isle of Man. Alfred had sold his confectionery business and bought a tearoom/ restaurant called the Swiss Cafe in Douglas. For Alex and Betty it was a cheap holiday, although they sometimes had to work for their keep.

When Betty's parents planned to move to Oxford, Betty decided to enrol at Oxford University to complete her degree. This provoked a crisis. 'I'll lose you,' Alex complained, agonising over what to do as he faced yet another desertion. In the end he persuaded her to marry him, but to keep the marriage secret, to be revealed only later when they had both qualified. On 15th January 1947, they went through a marriage ceremony at Blythswood Registry Ofice. Alex was twenty-one, Betty twenty-two. There were only two witnesses present: Alex' cousin, Victor, and Cecil Strachan. Alfred was ill with heart-trouble at the time and later that year, underwent major heart surgery. But Betty immediately became pregnant at Garronhead and had to give up her studies at Vet College even although she was well into her fourth year. Several times she had become sick on the journey into town and had had to get the driver to stop the bus. They decided they would stay at the cottage until Alex had completed his University course, a period of three more years and the child would be brought up in the country. In the meantime, life was fun. Alex had got rid of the shaky horse and cart and now had an unreliable motorbike, an Ariel 500cc - a veritable monster, of which he was very proud. The neighbours, including their doctor, were scandalised when Betty continued to ride pillion into the ninth month of her pregnancy. Their first child, Jacqueline Anne, was born on 15th January 1948. At twenty-two, Alex Trocchi was a father. He swapped the motorbike for an old Hillman camper; more in keeping with his new status as a family man.

While living at Garronhead, he had begun to fill the first of a large number of notebooks with ideas, sketches and thoughts on the use of language and commentaries on 19th and 20th century writers, as well as early drafts of poems. A manuscript, seventy-three pages long, titled 'General Theory of Literary Criticism', Alex' thesis, shows how seriously he was taking his studies. He was not merely working for the MA degree, he had made the conscious decision to be a writer possibly as early as his late teens, but this decision had assumed urgency during his war service. He was working on the first of several novels that were never to be finished. One was titled *The Men*. Another, including brilliant passages based on his childhood, remained untitled. He was reading a great deal of contemporary fiction and Orwell was a favourite, although his reading included Giono and other modern Europeans. A large number of short stories survive from this period. Some, such as 'The Curlew' delineate the relationship between a man, his wife and his best friend. In 'The Curlew', the narrator speaks: 'Do you know, I still love you after all these months? Queer isn't it? ... He was looking across the moor. It can't last long he was thinking ...' 'The Earthbound' is another such, in which the author, called Nicolas, is married to Judith, and in which Cecil Strachan appears

Passport photo of Alex Trocchi, c.1949
(Courtesy: Jack Robertson)

as 'Jo Christie'. This contains a wealth of detail; pots of thick, mealy porridge, iron bedsteads with creaking rubber-encrusted springs, a kitchen table with knobbly matchstick legs, two folding chairs and four tallow candles. These were their actual possessions at the time. Titles of poems written at this time were 'The Broken Ikon', 'A Dream of Cain', 'The Dull Green Jar' - which ends; 'once too, I caught perfection in a jar.' Others are 'Song' ('Be still my love, Betty/ on a bed of soft leaf/ the world may crack, Betty/ gape black with grief/ I shall still be your love, Betty - till death...'). Some of his early work contained no autobiographical material derived from life. 'The End Of The Holidays' is, for example, a 'conventional' short story exercise, though nearly all of his work is deeply personal, the narrator clearly Trocchi himself. One of the strongest pieces is 'Fragment From A Diary Of A Man Found Gassed In A Glasgow Slum' which shows clearly the first-person reminiscence/confession style that he would increasingly adopt. In a small notebook, titled, after Eliot, 'Butt-ends' the original idea for the novel that would eventually become *Young Adam* was taking shape, vastly different from its first published form in 1954 and its 'definitive' version in 1963. In April 1948, his conception of the novel was as a confession of a man who had 'god forgive me, served on a jury that convicted an innocent man...' The central character, not the narrator, was Jo Henfield (the surname was later dropped), a reporter from the *Lairs Gazette* investigating a sex-crime. That the idea took hold of him is obvious since the rest of the small notebook, approximately five pages, is taken up with notes on the characters. At the time it was just one of a great many other ideas in a notebook.

In the summer season of 1949, Alex had taken a job as a wine waiter in a large hotel in Oban. This had led to an amusing clash with the titular head of Clan Campbell for his initiation as wine waiter coincided with the start of the annual Highland Games. Unused to the subtle distinctions of the clan hierarchy, Trocchi greviously slighted the Duke of Argyll, believing that he was a mere piper! Worse, when the dinner was actually underway, anxious to make amends, Trocchi enthusiastically served wine to the gathering but by the time he reached the Duke - not a man to offend lightly - at the head of the table - there was no wine left. The Duke of Argyll had to do without, while his less eminent clansmen became convivial at his expense! Lesser insults had precipitated all-out clan warfare ... During the weeks of his employ in Oban, he phoned Betty frequently: 'oh darling, I'm missing you terribly. And the first of the six minutes will be used up while we frantically try to get closer to one another...' But despite his love for Betty, which was real and intense, his notebooks reveal that he was having relations with another girl, designated simply 'X': 'what meaning can I give to this relation? It is there, like the red leap of sun on the sea at night. It is part of my personal inventory; one alarm clock, two cases, one typewriter, relation with X ... just like that ... without a fragment of a reason. And I am already on my way down to see her...'

His Senior Honours final exam was imminent. He didn't bother to do any preparation for it. If he wasn't intelligent enough to pass without study, well ... 'swotting' was for the dullards. There were six papers; literary theory, pre-1700, post 1700, two Shakespeare papers and a paper based on the prescribed texts. This allowed considerable scope as to periods, from early English poetry to modern fiction. Unfortunately, while great things were expected from him; not less than a first-class honours degree, in the event he obtained only a second-class one. The reason was due to his prediliction for taking Benzedrine tablets to keep himself awake and active for longer periods. By an unfortunate error, he miscalculated the number of tablets before the Philosophy final and simply fell into a doze in the exam hall. He was saved by a very good mark in the English subjects, but it was a blow nevertheless. Many of his lecturers expressed disappointment over his unexpectedly poor performance though they were not acquainted with the reasons for it.

Notwithstanding the Second Class Honours, his father was so delighted that he sent a crate of lemonade to Alex's philosophy tutor, although Alex later explained this grand gesture as designed so that 'he could now speak of that philosophy professor with familiarity before friends and rivals...'

Chapter 4: Paris Letters

Despite the fact that he had failed to obtain a first-class honours degree, there was considerable sympathy for his position among the University staff in May 1950 and due to the influence of some of his tutors, who felt that he was 'really a first-class man' he was awarded the Kemsley Travelling Scholarship. This was an award to outstanding graduates to facilitate educative travel abroad. Alex and Betty, with baby Jacqueline, did not bother to wait for the graduation ceremony and immediately set off to Europe. The award totalled £400, and they visited Siena and Ventimiglia and toured Italy, Greece, Turkey, Yugoslavia and lived for a short period in Paris. Alex now planned to attend film school at the Sorbonne, one of the leading schools in Europe. He had various discussions and hoped to get a position as a production assistant with a filmmaker called Boucher. Failing that, he hoped to obtain a job with UNESCO or join Jack and his wife, Marjorie, in India. Then a more elaborate plan emerged and soon he was writing to Jack and to Alf seeking funds for two bicycles and a small trailer with which he and Betty were to circumnavigate the Mediterranean Ocean over a period of two years. He felt such an expedition would have considerable news value, not least since his patron, Lord Kemsley, owned four national Sunday newspapers that might feature the expedition. He would write a best-selling book about their adventures on their return. The trip was planned for the autumn. In the meantime, he and Betty were living at Gagny, a village suburb of Paris, in a former gardeners' cottage on the estate of Monsieur and Madame Lee. He wrote to Sir Hector Hetherington, administrator of the Kemsley Award, asking for more money to enable him to buy a typewriter and this was sent on to him. An unsolicited letter to *The*

Scots Review in Edinburgh had been published in the magazine in November 1950 and the Editors had requested him to send a monthly piece which would receive its own by-line; 'Paris Letter'. Trocchi's 'Paris Letters' ranged in subject matter over politics, art, philosophy, book reviews and sport. In March, he described the rugby international between Scotland and France, which he had attended; 'the most striking thing about the match was the bad sportsmanship of the French crowd. I have never seen a visiting team treated so badly ... they not only booed every time Scotland was awarded a penalty, but booed while the Scots player was kicking for goal.' In the same article he discussed communist art, a new film, *Sans Laisser d'Adresse* which he had seen, and compares unfavourably with its Italian version, (although of course he could not speak Italian!), he noted the award of the Prix Goncourt and the French ambivalence towards bullfighting; the authorities, he writes, collected a tax for each ticket sold, then formally fined the organisers for breaking the law. 'The fine, being reasonable, is paid in the same spirit of understanding as it is imposed!'

In the April 'letter' he comments on the French political stalemate by which, for several weeks, there had been no government in office. He brings to the attention of a wider public 'Le Pere des Grenouilles' - a man who makes a living out of swallowing live frogs and regurgitating them. Then there was the Cyclotrone, a new fairground amusement, the death of Andre Gide, an exhibition of German painting at the Petit-Palais, which includes works by Bosch and Rembrandt. He compares the prices commanded by various contemporary painters, and concludes - 'my interest is purely academic - I have no money to buy.' Alex Trocchi was well integrated into Parisian life and enjoyed much that it had to offer. He had rapidly acquired a command of the language - later, his translations of several French novels were to be nominated for awards.

He was writing regularly, almost obsessively and during the summer sold his first work; a long poem, of sixteen pages, classically entitled: 'How At Thebes Tiresias The Prophet Told' to Princess Marguerite Chapin de Caetani, the publisher of *Botteghe Oscure* a literary journal established in 1948 in Rome and described by Trocchi as 'the best literary magazine in the world.' The fee, he was later to claim, was $300, which would appear to be highly generous for 1951 - but then the author was prone to slight exaggeration of this kind!

Princess Caetani later had reservations about the erotic and even the scatological nature of the poem and printed it in part only. It is strong stuff, very good in parts, using an almost Shakespearean vernacular, and indeed, Falstaff, Henry V and John of Gaunt are in the poem, in the company of Aquinas, Ovid, Plato, Aristotle. It is a modern metaphysical poem, displaying an in-depth knowlege of the techniques of Donne and Marvell. Trocchi was later to declare that he had been Caetani's 'white-headed boy' for a while, but had fallen from favour. It is probable that he met her during his travels, although it is unlikely that an 'affair' of any kind took place since the Princess was considerably older than he was. Not that that would ordinarily have acted as any impediment to Alex. He had, as we shall see, few moral scruples when it came to pursuing the favours of women. Betty had several times reproached him already with her suspicions over his close friendship with Barbara Weise, an American sculptress, in Paris.

It was in Paris that he wrote the first drafts of many poems which did not appear until more than twenty years later, when his poetry collection was finally published. Many reveal Alex's background in, and love of, Classical literature, in particular, poems such as 'Wind From The Bosphorus,' and 'A Little Geography Lesson For My Sons and Daughters', roam continents restlessly like poetic argonauts. He had completed another novel, which remained untitled, except for a note on the cover 'in the manner of Dos Passos', and the first draft of another which was now firmly entitled *Young Adam*. This was his fourth, and he was already working on a fifth, to be titled *James Fidler*, which, unlike all of his other work, was written in the third person narrative tense (and clearly influenced by Joyce's *Dubliners*).

The trip around the Mediterranean was postponed indefinitely. While Jack agreed to 'invest' in the trip, Alf advised delay. Alex had recruited two other couples that were to travel with them. There would now be two cars. Bicycles were not suitable. The plans were

Alex, Betty, Jacqueline and Margot at Cap d'Ail, August, 1951.
(Courtesy: Elizabeth Creevey)

constantly being revised. In a diary of the period he describes the circle of friends that he had built up in Paris. Painters such as Ernst Fuchs and his wife Gerry, Russell Sully, Peter Ross, who was a writer, and Barbara Weise. He described himself as 'a long-haired, ill-clad creature, unshaven, an anonymous member of the army of foreign shufflers who walk Paris streets.' His shoes were down at heel and his last remaining suit, blue hopsack, was rent through in places. This and toothache and athlete's foot, did not prevent him from visiting exhibitions and studios, and drinking coffee in the bars around Montmartre. He read Stendhal, discussed the fashions of the day; Sartre, Jaspers, Heidegger, Kierkegaard and masochism ...

His family life in Gagny was entirely happy. He was looking forward to the prospect of a second child. One evening as Alex sat with Betty she told him to go into the city to have fun. She was nearly nine months pregnant and felt that the waiting was driving him mad. He went off but returned early carrying a large teddybear for Jacqueline, which he had won in a fun fair.

His writing was going well but a diary note of the period states: 'I feel I have assimilated all I can (need) for the moment in this part of France.' He had managed to acquire a leather-upholstered 1924 Ford Talbot - a beautiful car - through a complicated network of friends of Madame Lee. It was in Alex's nature to make complex the simplest transaction and he emmeshed his friends in his extremely elaborate and complicated schemes. If he had to acquire a car, he would not simply buy the car outright from A. Firstly, he would approach B, who knew A's friend D and arrange to be seen by C (A's girlfriend) in the company of B and D in the belief that this would lower the eventual asking price in the 'endgame' negotiation with A. (Later, of course, he would keep a secret tryst with C and then resell the car to D). When his friends complained of his behaviour he would dismiss the criticism with one of his many *bon mots*, of which he had already accumulated a great store, precisely for situations like this. 'Now, but really old man...' he would protest, with a languid movement of his hand and a flashing smile. It was difficult to be angry with Alex for any period of time. His charm was completely disarming, and he knew when to turn it on. Friends described him as like 'a young fawn' - very handsome and striking in appearance, and of course, he was tall and lean.

He could also be amusing, playing a comic/macabre act among friends in the style of the then well-known Scottish actor, Duncan MacRae, whom he did at times resemble.

The Talbot had only 40,000 miles on 'the clock' and Trocchi gleefully noted that 'the engine is in beautiful condition, the car is covered in leather and all the fittings are of brass.' It was a stately vehicle and rather an anachronism; its consumption of petrol was monstrous. It was unsuitable for the trip it was to make - even although the front seats could be removed and Alex and Betty could sleep on the floor, Jacqueline on the back seat and Margot in a carrycot slung from the roof. They also had a large old-fashioned army tent with them for emergencies.

Having acquired the car, the journey began. The second car and the other couples had called off at the last moment and Alex firstly had to drive to Dieppe to collect Betty. Betty had failed her test in England. Alex would have to do all the driving. Their plan was to obtain work at the grape picking in the vicinity of Perpignan, although having waited until four months after the birth of Margot Francoise, their second child, who was born on 30th May, they were already too late for the season. On the 4th of October: 'Camped outside Paris, mud, dripping water, mosquitos and the rain. Money short as usual ... Betty with her usual 'sang-froid' takes the future for granted.' At times, Alex would berate her: 'Why don't you worry more about money?' Later, he would accuse her of being mercenary. On the 16th surprisingly they were *still* in the Paris area, for he writes that he 'saw Paris for the last time for how long?' After this false start they were finally off on the 18th and arrived at Chartres where he promptly blew 300 francs on a reproduction of stained glass windows. They camped in the dark at Vendome and listened to the noise of fairground music across the fields and Betty sangs hymns to quieten the baby. They drove through Chateauroux, Limoges, Montauban, Toulouse and Narbonne, and then, between Cap d'Agde and Sete, the car broke down. Although close to the coast, they were still some distance from the grape picking area, indeed they had taken a detour into the Languedoc in the hope of finding work. They spent an uneasy night, 'the baby howling and unappeasable' and were woken by pneumatic drills. Betty went off on the back of a motorcycle to the nearest garage, six kilometres away. While she was away, Alex noted in his diary; 'I've been poor for too long and I am beginning to be sick of it ... with the flies and by candlelight it's rather difficult to work; a pity because *James Fidler And The Beautiful Albino* is coming along rather well ... In appearance and reality we have become vagabonds.' When Betty returned and the car was repaired, they drove to Sete and camped at St Jean de Vedas, where they endured thunderstorms and heavy rain. The trip was turning into a nightmare. Their financial plight was eased when, as Alex noted casually in his diary, 'Betty met an artist - Osborne (at Cannes) - he gave us 5,000 francs. God knows what we would have done without it!'

Ten days later, Trocchi writes that they have half-starved for the past three days on 700 grams of bread between the three of them. He has been constipated and lightheaded. He had had to sell his new typewriter to buy food.

The trip was not all bad however, and he did manage to get some serious writing done. They parked in a camping ground at La Rondine, Cap d'Ail, between Nice and Monaco, just twelve miles from the Italian border on a piece of ground owned by the Willmotts. Mr Willmott was a retired industrial designer and his wife Madelaine a former interior decorator. Both had retired to Cap d'Ail to become artists. On the very day that the Trocchi's money finally ran out, Mrs Willmott casually asked Betty if her husband was interested in working as a handyman/gardener. The offer was gratefully accepted and Betty was also employed, as maid and cook. They stayed for several months as 'working guests' and it turned into a real holiday. It was while at Cap d'Ail that the Trocchi's received an unexpected letter from Sir Hector Hetherington informing them that Alex had been nominated as the first 'Sir Godfrey Collins Travelling Scholar' - and was to receive £250. Sir Godfrey was the head of the publishing empire and Alex had high hopes that this new 'connection' might be very helpful to him in a literary way. Life was

Trocchi family at Newcastle, January 1952
(Courtesy: Elizabeth Creevey)

suddenly good again. Betty had learned to cook all of the recipes in the *Larousse Gastronomique* and both she and Alex would often stay up all night playing canasta with their hosts. At other times, there were trips to the 'Sporting Club', the Casinos of Monte Carlo and picnics in the countryside. The Willmotts had a wonderful private art collection of their own that included several Bracques, Picassos and Modliglianis. Living in such elegant company undoubtedly gave Alex his first, unforgettable taste of 'la dolce vita'.

But it had to come to an end and when the weather turned colder, Alex and Betty returned to Paris and from there to the Isle of Man. Betty had received a telegram informing her that her father was seriously ill - in Newcastle where her parents were then living. They left the children in Paris with a French couple, the Hellers, and returned to the UK. Alex made an appointment with Sir Godfrey Collins and 'created a great impression on him over an hour at tea in his office.' He also visited his own father. He had no intentions however, of staying in Glasgow for long and soon returned to Paris to await Betty. Her father did not die until February and Betty remained to arrange the funeral and the intended emigration of her mother and sister to New Zealand. Alex and Betty had planned to move to Majorca where they could live more cheaply, but in the meantime they wrote daily letters to each other, he, from Paris, she, from Newcastle.

Alex's brothers had also put distance between themselves and the family home. Alfred and his wife Marion were living in the Isle of Man while Jack had become Manager of The Angus Steamship Line in Calcutta. Alex had friends in Paris and that city was to become the base for the first of his serious literary projects and publications. Full of restless spirits, the city would suit him well. He established himself in Paris, for the second time, in late January 1952, resolved to make it his home and to walk in the footsteps of Henry Miller, George Orwell and Ernest Hemingway et al.

Chapter 5: Jane Lougee

Paris. The Seine. Art Galleries, discussions at crowded cafe tables on boulevards, the parks and fountains where the famous and talented mingle with tourists, prostitutes and millionaires. Paris has always been a city of the arts. In 1952, Paris was also a city of commitment. Four years of Nazi occupation had seen the destruction of all cultural certainty, waves of self-critical angst, the growth of extreme ideologies. Paris was the city of Camus, of Sartre and the as yet virtually unknown Beckett, all of whom had actively resisted totalitarianism. Paris nurtured the growth of existentialism. Trocchi was later to explain:

> 'I went to France, not London, from Scotland. I found the English attitude towards existentialism - French existentialism in particular - unsympathetic after the war. They had a very patronising attitude towards existentialism and Literature Engage. They thought of the term engage in the old 30s sense of 'commitment', whereas *engagement* could have the sense of refusing to be identified with either capitalism or communism. You could, in fact, be Engage as an outsider.'

From the outset it had been clear to him that writers should be involved in defining in human terms the reason and function of writing; what did it mean, what was the point of it all? For Trocchi, writing had already become a process of defining and exploring his own identity.

On 22nd January 1952, when Alex Trocchi became, for the second time, a citizen of Paris, there were some 12,000 expatriate

Americans living there, not counting the servicemen, or, indeed, the British who were certainly as numerous. Most of these were living on money sent from home and spent their days moving from one pavement cafe to the next in search of a good time. The young people, most of whom had been in the armed services and acquired a studied distaste for authority, consumed hashish, Benzedrine and even heroin regularly. Many saw themselves as latter-day Henry Millers or Hemingways ('Hank & Ernest') and made attempts at writing or painting. For the twenty-six year-old Alex Trocchi, Paris had 'that kind of atmosphere, that kind of situation, full of diversities, of contrasts, of new possibilities, in which the creative intelligence can produce its works, in which the critical spirit can live.' In Glasgow, he had experimented with whatever drugs were available, particularly benzedrine, and in a short story, written in Glasgow six years before, had referred to the addictive power of opium, alcohol, women, power and cigarettes, all of which he wished to enjoy. Whether this had been sheer bravado or not, he now found the availability of narcotics an incentive to emulate Coleridge, De Quincey and Baudelaire.

He was already acquainted with the meeting-places of the young intellectuals who haunted 'la rive gauche', the Left Bank of the Seine, just south of the Ile de la cite, imitating that earlier 'lost' generation of the 1920s and 1930s. Of outgoing nature and considerable personal charm, Trocchi found it easy to acquire like-minded friends of many nationalities. In coffee bars and bistros such as the Cafe Bonaparte, the Deux Magots, the Old Navy, the Coupole, the Boulevard, the Cafe Tournon, and in the Librairie Mistral on rue Buchet and Gaite Froge's *English Bookstore* at 42 rue de Seine, they scribbled and chatted and drank and argued. There were sexual partners to be 'picked-up', publishers who might be persuaded... drug dealers... parties, exhibitions, events.

Within two weeks of returning to Paris, Alex found himself invited to the opening of an art exhibition. Invitations to this kind of event were always welcome because of the free food. Among the guests was an American, Victor Miller, who was planning to start a small literary magazine, to be called *Manuscript*. He was looking for an assistant and found himself talking to a beautiful girl from Limerick in Maine, who was interested in the idea. This girl was spending the winter in Paris on an allowance of $100 per month. During the course of the conversation at the gallery, Miller was introduced to a young Australian poet, Alan Riddell, in whose company was Alex Trocchi. Riddell, although an Australian, had been brought up in Scotland and had, similarly to Trocchi, undergone a nautical training. He was also interested in the project, and a meeting was arranged in Miller's room in the Hotel Letitia a few days later. Although Alex had barely spoken to the petite American girl with the long dark hair, she had clearly made a big impression on him. At this second meeting, Alex himself emerged as the favoured candidate for the Editorship of the magazine which was as yet only a bare idea in the minds of half a dozen people. There was a row over the question of funding the project, and after the argument, Alex and the American girl emerged from the Hotel, hand-in-hand. The girl's name was Jane Lougee and she and Alex were to be inseparable for the next three years; their partnership was to lead to one of the most influential literary magazines of the post-war years. They were starting something new and important, something which would make them perhaps famous, certainly talked-about and everything else in their lives became consequent upon their need to be together, and working together, towards their joint aim. Although only 19 at the time, Jane had already been married in America, to a man called (?)Langhands, but this marriage had been over almost before it had started. Alex told her his own marriage had become intolerable, all romance had been dissipated. Betty, he claimed, continually insisted that he should get 'a job' to provide the means to support his family - which he had no intention of doing. She seemed not to understand his literary aims. These were convenient excuses, and anyway, were entirely untrue. He had written to Betty shortly after the meeting with Jane, saying that he loved them both and did not know which of them he loved the most. Neurotic, confused, manipulative, he seemed unable to make a decision. He seemed to want the decisions to be made for him.

Alex and Jane Lougee at Cap d'Ail, 1953
(Courtesy: Jane Lougee Bryant)

Betty, in Newcastle, was astonished at the turn of events. She travelled to Paris where she discovered that the children were desperately unhappy; Alex, it appeared was not visiting them: 'I can't bear to see them unhappy' he told her. This was outrageous. Jacqueline and Margot had been boarded with a French family, who spoke no English. Jacqueline was nightly wetting her bed. 'I can still hear Jackie's screams as we left,' Betty remembered. 'Alex was watching my reactions like a cat watching a mouse, manipulating, pushing me into a decision. I agreed to separate...' Alex even managed to establish a convenient scapegoat, Betty's mother. She was to blame for their 'separation', she was trying to take Betty away from him, she had never liked him ... He was desperately trying to provoke Betty into making his decision for him and in the end, she 'took off blindly for Rome, but once there had to get back to Paris to the children ... desperately unhappy.' In Paris, she discovered that the Lees were on holiday and took a room on Ile St Louis. She had been approached by the American magazine *Ladies Home Journal* to model for them and had modelling tests taken in Paris by *Vogue*. Then Madame Lee returned and spoke to the woman who was looking after the children. It transpired that this woman had assumed the children were bastards being farmed-out - thus her bad treatment of them - and that Jackie was *deliberately* wetting the bed because 'the lady didn't like me.' Betty had had enough. She took the girls and insisted that Alex drive them all to Spain. There followed an unhappy journey to Madrid. An apartment was found for the family, in Calle Rufino Blanco, luxurious, the wages of a servant being included in the rent. Alex's brother Jack had assisted with the deposit. Alex returned alone to Paris and Jane.

So what had gone wrong with their happy marriage? Betty considers that the lure of success with the magazine proved too great, for Alex was a showman and loved the prestige which the magazine gave him. Someone had warned him to be 'careful that you don't become notorious instead of famous' and he was obsessed with that remark. 'By God! He would be both!'

He had started to put the word around about the magazine and had begun to acquire poetry and prose from friends and associates. He contacted A.J. Ayer - rather an ego-trip this - to ask permission to reprint a section of his book. The question of funding and distribution became crucial. Victor Miller, it now appeared, had no funds whatsoever, and after some to-ing and fro-ing, wrote a handwritten affidavit from Bermuda, dated Palm Sunday, re-assigning the editorship to Trocchi. Alex had been busy, too, for, in a letter dated 28th April, from Jane's apartment in rue Lecomte de Lisle, he informed Miller that the magazine is 'about to come out and the printers want money.' He questioned Miller about distribution arrangements and demanded a written agreement that the magazine run for three years, twelve issues, and that, as Editor, he be paid 25,000 francs per month. He warned Miller that if no satisfactory answer to all the points was forthcoming by return he would seek another backer. He mentions the 'gradual degradation of Alan Riddell ... caused more or less by semi-starvation and the lack of a franc in his pocket,' (which he blames on Miller). Another letter of the same date is addressed to Riddell:

'Dear Alan,

Reluctantly, following a general vote of no confidence in you on the part of our contributors, I ask for your resignation as Assistant Editor. At the same time I must ask you not to represent yourself as officially connected with Mss in London or elsewhere.

The question only arose a few days ago when it was pointed out that while you were in Paris under my wing no harm, and possibly good, could come out of your being associated with Mss, but that, alone in London and representing the magazine there, you might do considerable damage.

Personally, I believe that the danger was overestimated but unfortunately I could not honestly say that it was non-existent. I do have doubts about your character and capabilities in relation to an international review, but, while you were in Paris, was able to defend you against criticism by pointing out that you were 'teachable'. After you had left and your critics came round against you in force recourse to that defence was impossible. I swithered for a long time over the problem... are you in London the right man to be going round saying "I am the Assistant Editor of Mss." and, putting personal feelings aside and considering the question solely in my capacity as Editor, I decided that you were not. Logue, Burford and Chester were unanimous in saying that if you approached them they would not think of contributing, nor can I think that you would have met with any success with Ayer. It was pointed out, and undeniably, that, apart from the Scots poets (none of whom we now intend to use), you had got hold of nothing. Anyway, there it is, and *qua* editor that is my final decision.

As for my personal feelings, I feel lousy about it, the more so because I realise what a difficult position I have created for you in Scotland. I can only say I'm sorry and assure you that I remain your friend if you can forgive me. And as for advice, swallow your pride, and wherever you are or may go, get on with your writing. I shall at all times be pleased to hear from you.

PS. You will, of course receive mention in the *editorial* for the thankless work for which you received very little from Victor Miller.'

The magazine was to be based in Jane's studio apartment in Auteil. Riddell had sought to reprint large chunks of Scottish poetry; the work of Hugh MacDiarmid and other writers of the 'Scottish Renaissance' whereas Alex wanted the magazine to represent a coherent philosophy and to take a position on the leading political and ethical questions of the decade, principally against militarisation and atomic weapon research. Riddell went on to found the Scottish poetry magazine *Lines*, which appeared quarterly into the 1990s although he died tragically young. *Merlin* never did represent any consistent body of thought, except that of its founder-editor.

One of Alex's closest Paris friends at this time was Christopher Logue, a cadaverously thin English poet in a dirty duffle coat, tight trousers and shoes which were to become known as 'winkle-pickers'. He described Trocchi thus;

'He was a handsome man. Broad, easy on his feet, with a gliding walk, body tipped forward from the waist, and usually talking in a confidential way to whoever was with him. When he drew himself up to look before entering the traffic his six-foot two surprised ... my photograph ... shows a face comparable to Burt Lancaster's, a man full of worldly confidence.'

The first meeting with Logue occurred on the staircase of a run-down hotel in the rue de la Huchette, just north of Ile de la Cite. Jane's father, Arthur Fogg Lougee, a Limerick Banker, arrived to take Jane on an extended holiday and, so, for appearance's sake, Alex took a room in the Hotel, amongst its residents, the Algerian street pedlars who sold carpets and nick-nacks to tourists. It is the hotel thinly disguised in the short story 'The Holy Man', whose denizens are prostitutes, German and French, a Hungarian rag-collector, a one-legged woman, and of course, the mysterious holy man of the title.

Another friend was the English poet and all round character Henry Charles Hatcher. Hatcher also lived for a time in the Hotel Verneuil and when he couldn't pay his bill, simply packed everything into his guitar case and walked out. American poet Austryn Wainhouse was working on a translation of De Sade's *Philosophie Dans La Boudoir* when Trocchi sent him a *pneumatique* (telegram) and they met several days later, after Wainhouse left a reply for Alex at the Librairie Mistral. Wainhouse regarded Alex as barely competent, but was aware of his conspicious charm and described him as 'a minor coquette' toying with the affections of everyone. His first impressions of Trocchi were of 'a great lean rascal in a raincoat, collar pulled up, over its rim a long nose claiming all the space between two little deep-set eyes, very blue, very winning and manifestly not to be trusted.' There were four other Americans close to Trocchi; Richard Seaver, Terry Southern,

Mason Hoffenberg and Baird Bryant. Southern, known as 'Tex' was a dedicated hipster and tried to give the impression that he had a mysterious if not actually criminal past by delinquent and irrational behaviour. He was generally monosyllabic - 'cool'. To add to the impression, he kept a pet owl in his hotel room. Other friends were poets and writers Alfred Chester, William Burford, George Plimpton, John P. Marquand Jr, (who, as John Phillips had already published a successful novel, *The Second Happiest Day*), Patrick Bowles, John Stevenson - who became the magazine's business manager - and dozens of others, upon all of whom Alex exerted a peculiar fascination. Baird Bryant treated Trocchi as a God, and hung on his every word. Seaver was to commit extraordinary sacrifices in the name of the magazine. For him Trocchi was a 'big brother' figure (and he christened his first son Alexander). Tex Southern envied his charisma; 'Everything he did had a Wagnerian grandeur', Marquand - the successful novelist - was made to feel excessive guilt for his bourgeois attitudes to literature and was given a prescribed reading list, also told that giving money (to Trocchi) was a salve to conscience. Trocchi later told him 'humility is not enough, John'.

It had been arranged that Alex would send money to Betty for the children and, of course, it was Jane's money that was being sent. Not that this was regular, for Alex' energies were centrally directed towards the magazine, which had now been named *Merlin* (by Christopher Logue) - a reference to Ezra Pound, not the great magician of Arthurian Britain. Jane had an allowance of $100 per month - but since it was this money which was being sent to Betty now in Mallorca - the money to pay for the first issue had actually to be brought from America by Arthur Lougee; money from the sale of Jane's car in America. At first, Mr Lougee had blamed Jane for breaking up Alex's marriage but Jane remembers having the impression that Betty was 'spineless' and Alex telling her that she had not understood his aims.

Meanwhile, Jane and her father toured extensively throughout Europe and even visited Glasgow. While Jane was away, Alex continued to hang around the cafes as usual and his current

Alex with Eugene Ionesco, Paris, Dec. 1953.
(Courtesy: Jane Lougee Bryant)

favourite was Café de Tournon on rue du Tournon on *la rive gauche*, where of an evening, could be found Christopher Logue, George Plimpton, Alabama writer Eugene Walter, William Pene du Bois (art editor of Paris Review) and Peter Mathiessen. While these argued politics or played chess, Richard Wright played pinball and the talk often turned to the subject matter of spies and the cold war. Mathiessen of course later revealed that he had been a spy for the CIA and the KGB! Alex may at this time have had a brief affair with an extraordinary and beautiful American woman, Theodora Keogh. Married to artist and costume designer Tom Keogh in a rather loose marital arrangement, she was, under her maiden name of Roosevelt, grand-daughter of the former American President. Whether there was in fact any sexual connection between her and Alex, Theodora, who wrote dark, sinister novels featuring lurid covers, portrayed in *The Fascinator*, (Olympia, 1954) a sexually-predatory, and diseased, sculptor preying on young girls - which is believed to be based on Trocchi.

On Jane's return, Alex was glad to move from rue de la Huchette into a room in the Hotel Verneuil. Shortly afterwards both he and Jane caught jaundice, from a meal in a cheap restaurant. Despite their illness the first issue of *Merlin* finally appeared on 15th May 1952, in an edition of 1,000 copies. 'Appeared?' Trocchi later remarked. 'The word is at once too weak and too strong. I who edited the mag., can vouch for all the toil and effort that went into it ...'

The magazine was sold in Amsterdam, London, New York and Paris itself, by street-sellers operating around the cafes and at cultural events. Colin Wilson, Kenneth White and Alan Sillitoe were three of these occasional street sellers who sold copies of *Merlin* for commission on each sale. Shortly after the first issue came out, Trocchi made a brief trip to Mallorca to see Betty and the girls, during which visit he introduced her to marijuana and proposed that they should leave the girls with Madame Lee in Paris and go on a journey through North Africa together. Betty declined the offer but some time after his return to Paris and to Jane, discovered that she was again pregnant!

For Alex and Jane, life was fast moving and great fun. They were often on the brink of starvation but thought little of it.

There were many days and nights of light-hearted arguments at pavement cafes on philosopy, the relative merits of Eliot, Pound, Yeats, Joyce, Faulkner, and Miller. Alex was fond of canasta and of pinball. One of his favourite haunts now was the Grappe d'or Cafe ... 'run by a mean peasant from Auvergne ... which had the finest pinball machine in all Paris... It was a gloomy museum of a room, illuminated by the lights of the boulevards ... sad, desperate and jealous by the Quais of the Seine, the absurdity of Paris traffic ... many of the poets and painters in Paris in the early fifties played pinball; few without feelings of guilt, as in all games, there is a kind of mystical confederacy between players, amongst those who knew how to abandon themselves entirely to it; joy, grace, tension, elation and between players, collusion. There is a similar confederacy amongst those who take drugs. In these things only the spoilsport is despicable.'

Christopher Logue had been consulting Alex regularly for advice on the precarious course of his romantic affairs, but in despair took himself off to Canet Plage on the Franco-Spanish border in the summer, leaving a note of his intention to commit suicide. He had fallen for a Brazilian girl, daughter of a prominent Brazilian family who was studying in Paris on a fellowship. When seventeen year-old Vera returned to Brazil with her mother, Logue decided suicide was his only option. A fellow resident in the Hotel Pantheon, a South African painter, Louis De Wet, (whose father was, incidentally, a Chief of Police) revealed that Logue had left. Austryn Wainhouse raised the alarm. Alex arrived and somehow elicited the information that Logue was headed for Perpignan. A quick whip-round among friends and Trocchi was on a train heading south. At Perpignan station he took a tramway for the five miles to Canet Plage and spotted Logue on the beach, disconsolate, bashing a tin of what Trocchi described as 'rat poison' (but in reality according to Logue, merely a concoction of sleeping pills) on a rock in a futile attempt to open it. He had originally intended to buy a boat and simply let the tide take him beyond rescue, an idea cribbed from Beckett's *Malone Dies*, but had had only enough money for a small tin of pills. 'Alex, I can't open this' were his first words. Then, 'Alex, what are *you* doing here?'

'I've come here to embarrass you,' Trocchi said, bending down. He picked up the tin, tried for a little while to open it and then slipped it into his pocket. 'Come, Christopher, let's go into the town ...' and, by using his charm, enveigled the forlorn poet onto a train, first-class, of course, bound for Paris, having sent a wire ahead. Logue was deposited with their wealthy friends, Clement and Matilda Heller, until the crisis had passed.

It was in the second issue of *Merlin*, published on 15th September that Alex spelt out his literary and political priorities;

'Some ways of talking about literature are more useful than other ways of talking about literature. All ways of talking involve the use of distinctions. That is alright so long as those distinctions are not allowed to harden, that is to say, if we abandon them as soon as they cease to be useful. Most of the traditional categories are merely distinctions, hallowed by antiquity, which have been allowed to harden, and which, in the hands of unscience, have become an inquisitorial rack to which the flesh of contemporary writing is to be twisted. James Joyce's *Ulysses* broke one rack for the intelligent; they saw that it did not amount to much to say that it was not a novel, the significant point being that it was obviously a great work of genius ... Since then there have been other instances of rack-breaking; instances, but the principle does not appear to have been grasped, even by the intelligent reading public. That principle may be stated simply: all categories are utilitarian; when they cease to be recognised as such, they become obnoxious.'

In the hothouse literary climate of the magazine, Alex Trocchi quickly became friendly with many major writers living in Paris, including Jean Paul Sartre. He had an arrangement with Sartre that *Merlin* could reprint what it wished from Sartre's magazine *Les Temps Modernes*. In its eleven issues, *Merlin* published Jean Genet, Paul Eluard, Nazim Hickmet (a Turkish poet who had had to flee to Moscow), William Sansom, English novelist and short story writer, Eugene Ionesco (one of the founders of the Theatre of the Absurd), Italo Svevo (whom Joyce had taught in Trieste), Arthur Adamov, Tristram Hull, Robert Creeley, Patrick Brangwyn, Daniel Mauroc, the Italian novelist Vasco Pratolini, the Scottish poet WS Graham, the Chilean poet Pablo Neruda - and of course, Miller and Beckett - plus a large number of young writers, many of whom have gone on to literary success.

There were enough writers in contact with the magazine for Alex and the others to plan a further venture and *Collection Merlin* was born. Under French law, no publishing venture could operate without a 'gerant' or manager who was a French citizen. Enter Maurice Girodias. Girodias' black Citroen stopped outside a pavement cafe for his meeting with the half-dozen writers of the *Merlin* group, and out stepped an elegant, flamboyant man in his early thirties. His father, Jack Kahane, had been the owner of the Obelisk Press which had published the earliest sections of Joyce's *Finnegans Wake*, Henry Miller's *Sexus* and *Tropic of Capricorn* but Girodias initially had no interest in the literary work of the young writers of the *Merlin* group. He planned to make a fortune by selling pornographic novels to the ready market of English-speaking expatriates in Paris. He had been attracted initially by Wainhouse's translation of De Sade. Girodias was 'a wide boy' in every sense of the word, charming but unscrupulous. Seeing the enthusiasm of the young writers for their 'pet' projects, which included publishing Logue's poetry collection *Wand And Quadrant*, Jean Genet's *Thief's Journal*, Wainhouse's translation of *Philosophie Dans Le Boudoir* and his novel *Hedyphagetica*, Girodias immediately saw an opportunity to get talent cheaply and agreed to act as their backer if they would write him pornographic books - to an agreed formula - for which he would pay. Seeing this as their chance to get *Collection Merlin* off the ground, the group readily agreed. It became a matter of honour as to which of them could turn out the most d.b.'s (dirty books) in the shortest time. Trocchi was to be the outright winner, for not only did he write eight books, he even wrote catalogue copy and 'scouted' further talent for Girodias' publishing house, the Olympia Press. But although Girodias has described himself as 'a second-generation Anglo-French pornographer', neither he nor Olympia Press can be so casually dismissed. In the six or seven years that the Press operated, it led an ultimately successful assault on the moral establishment of Europe and America and helped to end the concept of censorship and the banning of literature on the grounds of obscenity. Since 1933, when a judge had upheld that James Joyce's *Ulysses* was not obscene because of its literary merit there had been a lull in prosecutions under the obscenity laws in Britain, Europe and America. The next book to be subjected to international legal scrutiny was Nabokov's *Lolita* in 1955, followed by *Tropic of Cancer* in the USA in 1962 and John Cleland's *Memoirs of Fanny Hill* in Britain in 1964. All three were originally Olympia books. But that was in the future. The Olympia Press was founded in 1953 with the simple and undeniable aim of making money from English language pornography.

Meanwhile, the magazine (and Alex and Jane) moved from the Hotel Verneuil into a basement storeroom which Dick Seaver had found, beneath a curious Afro-Carribean antique emporium in the rue du Sabot. The emporium's owner, Oscar Meyer, had gone mad and was incarcerated in a suburban hospital. Seaver and his fiance, Jeanette, lived in the first floor flat. The attraction of this place was that there was no rent to pay. The basement had a concrete floor, on which a mattress was strewn. It had no windows and little furniture and a single gas ring on which Trocchi managed to conjure up terrific hot meals, on one memorable occasion, a meal which included African lobsters. His speciality was pea soup, made to his mother's recipe and Brendan Behan was among the visitors to testify to the quality of the soup. Behan often stayed for several days at a time, whenever he was in Paris, coming back drunk in the night and sleeping across several chairs. Once, he sang them a song written by his brother, Dominic, 'Zoological Gardens' which Jane particularly liked and which was not actually recorded until the 1960s when it became a staple of the folk music circuit. All life was here.

Chapter 6: Merlin and Beckett's *Watt*

There is an amusing - although entirely fictitious - description in Deirdre Bair's biography of Samuel Beckett of the meeting between Maurice Girodias and the enthusiastic editors of *Merlin*, headed by Alex Trocchi, in possession of a rather unwilling Samuel Beckett. The truth is more prosaic. One wet evening in the rue du Sabot as the friends sat around, drinking and talking, a knock at the door announced the arrival of the unmistakeable tall, lean, craggy-featured Irishman, who merely handed over the manuscript of the novel *Watt*. Beckett did not stay and after his departure, Trocchi began to read aloud from the manuscript, of the tragi-comical manouevrings of Mr Hackett ... Within a very short time everyone in the room had become thoroughly fascinated. There was a shared realisation that literary history was occurring, there, in that damp basement, and that they were all about to play a part in great events.

Dick Seaver had played a crucial role. Seaver had good contacts, one of whom was Patrick Bowles (who had originally introduced Seaver and Trocchi to each other in a cafe) and Jerome Lindon, the Director of the highly influential Paris publisher, *Editions de Minuit*. It was through Lindon that Seaver, and then Trocchi, first met Beckett. Seaver's interest led to him being commissioned to compile an article on Beckett for the second issue of *Merlin*. A copy of this issue was left for Beckett at Lindon's office in rue Pallissey, a street away from rue du Sabot, and thus Beckett arrived at the basement. Subsequently, Trocchi saw Beckett often and was regarded as a protege. Beckett felt that the young Scot had considerable talent and it was Trocchi who largely proofread *Watt*. Indeed, Beckett came to trust Trocchi so much that he ultimately allowed him to handle the business of the negotiations and the contracts for *Watt* and *Molloy* were actually put in Trocchi's name. Due to Samuel Beckett's death during the preparation of the first edition of this book, the author was unable to corroborate at first hand the detail of their relationship – and it has been pointed out that Beckett was famously unforthcoming anyway - but many remember meetings between Beckett and Trocchi at the apartment where Beckett lived with his fiancee. Jane Lougee attended several of these and Terry Southern recalled being taken to Beckett's apartment by Trocchi where the Irishman cooked them a breakfast of kippers.

Collection Merlin, under the imprint of Olympia Press, published *Watt*, Beckett's first novel in English in 1953, in its first edition, and later *Molloy*, Beckett's first 'French' novel, translated for the group by the author and Patrick Bowles. The publication of these two novels, virtually introduced (or re-introduced) him to the world's attention. They were followed by Genet's *Thief's Journal* translated by Bernard Frechtman, (the first-ever edition in English), *Hedyphagetica*, *Wand And Quadrant* and James Broughton's *An Almanac For Amorists*. However, when arrangements came to be made for the publication of *Molloy*, financial complications ensued. Beckett had returned to Ireland, to Killiney in County Dublin on family business and did not receive royalties that he had anticipated. Additionally, he had found fault with an extract that had been published in *Merlin*. 'My text is full of errors,' he complained, 'why did you not send me proofs ... I begin to weary of your treatment of me. If we cannot have ordinary relations, better we had none at all.' Of course, Trocchi had a reassuring answer: 'You were in Ireland and had left no specific instructions.' That was why no proofs had been sent. Nor had Trocchi known the name of his bank in Ireland. However, the money due would be paid into Beckett's account by the end of the week. But Trocchi was rather irritated: 'The cool tone of your last letter makes it difficult for me to say anything at all ... That you were able to get so many recriminations directly and by innuendo on one small page does credit to your literary ability but says little for what I believed was our friendship ... really, I don't think you have much to complain about in our treatment of you. The whole group has worked hard and loyally for a long time to

Reception for 'Merlin' publications, at home of Clement and Mathilde Heller, 5 rue Vaneau, Paris, 9th December 1953.
Back row, L to R: George Plimpton, Corneille, Richard Seaver, Mary Smith, Patrick Bowles, Gaite Froge, Jane Lougee.
Front row, L to R: Christopher Logue, Austryn Wainhouse, Christopher Middleton. Photo: H. Riemens.
(Courtesy: Jane Lougee Bryant)

advance your interests, and whenever there has been a possibility of friction we have subordinated our own interests to your wishes ...' It has often been said that a young writer needs a collossal amount of gall and ego to push him or herself to the fore and Trocchi had perhaps more of this than anyone else. Who else would have taken to task a Nobel Prize winning author, possibly one of the greatest writers of his day on the matter of his own proofs and royalties? But Trocchi had already developed the uncanny ability to make the outrageous seem impeccably reasonable, to smooth over all difficulties and that Beckett and he remained friends is testimony to that. Terry Southern was later to write to Trocchi, who, in 1958, was in America, assuring him that 'Beckett is... most fond of you. You ought to write to him from time to time, as he expressed great interest in how you are getting on.'

The days were never long enough, beginning about 9am when a small line of writers would present themselves at Girodias' office in rue Jacob for money. In theory, Girodias paid each writer 300,000 old francs per d.b., in practice this was paid in amounts of ten, twenty or thirty francs, and Girodias did not keep accurate records. It was a hand-to-mouth existence, a matter of survival. Baird Bryant wrote *Play My Love*, Mason Hoffenberg wrote (as 'Faustino Perez') *Until She Screams* and *Sin For Breakfast*, Christopher Logue penned *Lust*, under the psuedonym of Count Palmiro Vicarion, (and later *Count Palmiro Vicarion's Book of Bawdy Ballads* and *Count Palmiro Vicarion's Book of Limericks*). Iris Owens, as Harriet Daimler, wrote *Innocence*, *The Organisation* and *Darling*, Austryn Wainhouse translated de Sade's *Justine*, and his *Philosophie Dans Le Boudoir* also appeared from Olympia as *Bedroom Philosophers*. *Candy* (a spoof of *Candide*) was written by Terry Southern and Mason Hoffenberg under the joint pseudonym of Maxwell Kenton. Trocchi himself wrote seven novels under the pseudonym of Frances Lengel and collaborated with Dick Seaver on a translation of Guillaume Appollinaire's *Les Exploits d'un Jeune Don Juan* but left Seaver to complete it on his own, preferring to work on another Appollinaire work; *Les Onze Mille Vierges* published variously as *The 11 Thousand Virgins* and *The 11th Hour of Whips*, (since the title is a play on words) but generally known as 'the debauched Hospodar', being the supposed memoirs of a Rumanian Count. According to George Plimpton, 'late in the evening, on occasion, Trocchi would stand on a table in the Cafe Bonaparte and recite parts of the translation he had just completed - his Scottish accent softening the scatology so that the readings were more charming than startling. Friends would ask Alex in the street: "Is there to be a reading tonight? Have you finished Chapter 4?"' When the book came to be published, in July 1953, Trocchi adopted the psuedonym of 'Oscar Mole'.

Olympia Press, with its famous green covered paperbacks was to continue under various guises; as Travellers' Companion, Ophelia Press, Orpheus Press and with manifestations in France, other European countries, Britain and in America for a further twenty years, and it is undeniably true that its aims developed away from its original low-quality pornographic output. It is true also that Girodias was a shrewd businessman and acquired books such as *Lolita* by Nabokov, works by Henry Miller and de Sade, Burroughs' *Naked Lunch* and *The Ginger Man* by J.P. Donleavy, all erotic classics, and all procured from outwith the *Collection Merlin* group. True also that nearly every author he ever published sued him. In his autobiography, *J'arrive* (Paris, 1977), re-issued as *The Frog Prince* (New York, 1980), Girodias made some extravagant claims to literary fame and acumen, but it would seem obvious that it was this first contact with the literary writers of the *Merlin* group which created the stature of the Olympia Press such that it was able to attract work of merit. Neither should Paris itself be overlooked as a factor for Olympia's success; almost everyone who was anyone passed through Paris for a long or short time in the early fifties; Irwin Shaw, Stravinsky, Richard Wright, Genet, Hemingway ... even Jane Fonda ... so spreading its fame and notoriety. Only in Paris could one obtain some of the most interesting books of a new era, since there was, in France at that time, no censorship. Having been the first and most astonishing venture of its kind, Olympia was widely emulated around the world, its house-style stolen by a plethora of publishing 'pirates'. *Candy* for example appeared in up to fifty unauthorised editions selling a total of over fifteen million copies worldwide, with not one cent going to the authors or the original publisher. The story of the Olympia Press - its harrassment by 'the forces of reaction' and its struggle to fight off the 'pirates' (who even faked the Olympia catalogues) has been sketched in Patrick Kearney's *The Secret Record* (1966) and *Paris Olympia Press* (1987) and in the as yet unpublished second volume of Girodias' autobiography. Copies of Olympia Press books, whether forgeries or not, are now of course collector's items.

In such a cultural climate, other magazines too began to flourish; Sindbad Vail's *Points* and *The Paris Review*. Although these were produced from the same milieu as *Merlin*, they were not true rivals, although there was certainly some tribal rivalry among the editors of each. Sindbad Vail's father had been an influential figure in 1920s Paris; one of the original sixteen signatories of the surrealists' manifesto, and his mother was the famous Peggy Guggenheim, whose family had donated the Gallery of Modern Art in New York. He was, in fact, named Sindbad by his eccentric father to forestall any ambitions he might develop to be a poet. From such a privileged background, he was regarded by Trocchi as 'easy meat' and was manipulated unmercifully to obtain invitations to the Guggenheim's palazzo in Venice. Vail also kept his girlfriend well clear of Trocchi for fear (as he later confided to Terry Southern) that Trocchi would appear to 'suck the cervix clean out of her!' To Trocchi, Vail was a spoiled dilettante, and anyway why should *Points* have it so easy, when he, Trocchi, and *Merlin* had to struggle for every franc? 'Like, it was his duty to assist our venture ...' Trocchi might have said, and probably did.

Trocchi had perfected a masterful way of using people from bourgeois and privileged backgrounds. He infected them with a sense of guilt and embarrassment at their conspicuous luxury in his presence while simultaneously, by his benevolence and sheer bonhomie, would appear to overlook their obvious unease, inducing in his victims something almost akin to relief and a frantic need to earn his respect. He had some unexplained power, perhaps emanating from his dry, mesmeric voice, which exerted influence over his peers, such that most would quite willingly do his bidding,

Jane Lougee and Fuki at Hotel de Verneuil, 1954.
Photo: Lennart Olson.
(Courtesy: Jane Lougee Bryant)

or give him what he asked. John Marquand, whose father was a famous author, and George Plimpton, whose father was a Wall Street Corporation lawyer and US Ambassador to the UN, were particularly ripe targets. Especially since Plimpton had had the gall to start a magazine of his own! Admittedly, the *Paris Review* did not profess the high literary-mindedness of *Merlin* - they were not *engagé* - but published many of the same writers, and - to Alex's great chagrin - were funded by Prince Saddrudin Aga Khan! The *Paris Review* produced its first issue in 1953, Plimpton and Peter Matthiesson being its main movers. Interestingly, three letters exist which prove that Matthiesson had tried, while in London in July 1952, to become the London distributor for *Merlin* but had been somewhat abruptly rejected. He responded in September, describing this as 'somewhat sad news.' Had he been accepted to work for *Merlin*, it is possible that the other magazine may never have come into being. The magazines tended to come out within a few weeks of each other and there was constant vying to see which group could sell most copies. Initially, both magazines were distributed to the USA through the US Embassy, but when Trocchi reviewed a book by Sartre (derided by the Americans as 'that French commie'), *Merlin* was no longer welcomed, in what was now the era of Senator McCarthy. Copies were sold at the American Express in the Place Etoile, principally by Jane, often with her silver-grey Siamese cat, Fuki, sitting on her shoulder, scrutinising each prospective purchaser. Alex and Jane had a second cat, 'old poppa' Hetherington, named by Alex in grateful thanks for the taste of luxury and high living which the Hetherington Award had afforded him.

While the *Paris Review* crowd was generally more light-hearted about literature than *Merlin*, the latter group looked askance at a magazine produced by editors who seemed to spend their days at the Paris Races. Neither generalisation was, of course, entirely correct, and George Plimpton was more or less within both groups. Sadruddin Aga Khan's money was not enough to cover all the costs of the magazine, though the *Review* soon came under the wing of the establishment publisher, Plon. There were also accusations of CIA involvement and in one memorable incident, Marquand

Alex at Tossa de Mar, Spain, June 1954.
(Courtesy: Jane Lougee Bryant)

almost came to blows with Southern after Trocchi had accused Marquand of being in the CIA. Later, of course, it was discovered that Peter Matthieson had been in the CIA - *and the KGB*! - when his novel *Partisan* came out exposing his former double life. The *Paris Review* celebrated its twenty-five years of publication in 1983 and, although its nexus has long been New York, continues to produce issues under its eagle masthead.

There were many larger-than-life characters in Paris at this time; Ishmael (Cobra) Kelly, a negro from Alabama with a lazy Southern drawl was a successful con-man, customarily wearing a camel-haired coat and carrying an expensive attache case. He had a scheme for defrauding gullible tourists at the Eiffel Tower by pretending to record their voice impressions at the monument; tourists would be asked to record into a microphone and then would be presented with a record supposedly containing what they had said. Cobra Kelly later married the Princess of Holland, and appears as 'Fishbelly' in a novel by Richard Wright, a black American author who was another member of cafe society in Paris at the time. Another character with more than an element of the sinister about him, and one who appealed to Trocchi particularly because of that, was Kosta Alexopolous, a Greek sculptor, with whom Trocchi began to be friendly. The drug dealers from whom the expatriates obtained their drugs, principally hashish, though occasionally cocaine and heroin, were Arabs, some of whom Alex had first encountered in the rue de la Huchette. Drug dealing, notwithstanding the popularity of soft drugs in the city, was a very dangerous occupation, which only the Arabs were involved in at the time. The expatriate writers justified their use of drugs to relax from their creative efforts and viewed the danger as an added frisson.

Dick Seaver obtained a tutoring job at a US Army base and sent what money he could to the magazine. It was a job he hated but Alex had persuaded him that it was his bounden duty and a task for which the Realm of Literature (or the Republic of Letters?) would amply reward him. At other times, Alex himself managed to obtain some money by acting as a private English tutor, although he found this beneath him, resenting its interference with his other, much

Jane at Tossa de Mar, June 1954.
(Courtesy: Jane Lougee Bryant)

more important tasks. Jane was reduced to being a charwoman, for which she received 1,000 old francs per week. Unfortunately, she was unable to resist an avocado on the way home with her first pay packet. This cost all of 800 francs and, instead of handing over her pay, she presented this magnificent specimen to Alex. Once he had calmed down, he consumed his portion of the fruit, then, musing on the price of it, decided that he and Jane should travel immediately to the South of France, there to cultivate a grove of avocado with which to make their fortunes! Later, Jane worked as a remedial tutor for US Servicemen's children.

Although the first three issues of the magazine were printed in Paris, it was discovered that printing costs were cheaper in Spain - barely half of the French costs - so the fourth issue was taken to Majorca. Of course, cheapness is rarely a guarantee of quality so it was necessary for someone to go down to oversee the printing, and typical that that someone would be Trocchi. Trocchi had secretly discovered that the printing costs were even cheaper on the island of Majorca, so he decided to have a holiday on the difference between what the others thought it might cost and what he knew he could have it printed for. To make matters worse, he knew that Betty and the kids were there, and effected a touching reconciliation with his family. During this visit, Betty who had just had an abortion, again became pregnant. This, not surprisingly, did not endear him to Jane, still char-ing in Paris.

Trocchi had a good friend in Barcelona at this time; Shinkichi Tajiri, a Japanese sculptor who was the possessor of a powerful motorbike. Alex borrowed this machine for several days to pay a visit to Robert Creeley at Banalbufar on the island of Majorca, after he had dealt with the printers. His visit to Creeley is described in Creeley's novel *The Island*:

'He was tall, taller, had a crooked face with a strong nose, it was that one was first aware of, the beak-like strength of that nose, then the eyes, blue, sharp in no simple sense, set into the projecting forehead ... He liked the man on the instant, he wanted to be liked by him also ... '

While on the island of Majorca, it would have been characteristic of Trocchi to have visited Robert Graves at Deya, since the person who was overseeing the printing, Martin Seymour-Smith, was tutor to Graves' son, however, Smith did not dare to introduce Trocchi to his employer in case they did not get on, or in case Trocchi upset the poet and Trocchi himself was not particularly interested in meeting Graves, whom Creeley, for example, regarded as rather *passé*. Certainly there were afternoons spent in Graves' garden but Graves himself was in the family flat in Palma at the time.

It was necessary, on his return, for him to be suitably apologetic to all, particularly Jane – though whether he told her the full truth is very much in doubt - and he promised her a holiday in the South of France. He also promised that he would seek a divorce from Betty to marry her. This after getting Betty pregnant! Alex and Jane apparently also agreed that they would apply for custody of Margot and Jacqueline. The appalling smugness of this casual decision to deprive Betty of the one thing he had hitherto left her, the children, is breathtaking in its arrogance. This was the man who had abandoned his children to strangers while Betty was at home caring for her dying father! Now they would play happy families and to complete the act, needed the kids. Thanks and goodbye! Sorry for getting you pregnant! By the way Jane has quite forgiven me. As they took a reconciliatory walk along the Quai, Jane spied a beautiful Indian turquoise ring, and knowing that Alex had received money that day, hinted, somewhat obviously, that she would like the ring to seal their bargain - a sort of engagement present. But Trocchi abruptly changed the subject and they walked on. Nothing could be taken for granted with a man like Trocchi.

The rest of the group were irritated to discover that, of the edition of 3,000 copies, 1,000 sent to the USA never arrived, 1,000 on their way to the UK were lost when the boat sank! And, of the remaining 1,000 some never even made it across the Pyrenees. Those that did reach Paris only did so when Betty was recruited to collect the copies at Barcelona and drive them to the border. It then transpired that the printer had only enough fonts to set-up eight pages at a time and thus a rapid reprint was not possible. Consequently, the entire issue was a disaster.

Going on holiday was a timely idea. Alex and Jane set off by bus for the South of France and stayed with Clement and Matilda Heller for several weeks on their estate. They then travelled to Spain, hitch-hiking down through the central Massif. They found getting lifts no problem, but on more than one occasion, Jane found herself being molested by a Spanish lorry-driver while Alex feigned sleep. Furiously, she upbraided him afterwards. 'Why didn't you do something?' 'Like, I was afraid he'd kick us out of the cab...' For Alex, women's virtue even that of his own woman was a singularly disposable item. Virtue bored him. In a sense, their romance was growing a bit stale now that he had her in his power; Alex was restless for something vague and undefined.

They attended bullfights in Barcelona, sat on beachfront cafes at Tossa De Mar, Alex uneasily aware of the struggle which the other editors of *Collection Merlin* - particularly Austryn Wainhouse - must be having back in Paris.

There were about twenty-five separate proposed publications, with more unsolicited manuscripts arriving every day. On his return he was immediately plunged into proofreading *Watt* and advised Beckett to expunge some musical notation from the text. He was also faced with the problem of checking a large sequence of frog cries based on a furious sequence of Krek, Krik, Krak's, and told Beckett this was uncheckable. The book appeared late in the year. Beckett and Trocchi had much in common as writers. Both had created a literary identity from exposure to European literature, and both had been liberated by residence in Paris to create works that were in the vanguard of new European culture trends although rooted in representations of Ireland and Scotland respectively.

In early December, there was the *Merlin* party in the Hellers' Paris apartment in rue Vaneau. The guest-list included many famous writers, artists, and celebrities such as Richard Wright - a close friend of Sartre, society photographer Brassai, Max Ernst, Eugene Ionesco, the sculptor and artist, Alberto Giacometti, Sidney Chaplin, Max Steele, Arthur Adamov, Raymond Queneau, the brilliant French writer elected to the Academie des Goncourt in 1947, Jean Paulhan, Stanley William Hayter, Corneille - and of course the younger writers of the *Merlin* group and their partners.

It was a wonderful occasion and, apart from an unidentified bearded poet who became so drunk that he remained prostrate under the table for most of the evening, was a major success. A metal pin badge had been struck, and in the photographs taken at the party, even George Plimpton, whose own bird, strictly speaking, was an eagle, wore the falcon!

During this period, Alex was in the habit of keeping a diary or log and an entry picked at random, gives a flavour of his Parisian days:

Feb 9 1954 *Today, for example, has been a very interesting day: began at 1pm. when I was called to the telephone - Dick (Seaver), from his mother-in-law's, to say that he wouldn't get in till Thursday. In rather a bad temper, dissolved when I sat down to rewrite Y.A., (Young Adam) did five pages of the revision; what Gid (Girodias) nor anyone else will understand is that Y.A. is merely a 'neutraler', neither bad nor good, against which society comes: thus one sees society's categories break against neutral existence, crush it perhaps, but with society coming off worst (for its exposed absolutes) through criticism. That probably what caused Jane to call him 'mad' ... his lack of normal response.*

Today for first time in a long time sitting in a cafe with strangers, that's to say people I knew vaguely, not intimately, Gerry - Fuch's wife, some guy who talked like Porter Tuck (now killing bulls in Seville) but said he was French: very blase, wanted to impress, about his m .... ; got it in Tangiers, he said, 2 kilos of it, sitting there with a big bag of pot etc., ad nauseam, and another guy, didn't catch his name, an architect, an American (second we've met, or rather I, Jane not being there) who'd just come from Greenland ... all of us smoking some of the above French joker's pot, which I was pleased to accept humbly, and then all of a sudden who should come in but the model we saw in front of Elle last week, didn't realise she was an American, really very goodlooking indeed, and a friend of Fuch's and his wife's. She sat talking to Gerry for a while. Fuchs meanwhile sat. I sat and looked. She seemed very pleasant. Now there's a look about that kind of woman, quite quite unnatural, the face stylized, the make-up perfect in the stylization. Came away after saying goodbye to poor old Victor Miller (carrying a bundle and looking just like a tramp ... Things are looking up he says, God, poor bastard!)"

1954 was to be a year of change for the young writers. The publication, in February of *The Story of O* by Pauline Reage, in a new translation, had a big effect on Trocchi. Many myths surround this notorious book and it was long suspected that the real translator of the book, the real owner of the pseudonym of 'Sabine d'Estree' was not as originally believed, Baird and Denny Bryant, but Dick Seaver. His frequent and elaborate denials were finally overturned in an obituary written by his wife in the New York Times on 7th January 2009. The book, which Trocchi later described (to Djuna Barnes, in September 1954) as 'one of the most obscene and obstinately seditious pieces of writing since the Marquis de Sade,' led to outrageous experiments in sexual behaviour disguised as 'research' for such Olympia novels as *White Thighs* and *School For Wives*. Firstly, Alex insisted on having sex in a hotel room with a prostitute and insisted that Jane watch. He wanted to demonstrate that love was stronger than sex, that sex existed on a lesser level. He was struggling to define the meaning of sex and how it related to personality, experimenting with sexual jealousy, with 'possession' ... He then began to scandalise his friends by a series of 'experiments'. He enveigled Denny, Baird Bryant's wife to his room to spend the night. There was nothing at all furtive about it. Denny was delighted to acquiesce. If Alex had arranged it, then no blame would be attached to her, and Baird of course worshipped Trocchi. Dick and Jeanette Seaver and the others were 'horrified' at this casual sexual attitude and subsequently Sindbad Vail and Jane spent the night in a hotel room with a bottle of wine. Nothing happened but the intention was to provoke Alex, to ridicule the whole thing. But Alex went further. He had sex with Mary Smith and that really caused annoyance. Mary Smith was Gaite Froge's assistant in The English Bookshop, and was greatly flattered and confused by Alex' attentions. It was the actions of a cad to take advantage of this, and Jane threw a large quantity of china at his head, in individual pieces, in their room (they had moved upstairs, to the first floor flat which Dick and Jeanette had vacated on their marriage in June). Then there was 'the orgy' or a series of orgies; excited by the theme of *The Story of O* and the idea of a 'specialist brothel'. Alex decided to train some women on the finer points of sexual technique and either wanted to encourage wide-spread promiscuity, or make some money, or was it something else? It is hard now to know precisely what his motives were, but the facts are that he did 'sign up' a few women - friends, girlfriends, even wives - and at least one 'training session' took place. Trocchi watched while a nominated male made love to a female. He could not afford a leather whip and stood ready to correct any 'defects' with a wooden ruler! Trocchi approached Austryn Wainhouse to ask if his wife Muffie would be interested. 'I don't think so, Alex' he was told, and mercifully, he did not pursue the matter. On another occasion, at a party, Trocchi was greatly excited by the wife of a Dutch friend and stalked around the room with a French bread at his crotch, imitating a giant erection, extemporising in great detail on what he intended to do for this lady in a sexual way. His diatribe, accompanied with much leering, ended with the line; "I'm going to get my little finger into her cunt!" Suddenly, the Dutchman, who had not, until that point, understood what Trocchi was saying, leapt at him, causing a shower of sparks as several marijuana joints were knocked out of several pairs of hands. Trocchi came off very much second best from the fracas and later remonstrated with his friends; 'Like, why did he attack me?' He genuinely seemed mystified.

Christopher Logue returned from a long stay in Rome with WS Grahame (having sent the Trocchis some forty or so letters from there) and began virtually living in the flat. The situation was difficult, and Jane decided to leave Paris and return to America. She was doing so, ostensibly to be able to earn money in New York to ease the acute financial situation of *Merlin* - an idea with which Trocchi could hardly disagree - but she also wanted time and distance in which to think about her life and her relationship with

Alex. Before she left, the group attended their last big function together - the Quat'zarts Ball.

The Bal de Quat'zarts was held in early July by French Art students and was a wild affair. Its traditions date from the 1920s when it had been an imporant item in the Parisian social calendar. Members of the 'cafe society' could usually manage to get themselves invited, and on this occasion, Trocchi, Jane, Chris Logue and George Plimpton went as a group. The event started with a procession to the venue, usually marked by extreme behaviour and drunkenness - the students snatching food and drink off cafe tables as they passed - watched with bemused tolerance by the populace, and continued for twenty-four hours. The Police and citizens were remarkably tolerant of the wild antics and partial nudity was almost obligatory during the event. In 1954, the theme was Grecian and the group wore blue dye and scanty togas, Jane wearing only bikini bottoms. Once in to the venue, the Salle Wagram, the doors were locked and no one could get out until dawn. The orgy began. The only restrictions on behaviour were imposed by the 'cadre noir', students whose bodies were painted black from head to toe and who carried wooden clubs to separate 'unwilling' couples on the straw-strewn floors in the dimly-lit rooms. It was not an event for the faint-hearted! The music was provided - incongruously - by a military brass band playing from the second balcony, where they could not see what was happening below.

A traditional feature was 'le spectacle' for which each of the students' studios competed for a prize, awarded to the most spectacular. The first 'spectacle' in 1954 consisted of a spreadeagled naked girl, painted entirely blue, suspended apparently effortlessly in mid-air. But the studio that had invited the *Merlin* group had nothing prepared for their 'spectacle' and it looked as though the spotlight, when it moved in their direction, would illuminate an empty balcony. On discovering this embarrassing situation, with about ten minutes in hand, Alex announced that his group would put on a spectacle on their behalf, and one that would probably win the prize. This came as news to his friends. His idea was that Jane and he would engage in the act of sexual intercourse - naked - on the balcony while the others, like harem eunuchs, fanned the lovers with sheafs of straw. This was an outrageous idea, and daring, but, carried away by the loud music and the atmosphere of the event, the others readily agreed. Jane sped up the narrow stairs to the balcony. Alex took a preparatory swig from a wine bottle and prepared to join her. Unfortunately, in his haste, he knocked his head against the underside of the balcony and tumbled back down the stairs. He was out cold. Meanwhile, Jane, in the balcony was ready and was calling for him. The spotlight was just veering in their direction ... The tableau it revealed was an enigma which puzzled the audience; the rear-view of a naked woman looking away in expectation, while a single blue figure (Plimpton) languidly fanned her with a single sheaf of straw. No one could quite comprehend the symbolism. The spotlight lingered, and then moved on. When he came round, Alex was furious: 'Why didn't one of you take my place?' he demanded.

Jane left for America on 10th August. Alex moved back to the Hotel Verneuil, and by 5th November had moved to Montparnasse, in a tiny room on rue Campagne Premiere - which runs between the Boulevard Raspail and Boulevard de Montparnasse - at the instigation of Kosta Alexopoulos. They were the same age and had similar views on art and life. Alex was undoubtedly attracted by the criminal element of the Greek's 'hipster' character and his prodigious sexual exploits. They became close friends and Kosta employed his talents constructing a massive bed into Alex's tiny, fifteen-foot cube of a room, in which the bed - taking up half the space - was the centrepiece. Alex described this room as the venue for the 'violation' of Winnie, a 20 stone negress (although 'violation' implies unwillingness on her part which was not, according to friends, the case at all - Winnie is the basis of the giant negro woman on the billboard in *The Rum and the Pelican* short story), and the conception of *Cain's Book*. The bookcase, painted royal blue, was a structure of variable planes built to make reading efficiently possible when horizontal - which position he assumed when stoned. The room was planned along strictly cubist lines. His Underwood Noiseless portable sat on a packing case that served as a table while he sat on the edge of the bed. This was the writing environment for some of his best writing. But he was increasingly confused. He had been corresponding regularly with Betty and his letters are famous for their barbed endings; 'I really think you are very silly to put so many hundreds of miles between us.' As if *she* had been responsible for their break! Then again, ending letters with; 'Are you still beautiful?' or 'I hope you aren't starving.' Soon, she returned to Paris and the hospitality of Madame Lee. Alex began to see her again. He was supposed to pay $100 each month for child maintenance so that the girls could attend a private school in Gagny. But, with Jane gone, this was now beyond his means. Betty obtained a job as a nanny to an American Colonel's children and there was talk of Alex and her spending the summer at the Guggenheim's palazzo in Venice. There was a great deal of ambivalence on both sides. His letters to Jane continued to implore her to return.

Despite Jane's return to America, Alex obtained a decree of divorce in the 2nd Civil Tribunal of Bravos District, State of Chihuaha in Republic of Mexico on 3rd June 1954. There was no logic or design in his peculiar decision to stage the divorce at the Mexican Embassy in Paris. It wasn't cheap and cost £220 of which Alex paid £120 and delayed payment of the rest. Alex wrote to Jane promising that 'the lawyer who wangled the Mexican divorce has now announced that he can get us married by proxy in Mexico at another hideously large fee...' Trocchi would never do anything simply if there was a more complicated way available. He liked to cloak his activities in obscurity and byzantine complexity. He was once reported to have hired a taxi to take him from a cafe on one side of the rue de Reine to a cafe on the other side, just so that he could appear to have arrived from somewhere more important! It was more or less understood that his marriage to Jane had merely been delayed. In fact it was rumoured that they were already married, since he had not bothered to correct someone's congratulations on the event. He wrote thirty-three love letters to Jane from 20th August 1954 to 27th December 1955, some of considerable length, but learnt, indirectly, of her marriage to Gordon Griscom in December 1954. He completely disregarded this to write ('Will your husband read your letters?') and implore her to return. Yet, in December he informed her he was 'fast becoming the bull of Montparnasse. Six possible lays lay on my bed yesterday. The old bull, and one whom I don't want to put out of business is Alexopolous ...' He had taken Kosta's girlfriend, Liane, a beautiful Indo-Chinese girl, whose eyes, he told Jane, were 'as big as eggs - the 12 franc size.' He had also dallied with an American girl called Jane Flanders, who worked for UNESCO and he had 'tried what Johnnie Welsh sometimes takes (heroin). It's wonderful ...' He cooly admitted to Jane that he had 'fucked everything I could lay my hands on ... over Christmas and had learnt that 'the conquest of a new female, especially a beautiful one, was closer to hate than to love ...' This was only one paradox in which Trocchi was involved. Kosta Alex was his friend - so he stole Kosta's girl. He also put him into *School For Wives* as the arch-villain, the 'super-pimp' - under his own name - Alexopoulos. This was friendship.

Meanwhile, Betty had gone back to Spain for an abortion, having become pregnant on the single occasion on which she had, rather foolishly, succumbed to him in rue Campagne Premiere and without any shame he casually told Madame Lee she had gone 'for a dirty weekend' with someone else! He had informed Betty about Jane's marriage to Griscom thus; 'I have just received a telegram from Jane to say that she is married. I had my haircut a few days ago and the weather here is very good ...'

Jane left her husband in Silver Spring, Maryland and visited Paris for one week in January and they were together. In February, Trocchi discovered to his horror that he had gonorrhea, and wrote hoping that she had not been infected. He had lost interest in Liane and his other mistresses. He was increasingly restless, airing plans for extensive travel. He had Jane nearly persuaded to leave her husband entirely and suggested they meet in Laghouat in Algeria: 'I consider it essential that we go for a while right out of Western Civilisation. That is why I have chosen Laghouat.'

This romantic liaison - with Jane - or Betty - (the offer was made separately to both) did not happen. Instead, he went to the annual running of the bulls in Pamplona with another woman; Iris Owens, an American writer. He described this as two weeks of misery, in which he had been 'almost' in love and was rebuffed. He was trying to force himself to be in love so as to forget Jane and break her spell over him. It was a 'nightmare' he said, 'we didn't make love once. You and my writing,' he assured Jane, 'are all I care about.' He spent a fortnight with Sindbad Vail in Venice in August (Betty having declined to come with him!) and on his return, was shocked to hear that Jane and her husband had been in a serious car crash in New Hampshire. Jane had a split liver. Her marriage was already doomed - had been before the crash - and Alex may have had an inkling of this, for he continued to insist that they should meet in Algeria for a 'journey of unspecified time ...'

Betty had somewhat belatedly been taking stock of her situation. She felt she was being manipulated as a sex object. 'One minute he said he loved me and the children and the next he'd say that all that children need is good food and a roof over their heads and that my maternal concern was sentimental rubbish.' His reproachments now included the monstrous charge that she had been responsible for breaking up his relationship with Jane because of her refusal to let him and Jane have custody of the girls - Jane being unable to have children of her own. This was the bitter end and Betty decided to take the girls and join her sister and mother in New Zealand. Alex did not even turn up at the station to see her off. 'Go ... yet stay my flower, I die without you!' he had written in 'Poem For Elizabeth' in the heady student days of their romance in 1946.

Richard Seaver had become co-editor of *Merlin* and his influence grew, since Trocchi was increasingly absorbed with his own writing, his sexual exploits, and, undoubtedly now, the occasional heroin experience. Seaver disagreed with the increasingly didactic tone of Trocchi's editorials; the later editorials, as opposed to the early ones, are much longer - in the case of the Summer-Autumn 1954 issue, extending to nearly five pages, throughout the issue. The absolutism which Trocchi attacked was the splitting of civilisation into 'friend' and 'enemy', for the Iron Curtain had fallen across Europe and the Cold War - like an new Ice Age - had divided the world into armed camps each with the weapons of the apocalypse. The world trembled at the brink, it seemed, of Armageddon itself. He also attacked the moves within America towards totalitarianism, of which Senator MacCarthy was a leader. One of Trocchi's main themes, and a feature of the *Merlin* editorials is that art, and writing which does not constantly question its own validity is merely propping the barricades of cultural partisanship. Trocchi wished opinion expressed in literature to be clearly denoted *as* opinion and not masquerading as scientific fact. In one sentence he spelt out his belief; 'absolute linguistics imprison men within conflicting dogmatisms.' It was a theme that he was to elaborate in later work.

The writers of the *Merlin* group were aware of the political realities and, according to Seaver; could not remain neutral: 'for neutrality was the death of the soul. In the debate between Camus and Sartre that rent the European literary establishment, we clearly sided with the political scrapper over the detached philosopher, the *engagé* over the *non-engagé* We were not just different from our Paris-based elders who had filled the cafes of Montparnasse in the twenties, we were the extreme opposite: pure literature in the sense that a Joyce or Gertrude Stein understood it, experimentation as an end in itself, seemed to us impossible.'

The writers who saw their first work appear under Collection Merlin/Olympia imprints, were later taken up by Calder & Boyars or Peter Davies in London, Grove Press and New Directions in New York and other publishers of the international 'avant-garde'. In particular, the works of Jean Genet, Eugene Ionesco and Samuel Beckett were promoted to the wider world and given credibility and reputation. Ionesco's *The New Tenant* first appeared in English in *Merlin*, and a section of Henry Miller's *Plexus* appeared prior to its first publication, in the magazine. The *Merlin* group was one of the most influential, in literary terms, since their predecessors in Paris, thirty years before. This influence was not understood until years later, the nature of literary movements being that they are almost always retrospective. Trocchi's main contribution apart from his enthusiasm and organisational drive, which kept the magazine together, was his editorial work and his editorials but he allowed some of his own work to go forward in the magazine on occasion, sometimes using the psuedonym 'James Fidler'. Two short stories, *A Meeting* and *The Rum And The Pelican*, first appeared there, and, indeed, the second of these has never been republished. Some short poems also appeared. It is possible that Trocchi wrote other material in the magazine under other psuedonyms and there are several pieces 'under suspicion'. Appreciative testimonials to the value of the magazine were sought and received from Camus, Bertrand Russell, Stephen Spender and Sir Herbert Read: '*Merlin* is alone ... in its pages one can find the best experimental work in the arts that is being done on both sides of the Atlantic ... efficiently edited and well-produced ... it could fulfill a very important role in the cultural life of our time.'

In the middle of the next year, Trocchi found it necessary to write to the Editor of the *Times Literary Supplement* in London:

> 'June 10, 1955 *Dear Sir,*
>
> *I am writing to correct a false impression which arises from the reference to Merlin the Paris Quarterly in the article entitled 'Foreign Origins: Expatriate Writers In Paris' which appeared in the TLS on May 27th. It was stated that: Merlin unpublished for almost a year, is about to begin again, under the editorship of Alex Trocchi, Austryn Wainhouse and Christopher Logue. In the first place we should like to point out that Mr Logue has never been officially connected with Merlin, secondly that the implication that Merlin was in fact defunct and is now beginning again under new direction is quite unwarranted. The necessity for the 'relapse' was seen and prepared for by the editor and his associates last Springwhen a fund-raising campaign was planned. An especially large issue of Merlin was published meanwhile to fill the gap ... the future of the magazine seems secure ... Richard Seaver, my former assistant, is at present absent from Paris; for the time being Merlin is directed by Mr Wainhouse and myself. Mr Seaver will be the third editor on his return. No radical change in editorial policy is meditated, although, naturally, there is an evolution in this kind of thing.'*

Although Trocchi assured the public that the future of the magazine was safe, it was to have less than one year further of existence. Within a year, Trocchi would be in New York and *Merlin* would collapse. *Collection Merlin* also would crumble in his wake, leaving only litigation as one by one the published authors sued Girodias, beginning with Beckett, Miller and Donleavy, (Indeed, Donleavy now owns the Olympia Press). Girodias had obtained his literary material 'on the cheap' thanks to the assistance of the young *Merlin* writers and as with anything obtained cheaply, had not placed due value upon it. Without Alex Trocchi's benevolent presence to impose a check on him, Girodias had begun to adopt some rather sharp business practices with his authors. Girodias wrote in vain, on 22nd March 1956, to Trocchi requesting assistance: 'this fool Beckett ... has decided to sue me ... in order to break the contracts for *Watt* and *Molloy* ... my situation is very difficult ... you are the only person who is in a position to help me, by giving a personal testimonial covering your relations with the various parties ...'

Chapter 7: Trocchi's Erotic Paris Novels

Amid all the confusion, both physical and mental of the Merlin group and his expanding role on the party scene, Trocchi completed a number of novels which Girodias published under the imprint of the Olympia Press. Although most were bestsellers in their original imprint and in their numerous and often pirated US editions in the 1960s they were written quickly and were not intended to be long-term literary projects. Both author and publisher expected them to disappear after a year or two, yet these were the books that gave Trocchi his early reputation among his peers. These 'Paris novels' have been acclaimed as erotic classics and derided as literary pornography and the argument rages to this day on their overall merit or otherwise since new editions have appeared in the late 1990s. Between 1952 and 1955, Trocchi wrote six light novels which he described as *risqué* ... five; *Helen and Desire, The Carnal Days of Helen Seferis, White Thighs, School for Sin* (*Wives*, in some editions), and *Young Adam* - under the psuedonym of 'Frances Lengel' and a sixth, *Thongs* under the psuedonym of 'Carmencita de las Lunas'. He produced other books for the same publisher; a translation of Appollinaire's *Les Onze Mille Vierges* (Eleven Thousand Virgins) and a faked or 'improved' *Vol V of Frank Harris' My Life And Loves*. He also wrote catalogue copy and devised brochures. To a great extent, the early and crucial years of the Olympia Press owed as much to the talent and enthusiasm of Trocchi (then in his mid-twenties) as it did to its remarkable progenitor, Maurice Girodias.

Girodias was the son of the notorious bootlegger Jack Kahane who founded the Obelisk Press and became Henry Miller's first publisher. Because of the continuing problems of censorship twenty years later, together with the fact that he, like Miller, was a foreigner in France, Alexander Trocchi's (or 'Frances Lengel's) original agreement with Maurice Girodias of the Olympia Press was, of necessity, a verbal one. The tortuous story of the Olympia Press, its legal wrangles with the French Government and its own writers (particularly Trocchi) and of Trocchi's crucial role in persuading Girodias to publish the novels of Samuel Beckett, has been told elsewhere.

Trocchi's Olympia novels provide deft entertainment in a deceptively simple literary style. Sometimes, the plots of the novels are manifestly overloaded with Girodias' rigid strictures, but Trocchi was later to write of the first of these works; *Helen and Desire*: 'I can't help being impressed by the lightness of touch which I seemed to have been able to sustain throughout. Never again, with the possible exception of its sequel, *The Carnal Days Of Helen Seferis*, was I able to write so deftly and... if you will pardon the use of the word...so 'innocently' in the genre.'

The book commences with a letter from Major Pierre Javet to his friend Captain Jacques Decouer of the French Garrison at Mascara, Algeria, about a manuscript taken from an Arab prisoner. This manuscript within a manuscript begins...'It is dark where I am lying, in a tent, on a few sheepskins that they have provided for me. They have taken my clothes away from me and have given me the clothes of an Arab woman...' There then follows the story of Helen Smith. Born in a small town in Western Australia, she uses a local man, Tom Snaith to escape from the stultifying boredom and restrictions of life in a small town. The man expects marriage, however Helen has ideas of her own: 'Fortunately, he could not see my face. What a fool he was! The thought of marriage had never crossed my mind...that was my first experience of this kind of idiot male presumption - why do they assume that because we have need of their bodies we will be willing to submit ourselves to the drab pattern of their everyday existence? Such men should be housed in a stable after their toil, and, if it is a woman's pleasure, they should be loaned to her for her occasional enjoyment.' Helen leaves Snaith in a restaurant and catches a train to Sydney. There she meets another man who, in turn, deserts her, stealing her money. She is forced to submit to the advances of the elderly owner of the lodging house when she cannot pay the bill. She becomes involved with a seaman and is eventually abducted and sold into white slavery in North Africa where she becomes the property of one tribe after another.

As the plot unfolds, the reader is taken below the surface of the woman's thoughts, to explore all aspects of dominance and possession and the sexual act itself: 'Once again I have experienced the terrible joy of annihilation, the deliverance of my whole being to the mystery of sensual union, and this time with a male whom I would not recognise in daylight...I rejoice again in my separateness... I am not like those weak women who want to be owned by a man, body and soul...my life is my own...'

Years later, in an Introduction to a 1967 edition of the novel, Jack Hirschman was to comment:

'For a man to write a novel from the point-of-view of a woman is not in fact a novelty. The final pages of *Ulysses* attest to a relative degree of truth in the creation, by Joyce, of Molly Bloom. I don't believe it is an accident that both books possess a serio-comic touch - effected through the interior monologue and stream of consciousness by Joyce and through the technique of the 'found manuscript' by Trocchi. It's as though both writers understood that, to even begin to embody what is after all only an illusion of a woman, special effects were necessary.'

In *Helen and Desire*, Trocchi postulated the idea that individuals live for the negation of aspects of personality, a complete unanimity of body and mind: '...Here is a denial of personality which I have been at such pains to extinguish by my own efforts. Here is a positive and shattering assertion that I am coincident with the pleasure that is to be had between my thighs or at the nipples of my firm breasts. My wildest dreams then are become for these men who handle me as a matter of fact. Dualism is extinguished, mind obliterated by the refusal of these men to notice its existence. I am annihilated.'

Because Helen is treated as an object rather than a being with a sense of thought, she enjoys the vicarious freedom of considering the world with a sense of detachment, from a purely mental plane, unaffected by the activities in which her body indulges or the indignities to which it is subjected. The book chronicles Helen's travels wherever her body takes her, to wherever her body might be taken. Her picaresque journey began in Australia; the end of the Colonial empire. Or rather, in the time-lapse employed by Trocchi, she recalls her beginning as she reclines in the middle east of her destiny. Hirschman believed Trocchi had 'written a paean to woman...convincing in its display of intuition and perception. His prose, as well as the structured 'fragments' of the novel, unfolds like poetry. It is effortless. Excitement takes root in the pleasure of the flow of the words, even, careful, succinct. Nothing is fribbled away; the frantic is reduced to zero; the sensational is rendered null and void, and the imagination thereby honoured.'

The novel was an instant commercial success, indeed, Olympia had advance orders for 2,000 copies of this first edition of 1952. Immediately there was pressure for a sequel and years later, Trocchi was to write:

'When Helen, somewhere out there in the unrecorded time and space of the desert, was finally transformed into the kind of ultimate 'gland' of her sex; when she had finally attained to that voiceless, mystical carnality she hoped she would find in the vibrant extasis of objectivity...impossible notion: a feeling thing! Anyway, by that time, I, her creator, was finished with her. There she was and there for better or for worse she would stay, a desirable thing, in all its substance committed to its thingness... but... Frances Lengel was inundated with demands that her heroine should survive and return to the civilisation about which she had so many cutting things to say. "You must write a sequel!"... I felt, I suppose, as Rider-Haggard would have felt if he had been required to bring She back out of her lost valley into a flat in Belgravia. Various pressures, nevertheless, combined to force my hand, and, as soon as I had resigned myself to the idea of "bringing Helen back", all kinds of ideas came to me.

Obviously, the first problem was to locate her. And, indeed, that would have to be the main theme of the book since, without a great deal of tiresome repetition, I could hardly write an entire book about an endless and all but wordless series of anonymous copulations. This book, therefore, would have to be written from the point of view of the person who was trying to locate her... and so I found myself with my principal character, the king-bee in search of the flower, so to speak, Anthony Harvest. And, as Nadya was still intact... well, alive and well though without shame or chaperone, I should have no difficulty in getting things under weigh once I had engineered a meeting between that lush creature and my man, Harvest. There isn't much more to say. The book is light entertainment. It will either entertain or it will not. And, by the way, if it accomplishes nothing else, at least it may tear one more rent in that tough and superstitious fabric of sexual taboo so eagerly woven by Grannie Grundies, a cloth which has long defied the feeble efforts of reason, but which at length is being assaulted by the natural health of the generations.'

The Carnal Days of Helen Seferis was published several months after *Helen* in early 1954. It can be seen from Trocchi's own thoughts on the first two 'Lengel' novels that, although he was conforming willingly to the restrictions of writing for Girodias' sex-book market – and Girodias had tapped into a very considerable market (sales being almost entirely due to word-of-mouth publicity among the large numbers of ex-patriate American and British ex-soldiers in Paris) he had much larger ambitions for his 'light' novels.

In a letter in October 1952, to Christopher Logue, who was then in Rome, Trocchi announced that *Young Adam* was finished and sent off to London. He was later to claim that he had written it in 10 days, which must be untrue. He had been writing the novel for at least four years, having conceived it in 1948 in the tiny farm-labourer's cottage in Garronhead where he lived with Betty, as an undergraduate. Several earlier unpublished versions of the novel exist. He may have written the final draft in 10 days; that would seem unlikely, though not impossible. Richard Seaver recalls that it took him about six weeks. Publishers had apparently rejected the manuscript and since Trocchi was desperate for money he agreed to 'dirty-up' the novel for Olympia. Girodias was initially wary but it became the third 'Frances Lengel' novel, published in the same year as *The Carnal Days*:

Dear Alex,

When I read the two sections you gave me of the new version of *Young Adam*, I think I have been too much impressed by the quality of the book as a good book, and that has led me to forget the essential element of the problem, I mean the erotic parts.

I have just reread the whole thing rapidly, and I have been quite surprised to notice that the only erotic scenes included in the 2/3rds of the book consist in two very short love-making episodes with Ella, It is quite strange that this did not strike me earlier; I think this comes from the fact that the whole atmosphere of the story is very sensual. But I am afraid that this does not suffice; you know the rule: one scene per chapter, otherwise my clients will raise hell. They are not easily impressed by atmospheres and so on.

I think it is important to finish the book on a sexual crescendo, and make the last section really strong. But it would be wiser to divide the 30 pages which you still have to do to complete the MS as follows: 15 pages for the end; and 3 or 4 sexy scenes to be inserted at more or less regular intervals in the first two thirds. I also think that the two scenes with Ella are a little too short - they fall a little flat, all the more as they happen as a sort of conclusion to a long period of growing expectancy.

Of course, those additions have to be tactful; I wouldn't like the book to be ruined as a good book, and I suppose you wouldn't like that either. But it really does lack something still to make it a good sex book, and you can't put it all in the end.

I hope you won't resent my criticism. I know I should have told you all that before. Anyhow, we can discuss it next time you drop in. If you feel you can't make those additions right away, don't bother; it is much preferable to wait than to waste a good job.

Maurice Girodias.

Young Adam was published shortly after its revised completion. Unfortunately, only days later, Trocchi received a letter from a Boston publisher accepting the novel as originally written, and had to write and advise that the book was no longer available. The book was revised for its American publication under Trocchi's own name by Grove Press (with four stories) as *The Outsiders* in 1960, revised again for its first UK printing in 1961, further revised for the 1963 and 1966 editions, by which time Trocchi pronounced himself finally satisfied with the book. The Olympia version by 'Frances Lengel' in 1954 was vastly different from the book whose most recent UK edition appeared in 1983.

White Thighs appeared in the Olympia Press imprint in 1955 and later the same year from Keimeisha of Tokyo. The theme of the novel is sado-masochism. Once again, there is the quasi-biblical tone, as if the story was intended as a modern parable. The central character is entirely evil, guilty of the crime of murder, yet enjoys complete success throughout the book, as in De Sade's *Justine*. An English boy, brought up with rich relatives in America, Saul comes under the influence of Anna, his Governess - with whom he becomes sexually obsessed. The boy poisons his uncle when an attempt is made to have Anna sent away, and is himself sent to school in England. When he returns to claim his now-deceased Uncles's estate, he discovers Anna is married and promptly murders her husband. Their relationship continues until Saul comes under the power of his muscular female cook. In a dungeon in the basement they persuade the other servants to indulge in sadomasochistic fantasies. Saul soon tires of being dominated by the cook, whose imagination is somewhat limited and murders her also. At the end of the book he meets and becomes engaged to Vivian, a local girl. The reader is left wondering whether Saul will mend his evil ways and on the last page learns that whereas the other women had been essentially insecure, she possesses 'the insane courage of a disillusioned woman of thirty (and contemplated) the possibility of 'dying' to herself in subjecting herself utterly and irrevocably to another's will...'

White Thighs is dominated by dominance itself; it plays about with the idea of the master-slave relationship at the point where people cannot renounce themselves for love. In this, the book is an expression as old as history and as contemporary as the house next door. Kirsten, the woman to whom Saul becomes bound as a slave, is given almost deific proportions, for the hero's need for the pleasure of humiliation is so great that, the smaller and more insignificant he makes himself, the larger must the object of his pleasure loom. Indeed, such a scale is the measure of the book: all the women with whom he becomes involved are very quickly mounted and pedestalled, rendered omnipotent and therefore beyond his ability really to be humanly involved with them. Trocchi is able to sustain that incredible discretion, that tone... of the book's being a sort of common sense. It is a highly enjoyable travesty of the traditional English life involving master and servant.

The next novel, *Thongs*, again explored the themes of cruelty, lust and sado-masochism, set against the background of life in Glasgow's Gorbals in the 1920's. This novel, begun in early 1955, evolved from an earlier attempt to tackle a similar theme. This earlier version, titled *A Dynasty Of Razors* still exists in part. The first 33 pages were accepted in August 1954 by Atlantic Monthly Press, who sent Trocchi $250 as an advance. On 27th June, the following year, he informed his companion Jane Lougee that the money was spent and that he had no intentions of completing the novel. It is interesting to consider the changes subsequently made to this original script, some 80,000 words in length, considerably longer that *Thongs* and with a great many more characters.

Thongs begins with a crucifixion on an arid hillside in Spain. On the night of a full moon in February 1922 a small group of men nailed Gertrude Gault to a wooden cross and did not leave until they had flogged her to death. The novel commences with this stark statement: 'On a cold morning in February 1922 some gypsies moving across country between Madrid and Escorial came upon the naked body of a woman...' The reader is drawn to the corpse from a distance and, like a camera, drawn remorselessly nearer, with the gypsies, to it. Trocchi had written (in an early essay on Bronte's Wuthering Heights) - 'eroticism is, I believe, the approval of life even to the point of death.' This was his starting point for the novel and it involved a high degree of collusion between readers and perpetrators. Each reader would contribute to the enslavement of the victim.

After the horror of the opening page, the book reverts to the Gorbals in 1916, to Gertrude Gault's childhood as youngest daughter of John Gault, the 'Razor King', whose son, Gertrude's older brother, Johnnie, will soon brutally depose him. It is a violent tale of savagery and squalid sex - which never lapses into glorification of violence. The writing is ironic, graphic. Like Zola, Trocchi depicts reality, makes no comment in the passing. Gertrude Gault's initiation into the enjoyment of pain and her career as a 'Pain Mistress', renamed Carmencita de las Lunas (parody, perhaps of the Opus Dei, certainly of Catholic ritual) is described as the story moves to London. Trocchi later stated:

'It is my considered opinion that she not only consented to but demanded this terrible act of them... it was her own deep sense of destiny that drove Gertrude to become Carmencita.... despite the numerous passages of obvious merit it was not as good as it might be because I brought only limited energies to its making as a whole, though in certain phrases I found myself writing as well... as I know how.'

Thongs was by no means the first novel to describe the 'demi-monde' of the Glasgow razor gangs. A. McArthur and H. Kingsley-Long's *No Mean City*, written in 1935, had spawned a genre of razor-gang novels that had long become cliche. The razor-gang milieu in *Thongs* is incidental; merely a symbol of irrational, cultural violence within a broader context or is perhaps parodic of it.

There are significant differences from the earlier, unpublished text in which Gertrude Gault hanged herself from a lamppost, and in which there was no Spanish, or even London section - and no crucifixion. *A Dynasty Of Razors* had been a study of class and cruelty by a much younger Trocchi. He wrote in a synopsis: 'the plot is relatively straightforward. It bristles with violence and sex as does the terrible slum which is the geographical centre of the action.' Trocchi subsequently claimed to have lived on the edge of the Gorbals, although this claim was entirely without foundation. Interestingly, the novel's narrator is Willie Drummond, an intellectual who lives mainly abroad. Trocchi noted at the end of the synopsis that he hoped to have the complete manuscript ready not later that 31 December 1955. During the period between beginning the novel and that date, Trocchi must have decided that the 'victim of circumstances... daughter and sister of violent men, who suffered for their violence and finally, in desperation, hanged herself...' was compelling, for he removed most of the other characters and the narrator. The Glasgow section became compacted and the novel became, not a study of class and Glasgow razor gangs, but a confessional account of Gertrude's 'career' of masochism, and her attempts to become a purer, more complete victim... to move beyond the merely painful into Pain. He adopted yet another psuedonym - 'Carmencita de las Lunas' - for these were 'autobiographical' memoirs. Attempts by several famous film directors to film the novel foundered - as did many other attempts to film his other works. Trocchi himself wrote a film script based on the book but *Thongs* never made it to the cinema screen.

Olympia published an edited version of Vol 5 of *Frank Harris's My Life And Loves* in the same year, more than two-thirds of which was Trocchi's own work, based on the bundle of notes for the fifth volume which Girodias had bought from Harris's widow. This book was to fool the public for a number of years and indeed was regarded as the best example of Harris' work by many literary experts. Trocchi noted his dislike for the character of Harris and later described the work as 'a labour of hate' and confessed that he was 'taking the piss' out of the celebrated Victorian author and bombast.

The fourth 'Lengel' novel published by Girodias in that same year was *School For Sin*. This has been republished under the title

School For Wives in some editions, just as the 5th Volume of the Harris Memoirs was later titled *What Frank Harris Did Not Say,* or *What Frank Harris Did Not Write,* when their inauthenticity was recognised. Similarly, some editions of his novels have required to be retitled to avoid prosecution; *Helen and Desire* once appeared as *Desire and Helen* for example, to fool the censors.

School For Sin is the story of two young Irish country girls, Peggy Flynn and Doreen Connoly (sic) who, after numerous erotic adventures, (for which the convent had ill-prepared them), come into the possession of Mr Alexopoulos' and his rather unusual school, where Miss Durrell the beautiful instructress tells them and her eight other young girls 'it is not enough simply to be available' prior to a course of instruction in erotic techniques. Mr Alexopoulos, (and Trocchi used the name of his artist/sculptor friend without alteration as a 'revenge' for their rivalry over the sexual conquest of an Indo-Chinese girl called Lianne) is later revealed as one of a number of 'super-pimps' in a worldwide organisation run by the mafia. Alexopoulos is apparently drowned at the end - though with scope for a resurrection should a sequel be required - and both Peggy and Doreen get their men, Peggy a millionaire and Doreen a dashing detective. Hirschman stated in his 1967 Introduction that 'there is no-one in the English language who can handle such (sexual) scenes with greater realistic control.' Trocchi several times considered rewriting the novel, but by its re-issue in 1967, felt that it 'had gone dead on me,' and never did. The novel undoubtedly had its origins in real life sexual activities which Trocchi helped to organise, inspired perhaps by Pauline Reage's *The Story Of O.* But emotional instability and mental exhaustion convinced him that he must leave Paris and *School For Sin* was to be the last 'Lengel' novel. He departed for New York with a suitcase full of notes for *Cain's Book,* leaving behind the increasingly popular 'Lengel' persona, ignoring demands for new works in the genre.

Erotic or pornographic? A pornographer is someone whose depiction of sexual activity stimuates erotic rather than aesthetic feelings. Trocchi's Paris novels stimulate both erotic and literary sensitivities within a seamless narrative, unfortunately the title pornographer to which he clearly aspired at that time in order to *epatèr les bourgeois* has conceived a pejorative colouring more to do with debased, life-depressing commercial smut than the exhuberant and subtle excitement of Trocchi's sensual fiction.

It was not surprising that in 1964 Trocchi's name should appear on the cover of the first issue of *Penthouse*. He was listed as a supporter of *Playboy* too when that appeared. Both magazines emanated from the cultural 'underground' and, at the time, represented a kind of freedom of expression. Both were intended to be creative and imaginative and less exploitative than they actually became. In fact, Trocchi had not even been consulted about his name being on the *Penthouse* cover and as he later explained, did not complain so as not to give succour to the forces of moral indignation. He would certainly not support the degrading and repugnant gynaecological excesses of today's hardcore pornography.

Trocchi's Paris novels are clearly in the erotic tradition in literature in the company of such fellow-travellers as Aristophanes, Petronius, Boccaccio, Huysmans, Kleist, Appollinaire, DH Lawrence, Henry Miller and many others.

Alfredo Trocchi with Alf and Jack's mother-in-law outside Swiss Cafe,
Douglas, Isle of Man, 1955.
(Courtesy: Jack Robertson)

Chapter 8: London Interlude

The publication of the Paris erotic novels, albeit under pseudonyms, had given Trocchi a notoriety amongst the literary circles that congregated in and around Gaïte Frogé's English Bookshop at 42 rue de Seine. He had developed into the writer tipped by Richard Seaver as 'the most talented and prepossessing writer on the scene, the one, who, had a straw poll been taken, would have been voted most likely to become our generation's Joyce or Hemingway or - more likely - Orwell. Compared to Trocchi, who was only a year or two older than most of us, we were babes in the wood, fumbling towards knowledge or the hope of knowledge. He on the contrary was sure of himself, and his writing reflected it.'

However, in private, he was far from sure of himself. His reckless experimentations in sex and drugs had left him confused, bruised, out of touch with reality. He had immersed himself into a new group of young French men, a 'closed society, a clandestine group, which was to be my whole world.' This was the Lettrist International and Alex had joined after meetings with Guy Debord and Michèle Bernstein in early 1955. He was also, according to Debord, 'an active, founding situationist'. The Situationist International (SI) wished to effect a radical change in society and fervently denounced the better-known movement known as 'Existentialism' with which why they are often confused. Under the influence of this new direction and heavy drug use, Alex began to change his outlook. By the autumn of 1955, his letters to his brother and to Jane had become bilious tracts: 'I reject the entire system ... the answer is *revolution*. Not in the objective, idealistic sense, but there in the heart of every man ... a new attitude ... the Revolution has already taken place in me. I am outside your world and am no longer governed by your laws ...'

After five years in Paris, spiralling inflation and the Algerian War had made the metropolis less attractive and there were fears too about the Vietnam crisis and the threat of possible conscription. He had 'spent most of that last year in a small room in Montparnasse (rue Campagne Premiere) going from it to play pinball or to distract myself with a woman. This room has three sides and one large studio window which looked out over the projecting roofs of basement studios onto a high grey wall which cut off all views of the sky.' After the claustrophobic intellectualism of the S.I. (although Trocchi did not resign from the SI until Autumn 1964) he desperately needed to widen his horizons and to travel further afield. He did some travelling with a group of friends including Midhou; to Luxembourg and Holland in April, Spain in July, Genoa, Venice, Yugoslavia, Athens in October and November, before returning to Paris briefly.

It is interesting to compare the actions and nature of the wife/ex wife character (Moira) in *Cain's Book*, which he was already writing at this time, and speculate whether this was an accurate portrait of Betty, or indeed of Jane. The truth is more that it is a portrait of both of them, a composite - at times, one, at times, the other. He claimed to love them but had antagonised them both. Now he had persuaded himself that it was Jane whom he really loved, perhaps because she was out of reach. Jane was living in New York, where she was married to another man. In his confused state, he decided that he must pursue her. On 8th June 1955, a small package arrived at Jane's apartment in Greenwich Village, addressed to Mrs J. Griscom. It was the Indian turquoise ring from the Quai St Michel.

He was not in a good state of mind and friends describe him as 'disorganised on several levels' believing that his energy had been sapped by the work he had put into his d.b's. He was a man who had rejected almost everything, who struggled to escape 'the terrible modern negative of which Beckett is the most refined symptom, for it eats away not only one's art ...' He had even 'theoretically contemplated suicide.' Christopher Logue worried that there would be too much temptation in New York 'for anybody who is not internally strong. And believe me, Alex 'aint right now...'

he wrote to Jane Lougee, days before leaving Paris with Alex for London.

Before leaving Paris, Alex signed a contract with the Broadway-based William Morris agency, to cover all his works for three years, but this did not include those works already published or accepted for publication, which Girodias was entitled to reprint. He envisaged *Cain's Book* as the first of many works which would appear under the imprint of major publishing houses. He did not go directly from Paris to New York. He had, as he put it, 'hesitated' in London for some time:

'The bright and crowded days of my first long stay in Paris had come to an end. Suddenly it was as though I had nothing anymore, no wife, no love, no *Merlin*, not one shared certainty; I was alone and ... out of Paris ... unknown; and I came to and went from London like an invisible man. At the tail end of 1955 when I quit Paris after the decision to cease publishing the magazine I was still ... except amongst a few literati ... unknown. No complete work had appeared under my own name anywhere. *Young Adam*, written in 1952, had been rejected by virtually every publisher in England, and the manuscript was growing daily yellower in the drawer of a publisher in New York. I had written what I knew to be the first of a new genre of book in the English language and with the help of a few excellent friends I had for four years been editing the most discerning literary review in what I was beginnning to think of as the same goddamn tongue: would I have to follow my friend, Beckett's example, and take to writing in French? I kicked about London for a few weeks, was best man at the wedding of two of my friends, tried unsuccessfully to fall in love with a well-known actress, and for the rest fluttered like a moth against a glass or iron curtain of polite disbelief ...'

He arrived in London on 22nd December and actually stayed for some four months. The 'well-known actress' would hardly have been Jane Fonda, who, although in Paris, and peripherally involved in *The Paris Review*, was then virtually unknown, but may have been Ellen Adler (daughter of Stella), who was by repute the most beautiful woman in Paris at the time. He was, indeed, best man at the wedding of John and Sue Marquand in the Chelsea Registry Office. The wedding reception was held at Ken and Elaine Tynan's house in Mount Street, Hampstead. Trocchi was rather sceptical of Tynan - 'I don't like people who are more far out than I am!' he later confided to friends. The Marquands had been living in a flat at Cadogan Square, Chelsea and the cream of the London set were at the reception; Kingsley Amis, Iris Owens, St John Osborne, Charlie Sinclair, Mordechai Richler, Elias Canetti, Henry Green, Lady St Just (a former girlfriend of Tennessee Williams' - and the model for Blanche Du Bois in *A Streetcar Named Desire*). Other members of this set included Marcus Klein (whom Alex had met in Paris and was later to be Trocchi's partner in his Rare Books business in the Seventies), Michael Sayers, Kitty Epstein, 'grand old' Sir Matthew Smith and Ray Cortends. Cortends, like many of the set had lived for a while in Paris where he had obtained a room near the Pantheon from an old lady, rentfree, on condition that he spent some of the day winding yarn onto a spindle. Every morning this old lady would deposit a bowl of porridge outside his door and collect the previous day's yarn! Terry Southern would later write; 'these are sophisticated circles, Alex, and more than once I heard the fervent hope expressed that Grace Kelly's child would be some kind of pitch-black monstrosity.'

Trocchi stayed with various friends and began an affair with a woman called Janet, a schoolteacher in North Africa who was home on long leave. The affair ended and Janet had to have an abortion at St Mary's Hospital in Paddington. He saw a lot of his brother Jack who was working in London and living in Clifton Place. While living in a flat nearby in Chepstow Villas, he worked on several drafts of a screenplay for *Young Adam*, and the shooting script's margin is marked 'Film Geneve' - presumably an art-house film company interested in filming the book. Various other pieces of writing from the period ended up in *Cain's Book*. An extract, revised as a short story 'Dying', for example, although another, a five page piece, concerning his picking up a girl in a cinema and taking her to a French cafe in Soho, was discarded. He had a few friends in London, but really he was just marking time. On the 20th of April, he took vaccinations at St Pancras Hospital, and embarked on the steamship at Portsmouth, a harbour he remembered from his navy days.

Chapter 9: The Life of Cain

Alexander Trocchi was admitted to the United States of America as an immigrant on 30th April 1956 and paid the $2 landing fee to disembark at New York Harbour. His passport lists his occupation as 'writer' although he had published little under his own name. Among the scanty possessions in his single suitcase, 'taking up a disproportionate amount of space,' was a large envelope containing a mass of scribbled notes and loose typed pages which were, in time, to develop into his masterpiece; *Cain's Book*. Although the story of a junkie in New York, he had started the book *before* his arrival in America. Equally, he was well acquainted with heroin prior to crossing the Atlantic - but not yet an addict.

Jane was waiting for him when the ship docked at the harbour at Manhattan island. Her signature was required on his entry visa. They had a joyful reunion and returned to her apartment at West 11th Street in Greenwich Village. It was clear from the start that things would not continue as before; although Jane's marriage to Griscom had ended in December 1955, and she had left him (he was to die in 1956), she was now involved with film-maker Al Avakian; it seemed clear that her somewhat tortuous love affair was Trocchi was over. She allowed him to stay at her apartment for several weeks. She was working during the day at Brentano's Bookstore.

Through the small number of people aware of his literary reputation, Alex had *entrée* to the literary/bohemian circles of New York and quickly set about acquiring a network of friends. The *Paris Review* had, coincidentally, moved to New York, and now had an office in a ramshackle railroad loft in East 82nd Street. The magazine was publishing an extract of *Cain's Book*; an extract which

Alex on the scows, Hudson River, New York, 1957
(Courtesy: Jane Lougee Bryant)

included the line; 'Give me that spike quick or I'll slit your fucking throat,' which, when read by the US Customs censor almost led to the impounding of the issue. Luckily, the editors were forewarned and the magazine was spirited away from the warehouse before the marshalls arrived. The issue was held up for some time, but eventually cleared by order from Washington. Meanwhile, Trocchi availed himself of free accomodation in the *Review* office, in an alcove sectioned off by a discreetly hung burlap sack. Very quickly, however, he stumbled upon a 'live-in' job that suited him perfectly - a job moreover that underlined his position as an 'outsider', and did not commit him to anything, did not compromise his status - or his time.

Perhaps it was some romantic notion or other that led him in the first place to seek work as a scow captain with the NY Trap Rock Corporation. Scows are long, flat, barges with a tiny cabin at the front, and these were used widely throughout the waterways around Manhattan Island for a great variety of cargoes, chiefly building materials. The docks on the Hudson and East Rivers were virtually the same as when Budd Schulberg had portrayed them in *On The Waterfront*. Trocchi discovered that the man in charge of recruiting scow captains was a Scot, known, predictably, as 'Scottie' and so, when he went to see this man, passably imitated a dour Calvinist Glaswegian, implicity reliable, with 'experience in small craft' - which was not strictly true, but he did have navy training. He got the job. Later, he would fix-up his friends with jobs on the scows; ('tell the man you have experience with small craft...') among them Mel Sabre and Mason Hoffenberg, both heroin users.

He was experimenting heavily with drugs. One night he allowed a friend who was an experimental chemist to add something that he believed would potentiate the heroin. Unfortunately, this incompetent measured the dose of his 'little catalyst' (which Trocchi thought might have been scopolamine) in milligrams instead of micrograms, and Trocchi 'went out like a light.'

'My body, embarrassing object that it was, was carried here and there about Manhattan until finally I woke up in an uptown hospital. Fortunately, my friend, Eric Bick, the chemist, hadn't abandoned me, and just as I came to he entered wearing a black homburg and carrying a little black bag. He had been careful to empty my pockets of all identification before he left my body where it would be found and had followed at a distance when it was finally taken by ambulance to the hospital. Now, posing as a Doctor, he informed the intern that I was a member of a well-known family and had escaped from his custody. He had a very authoritative manner and his mutterings about 'scandal' carried the day (or the night) and he was able to usher me swiftly past a bored group of police and newspaper men and hospital staff, through the exit into a waiting taxi. And thank God for that.'

There were numerous other dangerous escapades. The New York State legislature had just passed a law offering the electric chair to persons convicted of supplying drugs to minors and the attitude of the press and public on the subject of drugs was one of hysterical over-reaction, given that the number of addicts in the US was only a few hundred. Trocchi stashed his heroin in an airtight jar, suspended below the scow in the water.

The worst sin of the drug-takers was perceived to be that their habit was 'downright un-American.' Coupled with this, most of the junkies were young, hip and dressed outrageously. Some of the most-un-American had beards. The music they listened to was loud discordant bop jazz and they read all the most obscene and far-out literature, most of it written by foreigners. Now that the McCarthy-ites had sorted out the reds they had the drug-pushers and dope-fiends right at the head of their hit-list; the new bogey-men, the faceless terror that stalked every back-lot in America. Because of this reactionary pressure, many young people rebelled and there was a swelling of the counter-culture. Some of the original hipsters from Paris were themselves now living in New York. The term 'hipster' was coined to explain this young rebel who lived for kicks. The hipster bible, Kerouac's *On The Road* had just been published, closely followed by *The Dharma Bums*. Nowhere were the hipsters more prevalent than Greenwich village and the Manhattan docks, where their monosyllabic hero, leather-jacketed Brando had defied the mob in *On The Waterfront*.

The job on the scows - which was only available because of a Union rule - afforded Trocchi a large amount of free time. It was the perfect situation for a writer, and he got paid about one hundred dollars per week for it. All he and the other scow-men had to do was accept a rope from a tug. They would be towed up the Hudson where the scow would be filled with stone and then towed back into New York. 'We were regarded as the lowest form of animal life on the waterfront. It was a job for no-goods and all kinds of vagabonds ... the men who unloaded the stone would be smartly dressed in blue shirts, they'd be tanned and look beautifully clean - the American crane driver is a real engineer. The scow captains were regarded as the rats of the waterfront.'

Sometimes at weekends the scows would be towed up to one of the little yacht basins along Long Island Sound. The hipster scowmen would take on booze, dope, food and women for the trip, and, while everyone else was in the city working, they would 'lounge around in the yacht harbours, sunbathing, writing, drinking beer, screwing, shooting up junk, or smoking marijuana. The loaders and unloaders would look incredulous at the chicks in hot pants hopping in and out of the cabin doors of the dirty old scowmen.' It could be very boring though, out in the harbour for long periods, often a month at a time, and in winter it could be as lonely as lighthouse service. What made it worse was the proximity of downtown Manhattan, whose brilliant galaxy of lights was tantalisingly near but unreachable, until a tender came out to take you in to shore. This view of the metropolis from the margins accorded with the 'outsider' stance that Trocchi had adopted. He was an outsider also - by choice - because of his drug-use. An emigrant with few possessions, he had removed himself from his cultural roots. Nor did he fit in to any writers' club, for he had rejected 'literature' and literary 'product'. His heightened awareness of these distances, his self-imposed isolation from materialist America in one of its most materialistic periods, gave Trocchi the detachment he needed to complete his masterpiece.

The winter of 1956/7 in New York was cold and there were heavy falls of snow. He received a letter from Terry Southern in early December. Southern and his wife Carol had moved to Geneva, and Carol had become a teacher at the UN Nursery School. A 'large number of Alex' old friends in Paris have been asking after him, including any number of young ladies.' Terry recounts stories of the frolics at the Bonaparte, the Cameleon jazz-club and the Taboo 'in that order of the evening to morning,' recounting that 'before the waiter arrived with Pernods for Carol, Charlie Sinclair, Midhou (an Arab painter and dope dealer who had travelled with Trocchi the year before to Greece), Mason and myself - the pompous heathen (Mr Hadj, owner of the Hotel De Ville) grabbed the check, before raising his own glass in a hearty toast, 'A l'Ecosse!' people at nearby tables taking it up, Wainhouse, Vail, Debord, Iris, etc, 'A l'Ecosse!' and others too, whether these last in a true recognition, or in some simple desire to be a part of things, none can say, though the fact does remain that for more than a full moment on this crowded Saturday night shouts roared up from the Cafe Bonaparte, resounding in the peaceful square, causing smart heads to turn on the terrace of the Deux Magots and, perhaps, even at the altar of God itself across the way, 'A l'Ecosse! A l'Ecosse!'

The correspondence that now began between Southern in Geneva and Trocchi in New York is wildly extravagant, crude in places, mordantly amusing in others. It was a correspondence written between close associates, but one which was possibly to be published, indeed in a later letter, Southern advises Trocchi to 'tone down' his letters and use fewer classical allusions and more four-letter words. Girodias, who is 'keen to do it ... is going to pay us plenty, a thou a page and more perhaps ... '

Alex' closest friends at the time were Mel Sabre, who had lived in Paris and had a heroin habit, John Welsh, a black American who had deserted during the war, whom he had also known in Paris (also a serious heroin user), and David Burnett, a writer, who was to edit collections of short stories and work with Trocchi and Seaver on several projects. Alex received a letter from Girodias early in the new year, which referred to a clamp-down by the French

Government. Twenty-five Olympia books had been banned by the French authorities and this applied also to export copies. Thus he was hardly in a position to pay Alex what he was owed, though he hoped to have *Young Adam* published in French.

Terry Southern wrote back denying that the story of 'L'Ecosse!' at the Bonaparte was made up. 'If I'd of made it up, I'd of had Beckett and Girodias there as well.' Later in the letter, Southern alludes to Trocchi's boast of his night murdering of cats and dogs and asks for the details, and also refers to another matter: 'You also say that you 'killed a *man* as I understand it, a train conductor. I assume this is not actually true, but is your idea of a 'joke' and I find myself a little dubious as to its taste ... '

In the hedonistic world of the Cedar Bar, the White Horse Tavern and the other watering holes of the Village 'scene', Trocchi was a familiar figure. His life had become almost predictable in its irregularity. He wanted to break out of the restrictions of his existence. Thus his claim that he had murdered the train conductor - in the opinion of this author completely fraudulent - was an attempt to shock. It was also the period when he experimented with homosexuality. There are two such episodes of sex with men in *Cain's Book* and undoubtedly he did have an experience of the kind. Later he was to pretend to an ambivalence, an omnisexuality, which, in the opinion of all who knew him, he patently did not have. Nevertheless, he was desperate to break new ground, wanted to leave no convention unflouted. He seduced Mel Sabre's wife, Dorothy, who had a wooden leg, and she began to live with him in his scow, becoming the prototype for 'Jacqueline' in his book. 'His wife had attracted me from the beginning. It came over me gradually that she was beautiful ...' It is not known what Mel Sabre thought of this arrangement, but the affair was short-lived. At another time, he lived with David Burnett in an apartment in Bank Street in the Village, a familiar-sounding address for the ex-Hillhead pupil! And this was his base for some outrageous sexual exploits. But this was tame stuff and Alex was increasingly restless. He roamed around the city on his shore leave, writing and living for several days at a time in the apartments of friends. He used Jane's flat often to write in during the day, although she, like many other close friends, were beginning to find his increasing drug-habit and his nomadic lifestyle inconvenient, and baffling. He wrote to Jack in January, his first letter to his brother since his arrival in America: "Groping in the dark, adopting extreme attitudes, using the most dangerous drugs, it has been for the most part a period of extreme alienation. I have touched bottom in my own private hell ... I have been Cortez, Don Juan, Hitler, Christ, Rimbaud, Narcissus, Onan - to the verge of suicide and now at the end of all the anguish and the ecstasy I feel I am ready to be a man ... I have never come nearer to self-destruction ...'

Lyn Trocchi: Miss Hicks from Hicksville, 1959
(Courtesy: Jane Lougee Bryant)

Chapter 10: Miss Hicks From Hicksville

Marilyn Rose HIicks was a beautiful twenty-one year old from Indiana, with brown-blonde hair and blue eyes. Marilyn, or Lyn, as she preferred to be called, worked in an office on 42nd Street as executive secretary for an advertising and marketing weekly called *Printer's Ink*. She had an apartment on West 15th Street, on the fringes of the Village. Photographs generally show her with short hair in a pageboy style. She had a tendency to be melancholy, vague and rather dreamy. She preferred black clothes, usually tight jeans and sweaters. Her parents lived at the time in Hicksville, New York State, thus she was Miss Hicks from Hicksville, the epitomé of a wholesome young lady from a respectable and conventional background. She had been educated at Smith Ladies' College, and her parents were hopeful that she would meet an eligible young man. Alex Trocchi, then thirty-two years old and a heroin addict was as far removed from their ideal of a prospective son-in-law as it was possible to conceive.

Lyn and Alex met at a literary party in the Village. Alex was already a star in the New York literary scene, charming everyone within earshot, as he had done in Paris, except that there was more than a hint of notoriety about him now, whispers of his amoral past and his Paris days of hedonism. He was immediately attracted to Lyn, as most men would be. She had a poetic soulfulness, a vulnerability, about her, and was not a brainless bimbo. She had read a great deal of poetry, even some of Trocchi's writing - in the *Paris Review*. The relationship continued casually for a time, Alex even taking her around to Jane's flat to show her off. Jane was not impressed. ' A showgirl' she thought, 'with a rather obvious glamour.'

In April 1957, Alex had completed *The Sacred Grove*, a long poem for 10 illustrations, which was never accepted for publication and remains unpublished, indeed, the manuscript appears to have been lost during the travels - and frequent changes of address - of the next few years. He gave up the job on the scows and planned to spend the summer travelling with Lyn. Firstly, he visited Jane to see if she would change her mind and come with him - instead of Lyn. When she refused, his mind was made up for him.

He acquired a flashy American car - a coupé, into which they loaded their bags and set off across country in beautiful summer weather. They drove down through Virginia, Kentucky, Tennessee and Texas into Mexico. It was almost a reprise of the journey through the South of France six years earlier with Betty in the monstrous Talbot, but this trip was a great success and, intoxicated by the heat and fun they were having, Alex filed a divorce action from his wife at the Officina Del Registro Civil, in Cuidad Juarez, just across the Rio Grande from El Paso. In the Mexican border town of Tijuana, on 13th August 1957, a few days later, Alex and Lyn got married, with two hired Mexican witnesses, in a 'quickie' ceremony. It was another bizarre joke. A Mexican marriage to follow *two* Mexican divorces, albeit that one of the divorces was in the Mexican Embassy in Paris. They drove down through Mexico to a small town on the shores of Lake Chapala near Guadalajara where they stayed for some months - long enough for Alex to pronounce on the quality of the mescalin and peyote. Then they travelled north into California, living for a time near the Mojave Desert. It was here that Alex, finding a plentiful supply of driftwood close at hand, began accentuating the tortuous curves and shapes in the driftwood and painting them with what could be described as 'Aztec' lines and designs in primary colours. The results, visually stunning and exciting also in a tactile sense, he called 'feelies' and later 'futiques'. The Trocchis then moved to the coast where they took an apartment in Venice West, Los Angeles, just a few hundred yards from the beach and settled in for the winter.

Chapter 11: From Venice West to Las Vegas

Partly due to the pleasant climate and the easy living, the Californian seaboard has always attracted painters and writers and quickly became one of the main centres of the Beat Generation. The hipster had given way to the new 'movement' - a new name coined by Jack Kerouac, and while the beats were descended from hipsters, this new movement had adopted the *mores* of French existentialism. Ginsberg and Kerouac were the leaders of this nomadic tribe which commuted between Berkeley, Denver and Columbia Universities with occasional sojourns into Mexico. The epicentre was the seedy waterside suburb of Venice West, between Santa Monica and Los Angeles airport, where Pacific rollers break upon the long sandy beaches and palm trees sway in a breeze which disipates the heat and the smog of the connurbation. It is pleasant, if rather hemmed-in by the urban sprawl.

While many of the beat writers and artists were very young, with all the exuberances and naiveties of youth, Alex Trocchi, at this time, thirty-two years old, had a lengthy literary apprenticeship behind him and a dozen books. He had a degree, had survived one marriage and was into his second, had fathered two daughters. He had a cult reputation among his peers as one of four founders of the Situationist International. If any single person could be said to have founded the beat community at Venice West, that person would be Trocchi. All the important beats (the term was coined to mean 'those striking a beatitude') stayed at one time or other in the community, early residents included Ginsberg, Kerouac, Gregory Corso, Gary Snyder, Philip Whalen, Herbert Huncke, Neal Cassady and Michael McClure. It was in Trocchi's apartment, on the second floor (apartment 5), at 51 Brooks that McClure's

Meat Science Essays and Ginsberg's *Kaddish* were written. Ginsberg described Trocchi at the time as 'the most brilliant man I've met, another Neal Cassady...'

The beats experimented with drugs, did action paintings, some, like Wallace Berman, distributed 'found' objects, circumventing dealers and agents. Beats studied religions - especially those from the 'mystic' east, and fantasised about the lives of red Indians; i.e. Kerouac's *Big Sur* and *Poems of Holy Madness* by Ray Bremser. They were romantics, dada-ists, symbolists, surrealists, oriental mystics, cosmonauts of inner space, existentialists, anti-academics, nomads - and they were none of these things. Essentially, they were mixed-up middle-class American college students who wanted to get out of the rut, to escape from the collective guilt of the Korean War and the H-Bomb - who wanted something to believe in, something to belong to, something to live for. Such quintessential figures as Jim Morrison and Ken Kesey knew Trocchi at this period, and were, to some extent, influenced by him and spent time with him.

The rent was a mere $26 per month for the three rooms. The building was dangerously ramshackle and infested with cockroaches. The house no longer exists; it was pulled down long ago for reasons of public safety, but stood on the ocean-side of the junction of Main Street/Electric Avenue and Brooks. A piece of cardboard from a shirt box was tacked onto the door, with the legend 'Musee Imaginaire' written in large black Gothic script upon it. What went on behind that door is described in a chapter of Irving Rosenthal's spoof biography *Sheeper* (1967). Inside 'Trocchi's Pad' a large number of people are engaged in frenetic activity, the rooms are a market place, everybody talking double time, talking drugs and trading drugs by auction. A toothless painter, cackling quietly to himself, works furiously on an easel, on which is stretched, not a canvas, but a ladies summer coat. The apartment is carpeted with drawings and manuscripts. Astrological signs, animals, Greek and Hebrew letters are painted on all the walls. A bed, dismantled, and an old fashioned fridge-freezer have been conscripted for culture, and with chairs, lampstands and drawers, now resemble discarded items from a theatre props room. 'Everything functional had been drafted into the service of art, taken apart and reassembled, and many things looked subjected to more than one transformation, as if the lust to create had been so overpowering as to become cannibalistic, or as if each object of art, once created, became as stupid as a lamp or bookend, and had to be destroyed and built anew.' The inmates of this chaotic world took frequent fixes, watched others fix, argued and fought amongst themselves. Paranoias of police raids swept the apartment - the blinds were lifted and eyes peered out to look for cops - to be replaced by new paranoias. Everyone was talking, creating, destroying, recreating, arguing, and in the midst of it all, undeniably in command of activities was Alex Trocchi, large and genial, orchestrating the creativity and the disbursement of heroin. It was an astonishing insight into the 'creative chaos' of Trocchi's life. But Rosenthal was there by appointment. Ginsberg had sent him with an introduction, and he was in awe of the proceedings: 'The play of truth and moral beauty in that apartment was like lights, and Trocchi's Scotch burr scratched my heart, and for months I judged everything I saw and did as inadequate and cowardly compared to what went on in Trocchi's pad ... I used the honesty I gleaned at Trocchi's pad, there among rats and amphetamine heads, as a model for my own life as an artist.'

But the romantic picture of carefree creativity had a sordid side. Lyn had not managed to obtain work as a barmaid and they could neither afford to get a California driving licence nor to get the flat tyre fixed. Money had become an acute problem for the Trocchis. Whether it was Lyn or Alex who initially suggested an easy way to acquire some, they moved, in April 1958, to Las Vegas, whose famous casinos were doing business on a scale rivalled only by the girls who walked under the streetlights on Las Vegas Boulevard - 'The Strip'. Lyn had already noted in her diary her private thoughts about prostituting herself. It seemed an easy answer to their money problems. She wanted to be useful, to come up with a practical solution that would please Alex. Outside Caesar's Palace, the Flamingo Hilton, the Silver Slipper and the Stardust Hotel, rows of gleaming American blondes raked in the money as fast as their one-armed metal counterparts inside. Lyn Trocchi joined their ranks and briefly became a hooker.

Las Vegas resembles nothing so much as a frontier town grown rich, with neon lights flashing out in the desert night. Lyn lingered inside a casino called the Sands, but no-one tried to pick her up and she found herself quite unable to give anyone the eye. She bought a pair of high-heeled shoes and discovered, in her motel room, that they were both for the left foot. At other times, she danced in a sleazy night-club wearing silver spangles the size of half-dollar pieces gummed to her nipples and black satin stretched over a tiny piece of cardboard at her crotch. Her piece of cardboard was shaped like 'spades', and there were three other dancers; hearts, diamonds and clubs. Each carried a poodle which had been dyed pink as part of their dance routine. She got the job due to the fact that she could wear size 7½ shoes - the only pair available - and it paid $120 per week, minus twenty for rent. She was supposed to live on the premises, but managed to spend most nights with Alex, who was staying at the El Tovar Motor Court over on 5th Street, where he spent most of the time lying on the bed in a junk haze. The casinos and the nightclub were open twenty-four hours a day. Nothing ever closed. Alex loved Lyn and trusted her. He had her on a leash. She would always come back to him. She debased herself for him willingly. Like the plot of some Olympia Press novel, this morally repugnant scenario dispels any other explanation than the stereotypical junkie pimping his woman for junk. And Lyn was pregnant at the time. Later, Lyn confided that because she was beautiful, her 'Johns' would often simply sit and talk to her, and she would not have to do anything except listen. She had become pregnant before their arrival in Los Angeles, and soon it began to show. The baby was due in October and they decided to return to New York, where they had friends and where Lyn's parents were. Their year and a half on the West Coast had not been productive from a literary point of view. He had written nothing. A short letter to Terry Southern, dated August 20, from Jane Lougee's apartment at 333 West 11th Street, New York, announces their arrival. Alex notes in that letter that he hoped to become a registered drug addict, with a guaranteed supply of heroin substitute. Southern's reply, enclosing a copy of his first 'serious' novel *Flash and Filigree* (published by Andre Deutsch) which Alex had praised, congratulates him on his marriage and impending child and asks for the truth or otherwise of a story which Girodias was telling, that the child, regardless of gender, was to be called 'Cain'. Southern had looked up Samuel Beckett and had been well received; 'he is a grand old man and most fond of you. You ought to write to him from time to time, as he expressed great interest in how you are getting on ...' He also informed Trocchi of a large number of requests which Girodias had received for signed photographs of Frances Lengel ...

Chapter 12: Hard Times In Hoboken

One of the first events which the Trocchis attended upon their return to New York was the wedding of Jane and Baird Bryant at City Hall on Broadway. Alex was the best man and had to scrabble a suit. Then the Trocchi's had to find accomodation. They moved to a loft in West 23rd Street, between 6th and 7th Avenue. 'We inherited it from Johnny Welsh and Al Avakian when they split up, (it was) a superb big place which could have been palatial if we'd had some money to spend on it. Even as it was with some of our own artefacts it was quite impressive. The only thing: it took a helluva lot of heating in winter. And it was November. Late November and the beginning of a very cold winter such as New Yorkers from time to time experience ...' On a very cold night, Alex took the subway to the Bronx to the flat of their 'connection', Wolfie, a Puerto Rican heroin dealer. It was a long, boring, miserable and highly dangerous trip. He had a premonition of disaster - proved correct - for, notwithstanding the cold, miserable weather, the ever-vigilant New York Police Department had Wolfie's 'pad' under surveillance and raided the apartment shortly after Trocchi arrived. They were all frog-marched to the elevator and arraigned in the Bronx, at Concourse Boulevard. When Alex did not return, several hours later, Lyn phoned George Plimpton who contacted the Police, found where Alex was being held, picked Lyn up and drove to the precinct to bail him out. Luckily, Trocchi was somehow able to prove that he was simply an innocent visitor to the apartment and did not have any drugs on his person. He was not charged. It was a narrow escape.

Practical realities were now crowding in upon the Trocchis with the necessity of providing for their forthcoming child, and a new apartment was found, the cheapest possible, in Newark Street, Hoboken, New Jersey:

'The room had a bulging, uneven floor covered by a frayed red carpet, and everything in it, from the wobbly chair with one wooden arm missing and crinkly black stuff protruding from a gaping tear in the seat, to the three-legged, pale blue chest of drawers whose top was littered with hairpins, spilled powder, old bottles and innumerable spent matches, had a sad, seedy, dilapidated look. When the gas fire went out, the air in the room became cold, stale and clammy.'

A telephone was installed on 18th September, and on 2nd October, Lyn was taken to New York Hospital in East 70th Street, Manhattan, and early the next day, was delivered of a boy, whom they christened Mark Alexander. Jane Bryant was named as the baby's Godmother. There appears to have been some disagreement over the name, for later, Lyn was to attempt to amend the birth certificate to read 'Marcus' and not 'Mark'. It could have been worse – Cain! On 13th April 1959, six-month old Marcus was taken to the Hoboken Baby Welfare Center for a Diptheria vaccination. But domestic life was far from blissful as Alex was later to write:

'Lyn was slim then, in an old pair of jeans with a baby tucked under an arm. She looks marvellous in the photo, the sort of girl anyone would envy, a Goddess in blue jeans ... but she was a hateful mother and ... didn't love the child for some time. She does now. The picture that comes to her mind when she contemplates suicide daily is her watching him (Marc) neatly folding and placing his clothes on the bed. Two shoes with the socks in, concentrating, tongue protruding - in a children's home - after her demise.'

There was also 'the bug war.' Lyn, now also a heroin addict, became obsessed with quite mythical 'bugs' that crawled upon her skin and sat for hours obssessively picking at them. Needless to say she soon became a mass of scabs and there are considerable passages among Alex's papers which describe the growth of this obsession. Alex later claimed that he had gone to the lengths of buying a microscope to prove to her (and to himself) that these bugs did not exist.

The necessities of supporting the family - his second - drove Alex to take some rather unwise literary decisions. He was in no position to turn down work or book contracts, and subsequent legal entanglements date from this period in New York when he was struggling to earn money and of course trying to satisfy his drug habit. He had written an essay on George Orwell, published in the *Evergreen Review* the previous year. The essay refutes Orwell's assertion that where he lacked political purpose, he had written lifeless books. According to Trocchi, no estimate of Orwell's work could be further from the truth.

'His purpose was seldom so much political as humanitarian (or moral) and where he tried to make it so, as in Road To Wigan Pier (1937), the result is an unsuccessful medley of firsthand description, time-staled statistics and naive political exhortation ... for all his polemical brilliance Orwell was not a profound thinker. There is something 'occasional' about most of his writing, it is riddled with contradictions ... he was too concerned with sociological currents - he never concerned himself that everything is filtered through the prism of self and stopped short of total revolt against all abstractions with which society traps, labels and affixes status to the individual, preferring instead to concern himself with 'socio-economic vectors','class-oppression' and all the other abstractions of the 'socially-conscious' ... thus, he is of little interest for those of us who come after him, but then,one gets the feeling in spite of his constant references to politics that he was fundamentally unpolitical, that if he hadn't lived when ... it was fashionable to be 'socially-conscious', the superb, poetical element ... present in all his work would have made him one of our models.'

This concise and deeply felt essay subsequently became a popular crib for Literature students in America. Trocchi had mainly good things to say about Orwell and believes that his support of Henry Miller, whom he had met briefly in Spain, (referred to in *Inside The Whale* (1940) - and his claim that good novels are written by people (like Miller) who are not 'frightened', was accurate.

He reviewed *The Other Alexander* by Margaret Liberski and *The Devil In The Hills* by Cesare Pavese at some length in the magazine *Nugget*, and took on the task of translating the massive (1,000 page) French novel *La Gana*, by Jean Douassot. He was later to state that this was one of the best modern novels he had read and took on the task out of admiration, although it was known that he practically rewrote the book, working at the fast pace of about twenty pages a day. *La Gana*, according to a handwritten note in the Trocchi archive, is 'the uncompromising and imaginative account of the life of a caretaker family in the basement of a block of flats in a declining middle-class Paris suburb, seen through the eyes of a 12 year-old boy ... it's shocking and gentle and really a fine piece of work.' Unfortunately, due to the size of the task, the book was to remain un-finished until 1974. Nor was this the only book he was working on. Despite the failure of publishers to recognise the brilliance of *Young Adam*, he was engaged in negotiations with Castle Books of New York for the publication of a revised edition of the novel with some short stories in a 'portmanteau' edition, under the title of *The Outsider*. He was writing obsessively, changing and enlarging the scope of *Cain's Book*, and signed a contract with Grove Press of New York on 26th March 1959, receiving an advance of $550 with a further $200 to come on publication. The publishers' deadline was 30th June, the novel was scheduled to appear firstly in hardback and then in a paperback edition. Grove Press inserted a clause giving them options to publish either or both of his next two novels. Trocchi's co-editor at *Merlin*, Richard Seaver who had returned to America in 1957, was now his editor at Grove Press, overseeing the publication of the novel which they had discussed in Paris together.

The long poem, *The Sacred Grove*, written the previous year, had been inspired by his researches into ancient Greek mythology, and his highly literary mind, fond of hoaxes and japes, as he had already demonstrated with his fifth volume of the Frank Harris Memoirs, (firmly accepted as authentic in literary and academic circles), now conceived a further project with which to hoodwink the 'Aunty Grundies' of the establishment. The legend of the Poettess Sappho who lived between BC 620-570 provided ample opportunity for his creative skill. Relatively little was known of Sappho and only one twentieth of her poetry had survived. Her themes were intensely personal; her sexual affairs with men and women on the island of Lesbos. An aristocratic lady absorbed with the pursuit of physical beauty, entirely disinterested in politics, she used the hot climate and the fierce gales of Lesbos as symbols of her own violent passions. The distinction of her poetry rests in its total freedom from sexual shame or guilt; one of its most attractive features as far as Alex Trocchi was concerned.

He obtained the few surviving prose poems, some of which are mere fragments, and added to these, contriving entirely new events and affairs in the style, producing a sort of poetic memoir of her life. He did not admit to writing these himself of course, and the book was to be marketed as 'an amorous odyssey', *The Autobiography of a Strange Woman*, translated from the mediaeval Latin with Alexander Trocchi as its Editor. In the foreword, Trocchi referred to the 'most unsatisfactory history of the book from a scholarly point of view,' and describes how;

> 'A few years ago a manuscript in Latin was discovered in the town of Soller, Mallorca, in the Balearic Islands. An old gentleman, a one-time scholar of Latin, made a rough translation from which the present work has been prepared. The original manuscript was mailed in Italy to an address in the United States by the translator just before his death. It never arrived at its destination. Considering the dates involved, it is interesting to speculate whether the missing manuscript (if we can believe that it actually existed) does not at the moment lie at the bottom of the Atlantic Ocean, somewhere within the barnacle-encrusted hull of the much lamented Andrea Doria ... in presenting this prepared version of what purports to be the authentic autobiography of Sappho of Lesbos, the present publishers make no historical

claims watsoever. In their view, the doubtful authenticity of the work - the fact that the original was in a mediaevalised Latin and not in Greek of the Aeolian dialect - does not in the least detract from the extraordinary sensuousness of the poetry ...'

The volume was destined to become one of his most popular works, publishers exploiting its sensuality and lesbian aspects. The volume has been kept continuously in print, its book jackets draped with semi-naked blonde models, dressed like Victorian prostitutes although nude photographs of Lyn were taken for the cover of this first edition of *Sappho of Lesbos*. The original Sappho was small, dark, not very good-looking and possibly even crippled. Unfortunately, Castle Books became fearful of litigation under the obscenity laws after the book was printed and most of the edition was destined to gather dust in their warehouse. In 1971 Tandem Books published it in Britain. Had it appeared as intended in 1960 it may have succeeded as the highly successful worldwide literary hoax which Trocchi had intended.

Castle Books employed Alex on a week-to-week basis, paying $100 per week, for which he had to do rewrites of other authors' manuscripts, for Castle Books were 'pirate' publishers, one step ahead of the law. The contract for *Sappho* was irregular and neither Alex' nor his estate seem to have ever received royalties from any of the numerous UK and US editions which appeared and continue to appear. In the meantime however, Trocchi noticed that Castle Books had printed a 'pirate' version of *Helen and Desire* with the title merely changed to *Angela* and the name of the author to 'Jean Blanche'! A row developed, during the course of which he discovered two other 'Jean Blanche' novels in $2.50 hardback editions; *Return of Angela* and *Seed of Desire* which were his own *Carnal Days of Helen Seferis* and *Young Adam* retitled. It was barefaced theft! Alex felt that he had to protect the *Helen and Desire* title in particular so that a proper American edition of the novel could be sold later. He had hopes that Grove Press might handle that deal and did not want to ruin it by letting Castle Books bring the book out, even in a retitled form, so he offered to adopt their psuedonym of 'Jean Blanche' and rewrite *Angela* (*Helen and Desire*), to create a novel which would be in reality a different property. This would not be unfair competition for a later American Olympia edition of *Helen*. In return for this, Trocchi was given $400 to surrender his rights to the edition of the three books, and given a promise that they would not be re-issued. Thus, there were *two* contracts for *Angela* - the first, in which Trocchi disclaimed all rights to the renamed *Helen and Desire/Angela* by 'Jean Blanche', and the second, in which Trocchi, using the psuedonym 'Jean Blanche' had actually rewritten *Helen and Desire* as *Angela* for a cash fee of $400 ... Castle Books seem to have had an unenviable reputation for sharp practice, but many of Trocchi's dealings with publishers have been unfortunate. Almost every contract he ever signed worked out to his disadvantage, and there were many instances where there were no actual contracts signed at all. Publishers took advantage of his 'illness' - daring him - almost blackmailing him - to complain publicly. In later years, Alex was to attempt to persuade publishers to do book deals face to face in verbal agreements - in desperate attempts to get better treatment.

With his usual dynamic charm, he befriended Frederick Fell, a publisher with a reputation as a purveyor of rather lowly fourth-rate material, chiefly the 'self-help' type of book. Trocchi somehow persuaded Fell to declare himself for literature and got two projects accepted. The first was the excellent translation by Dick Seaver of an account of the evil experiments carried out by *SS Obersturmbanfuhrer Mengele* at Auschwitz. An extract had appeared in *Merlin* but a large number of publishers had rejected the manuscript as being too depressing. Trocchi also obtained a contract for a collection of modern fiction; *Beyond The Beat*, later retitled *Writer's Revolt*. Alex, Dick Seaver and Terry Southern co-edited the book, whose aim was to break down the 'beatnik' tag with which many writers were being labelled. It was to be an anthology of modern fiction from America and Europe which transcended the narrowness of the categorisation process. It included a large section of Ginsberg's *Howl* and Burroughs' then unpublished *Naked Lunch* plus work by Genet, Hesse, Baudelaire and Artaud. The book was a great success.

Chapter 13: Literary Outlaw

Thousands of miles away in New Zealand, Betty Trocchi, unaware that Alex had remarried two years before, and was now the father of a son, had raised an action for divorce in the Supreme Court of New Zealand at Wellington, alleging at least three years separation and desertion. She needed a British decree of divorce for legal purposes and claimed that the verbal agreement in 1952 and the written agreement in Paris on 3rd June 1954, showed the irretrievable breakdown of the marriage. After a hard struggle to make ends meet, Betty was working as a Child Welfare Officer and later became the Secretary of a charity organisation.

The action was undefended - hardly surprisingly, as Trocchi was unaware of it - and granted, being served on Alex at Newark Street, Hoboken, together with a bill for costs. The legal niceties were not acknowledged by Alex until 1961.

He was leading an irregular, dangerous and sordid life. Some of the worst aspects of his personality had begun to surface. Reading of the death of John Marquand's famous father - which made the front page of the *New York Times* - and believing that Marquand must have come into money, Trocchi contacted him with the 'old pals' routine. On being assured that John and Sue had no money, he persuaded, bullied or cajoled them into selling all their furniture and giving him the money - which promptly went into his veins and not, as they had imagined, towards paying his rent. Plimpton, Matthiesson and other friends were harrassed in a similar way. He would threaten that he would have to put Lyn 'on the street' if they could not come up with money. They often did. 'Humility is not enough, John,' he would say, as he mercilessly played upon their decency, their middle-class guilt, their frendship and their sheer good nature. Lyn undoubtedly *was* put 'on the street' on a number of occasions. When Marquand paid money direct to their landlord, Trocchi was furious. 'Like, do you not trust me, John?' he would say, or 'why don't you just turn me in to the cops and be done with it?'

The American authorities, responding to a massive increase in the number of drug addicts, imposed the death penalty for anyone found guilty of trafficking in drugs. The media, happy to have found new scapegoats whose lurid activities helped them to sell more papers whipped up hysteria. One novel about the addict in America was Nelson Algren's powerful *The Man With The Golden Arm* later made into a film starring Frank Sinatra in a 'straight' role which won him considerable critical acclaim as the addict, Frankie 'Machine' Majcinek. This had appeared from Doubleday & Co in 1949, four years before *Junkie* by William Lee, the psuedonym of William S. Burroughs. In 1959, Burroughs published his *Naked Lunch*, which, with the Algren novel and Trocchi's own *Cain's Book* are the greatest novels ever written about heroin addiction. Unlike Algren, who was never an addict, Burroughs was, or had been at various times, and his researches were eventually to lead to his close association with Alex Trocchi.

The publication of *Cain's Book* was announced on 25th April 1960 but circumstances were too far gone for him to be able to take advantage of this long-awaited event, and in fact, he did not even attend the launch party at West 11th Street. Grove's first edition was a hardback one, with a cover price of $3.95 but was rapidly printed in paperback in their Evergreen series. It began to sell well. The reviews were extremely good. The paperback edition was able to carry the endorsement of Norman Mailer: 'It is true, it has art, it is brave. I would not be surprised if it is still talked about in twenty years ...' Later, the first UK hardback edition would carry fulsome praise from Samuel Beckett.

A useful device which Trocchi used on the New York streets to escape detection during his drug-buying trips was a 'portable pulpit' of the kind used by religious orators. If there was any sign of the police, he would unclip the wooden pulpit which he carried by a shoulder-strap, and, flourishing a Bible, would commence a fiery sermon, masquerading as a latter-day John Knox, with traces of a good Scots burr in his oratory. Trocchi must have enjoyed the irony of impersonating the narrow-minded 'Holy Willie' Calvinist of small-town Scotland which his entire literary career had fulminated against! For here, on the streets of Manhattan he was the Very Reverend Bowleggeds of Grundy. It is not known if he made any converts and despite these elaborate precautions, Trocchi got into further trouble with the police authorities and spent several periods in 'The Tombs' - the New York Police Cells:

> 'I ran foul of the law all the time and it was an insane position ... I was arrested and thrown into the Tombs again and again. It's very uncomfortable, especially on the floor where they keep junkies. You're climbing over each other like monkeys in a tiny little space and herded in there with all those sick and half-sick people who don't have the drug. It's rather amusing actually, how little pain there is in that day, the floor and the prison ...'

On another occasion, when their flat was raided, Lyn boasted to friends of her success in hiding the drugs; she had hidden her syringe inside a baby's turd, floating in the toilet bowl. Trocchi also boasted to friends that he had 'cooled-out of a bust' by having Lyn 'make-it with the fuzz' in the back of a police car. Was this bravado? They were living dangerous, reckless lives in St Mark's Place, in the Lower East Side, a notorious drug area. One day their Puerto Rican neighbours saw young Mark staggering about, covered in what appeared to be blood, and thinking that the Trocchis had done terrible deeds - which they were quite prepared to believe - they called the police and the Welfare Department. It was soon discovered that the 'blood' was red paint. The Trocchi's had been doing some action painting and Mark had participated enthusiastically. The disappointed Welfare Officers had had to leave empty-handed. The child did not have an easy time. He would see all these men and women 'on the nod' sitting on the steps who would not or could not play with him. They just sat and stared at nothing, didn't even smile or speak to him. They had none of the normal human responses.

In April 1961, the crisis came. It had been long delayed. Alex was charged with supplying drugs to a minor. It was a charge that could be made to stick. What actually happened was that a prescription with his name on it was found in the possession of a sixteen-year-old girl. Trocchi had not known that she was only sixteen, nevertheless, under New York State legislation, it was the electric chair for him, if proved guilty and the evidence - that little piece of paper - was overwhelming. He couldn't talk his way out of this. Sitting in the cell, lower A9, on the 10th floor of the Tombs, Trocchi used the only pieces of paper he had on him, his Health card, a letter about Mark's vaccinations, and a letter from a friend relating to the review of *Cain's Book* in the *Herald Tribune*, plus their respective envelopes to make into a little booklet, on which, with a very blunt pencil, he scrawled the story of his arrest:

'... all sounds are metal sounds and male voices, ON YER FEET! The ironic part of it; this time (again) I am not guilty. I simply walked over to George's on Stanton Street on Tuesday to borrow a quarter for a telephone call and bus fare, was there 10 or 15 minutes, when, opening the door to go about my legitimate business, I was pushed back into the apartment by two gunmen, one black, one white (Irish red bastard), detectives from the precinct on Delancey Street. In the apartment they found a large jar of amphetamine belonging to - claimed by George. Gaston, Karen, a double bass and myself, junkie by his marks - thus presumed guilty of congregating for an illegal porpoise. Nothing I could say etc. No assurances - And the lousiest part of all I was unable to contact Lyn in our hideout for fear of jeopardising her so I don't know after three days if she knows what's happened to me. Perhaps she thinks, my poor lovely darling, that I walked out on her. Told my lawyer last night where to find her. He may have done so - So with Lyn presently out of the picture I have been virtually deserted. Dear Barney (Barney Rossett, owner of Grove Press), my publisher, concerned only for 'literature' (and am not I an unproductive one?) and not for the justice or injustice of my incarceration has, according to my lawyer, washed his hands of me! May his hands remain as rich as they are now - goddam blast his measly soul! Dick Seaver, *mon editeur et ancien ami est alli (allons?) a Paris* - God bless him. Lyn, Lyn, Marilyn, in prison out, in prison in, I shall always love you!'

Once again, George Plimpton came to the rescue. Poor George, whose father was an eminent Wall Street lawyer and UN Ambassador, had to put up the enormous bail of $5,000. He had no option; Trocchi would have made him feel guilty for the rest of his life if he hadn't. Plimpton wasn't naive - he was - is - simply a gentleman through and through. It was against his nature to let a friend down. Thus was the bail money found. Trocchi subsequently described the impossibility of his making even the slightest move now without the police jumping on him. He was being watched night and day and believed that the State would be quite happy to make an example of him. Unfortunately, he was an addict - hooked - and there were certain demands that simply *had* - even on danger of death - to be met ... His life expectancy was very short. With his need for regular supplies and his wide circle of friends, it was only be a matter of time before he, and they, were all in the hottest seat in the land. Trocchi had no time for writing. His life was on the line. He had a point to make. So, in the face of this terrible danger to his life, what did he do? He appeared on nationwide American television, on an NBC programme discussing drugs, and *gave himself a fix, live in front of the cameras* ostensibly for demonstration purposes! It was simply too much. He was Public Enemy Number One. It was he who became the one known and hated face of the erstwhile faceless terror that haunted the hearts of every decent American Mom and Pop. He was the maggot inside the American Apple Pie.

Relations with his parents-in-law were at an all-time low. Initially he had persuaded John and Sue Marquand and George Plimpton to come with him to Hicksville in the hope that Morris and Betty, Lyn's parents could be persuaded that Alex was really a decent sort. The Hicks did not understand Trocchi nor did they understand what their nice daughter could see in him. Now they were battling to break-up the marriage and to persuade Lyn and Mark to leave him to his fate.

Alex, Lyn and Mark made a fateful trip to Hicksville by train. On the way back, after several hours without fixing, Alex and Lyn attempted to take advantage of their semi-rural location. Believing that none of the locals would know exactly what they were doing, they began to fix on the station platform while waiting for their train. Unfortunately, FBI men, who had trailed them from New York, were observing them. Just as the train was arriving at the station, the Feds made their move. Too late, the Trocchis saw them approaching. Lyn was holding young Mark and could not run. But fear of the death sentence lent wings to Alex's feet and he caught the moving train as it pulled away for New York City. He looked back in horror to see his wife and child being hustled away.

Somehow, Alex evaded capture at Grand Central Station and reached the safety of the Phoenix Bookstore on Cornelia Street, a favourite meeting place for all the writers of the day. A friend from his days in Mexico, Ned Polsky came over to offer support. Diane Di Prima was working there at the time:

'I can't remember whether he called Larry Wallrich (the owner), or whether he just appeared at the bookstore, but I do recall very clearly that he was suddenly quite present, and ensconced in the back of the store (where we had a single bed, some cooking facilities, and - in the hall - a 'john') for several days. I was actively engaged in making calls from the store - with Larry's consent and on his time, bless him! - to raise money to help him leave, and in making jaunts to various spots to pick up whatever people were willing to give. I don't specifically remember collecting from Norman Mailer, but that seems quite likely, as Norman was part of the Cedar Bar 'scene', and one of the more successful writers in our little world.

People also came by to bring Alex dope, and although I considered myself quite sophisticated, I was quite shocked at the sight of him, stripped to the waist, looking over his torso for a vein that was sound enough to shoot into. I also remember bringing him food, from the restaurants nearby.

Alex was quite distraught, and upset about a woman he'd been with, who, as I recall the story - incoherent even then - had been busted. He was upset about leaving her behind, and in jail ...

He was, at any rate around the store for at least two or three days while we got money, and ticket, and whatnot, and then he left ...'

Ned Polsky, who had been buttonholed by Alex's lawyer, relayed the message that he had to show up for the trial but that his chances of avoiding conviction were slim if not non-existent. It seems that there were other charges pending involving forged prescriptions for demerol. Trocchi decided flight was the only option. Jane and Baird visited the store and Trocchi was given Baird's passport. Before he made his escape, he called at George Plimpton's apartment on East 72nd Street. This was taking a risk and Plimpton was not in. Alex got into the apartment however, and dressed himself in Plimpton's clothes. Plimpton, a man of some sartorial elegance, was famed for his Brooks Brothers' suits, and Trocchi, feeling no doubt that it was the least George could do for him, wore not one, but *two* of these expensive suits; one on top of the other. After all Baird Bryant was a deal heavier than he was, and a man with two suits on is less likely to have his wrists examined for needle-marks ... He also 'borrowed' a suitcase and some other essentials. Then he set off for the Port Authority bus terminal on West 40th Street, a twenty-five minute walk.

It had been decided that taking the bus on the shortest route for the Canadian border, and Montreal, was too risky and so he had a ticket for Niagara Falls - a long, 12 hour, journey, and, posing as an American tourist on a holiday visit, managed to sleep for some of the time. It was an anxious time for him - if caught, he would almost certainly face the electric chair - he had no defence now that he was in hot flight, it was a confession of guilt. Meanwhile the New York Police Department had put out an A.P.B. for him, and the FBI had relayed his identikit picture on the wire service to all the border checkpoints. His chances of escape, even with his friend's passport were not good.

Trocchi woke in the early hours of the next morning - or was awoken - by the rough hand of an American customs officer shaking him. They were at the border at Niagara Falls, almost within sight of the Horseshoe Falls and Canada. It was a tense moment. They were asking him his name and perhaps they had already seen his likeness on the wire service from New York under the name of Trocchi: fugitive from justice; arrest on sight. Such was Trocchi's fright that the name he was supposed to use had escaped his memory - then he had it: 'W. Baird Bryant' he muttered. The customs officer was instantly suspicious. 'What do you mean - W. Baird Bryant? What does the W stand for?' 'And oh,' Trocchi recalled later, 'just for a minute I couldn't remember. Suddenly out of the blue God gave me the name. It was Wenzel.' And he eased the tension when he added 'And if you were called Wenzel you'd say W. Baird Bryant.'

From Niagara Falls, Trocchi took a bus to Montreal. He had escaped from danger, or as he later put it; '... I had spirited myself across the Canadian border a few hours ahead of Anslinger's Athletic, or Hoover's heavies.' Without a supply of heroin, and since he had been unable, for obvious reasons to take any with him on the bus, he was already experiencing acute withdrawal symptoms. And of course, his wife and child were still in New York - in jail - and a source of apprehension. Would the police give Lyn a hard time to find out his whereabouts? All of his papers, manuscripts and books were back there with her. He was a fugitive in every sense of the term. A *real* outsider!

At Montreal the then young, virtually unknown poet, Leonard Cohen, met him at the Voyageur terminus. Montreal was to be rather a blur to him, though he was to describe Cohen as his 'guide and good friend during four nervous days waiting for a steamer.' Cohen had been deputed to meet him and bring him back to his flat in Mountain Street. As soon as they got into the apartment,

Trocchi produced a chunk of opium and began to dissolve it in water in a pot. He shot up with the solution and offered Cohen a lick, then they went out to a Chinese restaurant on St Catherine. Cohen suddenly went blind in the middle of the traffic and collapsed. Despite this, the poet and song-writer was in awe of the writer's fervour and intensity and also 'his madness, his bent for destruction... as a messianic figure.' He later wrote two poems about Trocchi and delivered his oft-quoted remark that Trocchi was 'the contemporary Christ.' As for Trocchi himself, he was not looking forward to the next stage of his journey back to Scotland, ten years after he had left to go to Paris.

Chapter 14: *Young Adam*; Comparisons with Chekhov

THE voyage across the Atlantic around the northern tip of Scotland to Aberdeen took thirteen days. Thirteen interminable days of increasing anguish - of 'cold turkey' - only partially alleviated by copious draughts of Demerol. He had accumulated enough Demerol to fill a small hip flask; 'enough to kill a number of elephants.' Consequently, he was aware of little on the voyage and spent most of the time flat out on his bunk in steerage. He was running out on his wife, his son, his friends, his sources of income, leaving behind his books, his papers and notes - everything. Lyn and Marcus were in jail. His situation was a nightmare and every second's churning of the propeller screws was taking him further away from any prospect of doing anything about it. He wanted oblivion from the mental anguish of thinking about it.

On arrival in cold, wet, misty Aberdeen, he took a train to Glasgow. He was met at the railway station by Don Cumming, a schoolfriend whom he hadn't seen for years. A few minutes later, Trocchi excused himself and went into Boots, the chemist, before returning with Cumming to his home in Pollokshields. Don's wife cooked steaks and Trocchi disappeared to the toilet for an inordinate period of time. 'What's taking him so long?' asked Cumming's aunt. Don explained that Trocchi was a drug-addict. 'Poor devil,' the aunt commiserated. After the meal, Don showed Alex around the garden. 'It's great to be back in Britain,' Trocchi enthused. 'Like, here, you can get drugs just by going into a chemists and asking for them!' Later, when Don asked Alex if he'd like a whisky, he declined: 'No, old man, I'd rather have a fix,' which he proceeded, there and then, to take. There was not going to be the same police pressure on him in Britain, which did not yet have a drug problem, nor a noticeable number of addicts. A few days later, he travelled to the Isle of Man to stay with Alf and his wife, Marion, and their three children, Alan, Norma and Penny. Alf's restaurant, the Swiss Cafe in Queen's Promenade in Douglas was busy in the summer months and he now had several other cafes on the island.

Alex needed money to bring Lyn and Marcus over to the UK. He began a letter-writing campaign to influential friends in New York to enlist their help on Lyn's behalf. He wrote to the editor of *The Village Voice* from Paris, where he went to visit friends. Lyn had been imprisoned because she was unable to meet bail of $2500 for a charge of forging prescriptions to obtain narcotics. Alex felt they were victimising her because he had escaped but Lyn was released several weeks later and moved to her parents' new home in Stamford, Connecticut.

There was a lengthy period before he began to receive correspondence from America. As well as negotiations about foreign editions of *Cain's Book*, Alex was involved in protracted correspondence about a *Young Adam* film, from which he was hoping to get a $10,000 advance plus 5% of the box office takings. There was even talk of a prior TV production in America.

Trocchi travelled direct from France to the Isle of Man and intended to remain there for the next couple of months. He signed contracts for the first UK printing of *Young Adam* with Heinemann before his departure. And now, at last, there was to be a British edition. The edition was a greatly revised version of the volume which had appeared under the Olympia imprint in 1954. He had restored many of the passages that he had had to 'dirty-up' for Girodias. Unfortunately, Heinemann were to give him the 'first-novel' treatment, unaware of the good reviews which *Cain's Book* had received in the USA, indeed, they seemed entirely unaware of *Cain's Book* - or chose to ignore it. They were certainly unaware of a long article in the *New York Herald Tribune* in which Trocchi had been compared favourably to Chekhov. As Trocchi was later to write, sadly; 'Years ago, I should have thought that such a comparison in such a place would mean a Rolls-Bentley (at least), four mistresses all six feet tall with rose-petals grafted on the insides of their thighs, etc, Helas!'

For many, *Young Adam* is Trocchi's most accessible novel. While *Cain's Book* attacked the basic structure of a novel and masqueraded in part as autobiography, documentary, or manifesto, *Young Adam* was the first of a new type of novel, albeit one which derived some of its solipsistic structure from Simenon but recognisable *as* a novel. It, too, attracted fulsome praise from critics. The *Glasgow Herald* found it 'a novel of unusually compelling quality and revelatory vividness'. 'Compelling', 'Very subtle', 'A masterly achievement', 'extraordinary writing', 'has power ... and flashing insights into human motives', 'an unconventional masterpiece' were some of the comments reproduced on the cover of a later edition. Trocchi was compared to Simenon and more often to Camus. Critics detected a similarity between the main protagonist, Joe (whose surname, originally Henfield, later Taylor, was dropped altogether from the Heinemann edition), and Mersault in Camus' novel *L'Etranger*. Both characters/personae share a lack of basic social responsibility, and their 'outsider' perspective. Mersault is an outsider as a Frenchman, a northern European amid the Mediterranean culture of Algeria, Trocchi's character is an exile *within* his native land. Trocchi disliked the Scotland he saw for its introverted parochialism and wished to change it. It has been suggested that he never came to terms with his Scottishness but he did - on his own terms. He was proud of being a Scot, and never denied it, or pretended to be anything else. In a sense, he never left Scotland, he merely took it with him around the world. He came to feel that he was not merely a Scot, he was the *only* Scot with a true sense of the value of Scottishness. His theme of being an exile within was an important direction for fiction.

Both *L'Etranger* and *Young Adam* reveal a deep sense of the powerlessness of individuals in society. Few critics remarked the strong links with the writing of Samuel Beckett. There are 'clues' throughout the book, which owes something in structure to *Molloy* - indeed, it is almost as if the character of 'Molloy' himself is seen at one stage, in the sighting of a tramp in the distance, and the noting that this was 'a connection somewhere with someone. Something vaguely familiar ... ' reading the passage which follows this, Beckett scholars could be in no doubt that this is a private joke of Trocchi's, a planting of flags. Personal identity and social responsibility are the prime subjects of the novel. Its 'hero' is entirely alienated from what he sees as the spiritual sickness of a second-rate and parochial backwater. The Forth-Clyde canal, where the action of the novel takes place, cuts through the centre of Scotland, and its use as a metaphor is deeply symbolic. It is a murder novel, a thriller, but although there is a woman's body and a man is sentenced to hang for the crime of murder; there has been no murder and the man condemned to hang, the eponymous Daniel Goon, had never met the victim. The novel does not follow any chronological pattern, does not begin at the beginning, and does not, in a sense, have any definable ending; the last words being 'and the disintegration was already taking place.' There is no attempt to focus on what, precisely, is disintegrating. In technical terms, this is a post-Joycean novel, a work conscious of the widened horizons of literature. As one reads, one is aware that there is more going on than can be gleaned from the first reading, and which afterwards lingers in the mind.

Trocchi had reasons to feel aggrieved, despite the success of the novel, in all but commercial terms (the sales were only moderate), when he was requested to change the ending of the film script so that the 'hero' or narrator got caught. 'What you are asking me to do is to turn a great film into a 'B' feature ... but I got $350 more than I got from you from some poor little amateurs who wanted to do *Cain's Book*, cutting nothing of the message ... don't fuck about with me any more ... ' He accuses the film producer, Don Getz of wasting four months during which time he had let Heinemann bring out *Young Adam* in their 'soundproofed edition,' without effecting any sort of tie up with the film. 'Quit stalling, Don! HOW MUCH MONEY?'

Lyn had been released on two years' probation and Alex was relieved, considering the charges, that she had escaped a jail sentence. He hoped that they could be together by early October and asked her to begin collecting their possessions together from the various friends' homes where they were deposited. He wrote to his Betty a few days later at last acknowledging the legal writ served on him by the New Zealand court for failure to pay maintenance;

'... my finances are non-existent. Betty, when you went to New Zealand you went in the full knowledge that I couldn't undertake to send you money out there. At that time you once again refused to share my life with me ... I would have to get a job. I will always wonder how you expected me to take myself less seriously than, say, Gauguin, whose purples and greens used to excite you so much. You changed, my dear, not I. I couldn't beg you to stay in Paris with me ...'

He had decided, years after the fact, that the *real* reason for the break-up of their marriage had been her intolerance of his writing. As we have seen, that is untrue. But it suited his purposes because he didn't want to send her any money. His financial situation, as ever, was desperate. He travelled to London in early September and visited Bertram Rota's bookshop in Covent Garden. While other writers make money from their published work, Alex was reduced to selling off his manuscripts and letters for cash. He even managed to sell one of his own watercolours for £50, and returning to the Isle of Man, he received £15 from the Olympia Press. He was to complain bitterly about payment in such small and infrequent amounts. Possibly it was Girodias' method of assuring Alex that despite rumours to the contrary, Olympia was still very small, very poor. Olympia in fact was virtually bankrupt. Instead of using the large profit which he had made from *Lolita* which had won its legal battle with the US Customs, Girodias had thrown his money into an ill-fated nightclub venture, 'La Grande Severine' in Paris. The French authorities had begun to harrass him. He was to appear in numerous court cases and be ultimately forced to leave France.

Alex returned to Glasgow and obtained accommodation at West Princes Street. He was annoyed too about the disappearance of his own personal library. 'I had about £2,000 of books when I first set out on my travels about 11 years ago. I left them with an old schoolfriend in Scotland, (Cecil Strachan) one of the finest small private libraries I have ever seen. I visited him a couple of months ago and he denied ever having had it. It seemed to me at the time to be as incredible as a man walking down the street carrying a five hundred pound anchor without being aware of it ...' He was so taken aback about losing all his books that he wrote to Betty complaining about Cecil Strachan. He never did discover what had happened to the books.

He wrote from Glasgow to Don Getz on 14th October; 'Here I am in Scotland whose narrow cultural world I should be bestriding like a collossus as the poet said; on the contrary, rather seedy looking and desperately short of cash ... I sit day after day in a half-furnished room waiting, and turning on, and waiting ... I'm pretty despondent about the film ... I don't know if it has fallen through ... '

Frederick Fell, no longer under the spell of Alex's charm, had decided to sue him - for some reason unknown - and had managed to block all his American royalties. This was a major harassment because Fell's company, New American Library were handling the rights to *The Outsider* - which included the sale of *Young Adam* to Pan Books, who produced a second British issue in 1963. Trocchi's problem was that 'monies are going to go for me from England to N.A.L. in America where they will be blocked and, who knows? seized and Fell upon. Did you hear my scream? I find it difficult to understand how a court can order my money to be blocked without my even being informed.' Alex furiously defended himself against the claims of N.A.L. and Fell. But soon, the US Government, informed by the I.R.S of his fugitive status, impounded all his earnings. He tried everything to relieve the pressure; attempted to get Grove to send him pre-dated cheques, tried to obtain copies of contracts to prove he had the right to allocate 'foreign' (i.e. UK) rights to Pan Books. He worked frantically to raise money to bring Lyn and his son over, away from the clutches of her parents, even if this had to be done in a clandestine manner. He attempted to get Don Getz or Dick Seaver to hold her passport on her behalf out of the reach of her parents. Lyn, on the one hand, seemed to have given up the struggle. She had managed to get a job and was doing publicity work for her local radio station in Stamford, Connecticut. But Alex was finding their separation increasingly hard: 'I am cut off from every sympathetic soul, unknown, unemployed, regarded all round (if at all) with a canny suspicion, sometimes even disgust ... my doctor for example fairly astounded me by announcing in great anger that he regarded my writings as 'obscene and feelthie rubbish, enough to disgust the most broadminded man, scandalous ...!'

He sent Dick Seaver a collection of poetry, prepared to accept whatever fee and royalties Grove could offer, though he hoped that Seaver could arrange for it to be bought, or the advance paid, by their British subsidiary. In the event, the collection was not substantial enough for publication. London publisher, Andre Deutsch, had expressed interest in *Cain's Book* and was prepared to offer a £400 advance for a UK edition, but his lawyers advised caution. Deutsch was prepared to go ahead if he had no trouble with a Mailer book, *Advertisements For Myself*, which he was preparing. There were to be German editions of both *Adam* and *Cain*, and the possibility of a Japanese edition of *Cain*, using the translator who worked for Mailer. Alex had a good recommendation from Mailer himself.

'Oh, Dick, I am so lonely. It was her (Lyn's) mother who turned us in, kidnapped our child, blackmailed us with threat of exposure to let her keep him (just for a while, dear!) opens her letters and gets her hands on any money, and all the while finks to the probation officer if Lyn as much as stays out late at night. Lyn is lonely and afraid, and I, friend, am going out of my mind with anxiety ... I have sent Lyn a great deal of money, Dick, far more than she needed to come over ... I have been expecting her any day for the past two months ... And now, this morning, I have another sad little letter in which she tells me she had blown all the money (again) and hasn't yet obtained her passport.'

Don Getz agreed to assist Lyn to escape from America and Alex began sending letters for Lyn to him, so that her mother would not intercept them. These contain instructions for her:

'Do and only do what you are told ... the idea of you leaving Mark behind is preposterous. When you come you'll bring Mark with you. If you are in a hysterical state I am not. I am in my own country and I am more than a match for all the Hicks and fuzz from N.Y. to Los Ang ... All right. You will choose your day, a day when you can be alone with Mark, and you will go straight to the airport in N.Y ... forget Canada, forget it *now* ... and take a fast plane to Prestwick ... I've been telling you for over six months that you CAN get a passport ... Get the passport ... When and ONLY when I know you have a passport I shall send you tickets, to Don I hope, open date tickets ... you will have to book seats about 24 hours ahead. Tell no one of all this nor of the film business except Don. NO ONE.'

Don Getz planned to travel to Glasgow in mid-December to check-out Glasgow locations for the *Young Adam* film and wrote encouragingly that Lyn's passport was ready to be collected. He hoped that, by the time of his Glasgow visit, the Trocchis would be *en famille* in Glasgow and able to entertain him. He was attempting to get £2000 cash for Alex from the film deal, (somewhat less than he had promised), and he reported on a new proposal to make a film of *Cain's Book*. Alex was relying on the film advance to pay Lyn's fare but this was delayed until January. His correspondence became more and more desperate, for he wanted to allay rumours that his wife had deserted him.

But there was desertion of another kind. A friend had called at his rented room in West Princes' Street. An old woman had opened the door. 'No, he's not here,' she said. 'He's in London.' And then added: 'But I've still got his suitcase!' Alex thought nothing of this kind of behaviour. There are probably landladies across the land for whom the name Trocchi means 'bad debt'! 'Paying rent is for the birds, old man!'

A second film option for *Cain's Book* had been taken by a English producer named Mickey Knox. Alex wanted to interest

Knox, feeling the writing was visually powerful and that it wouldn't be difficult to rewrite the plot in a more dramatic way. For this reason he delayed replying to Carl Esser an American theatre actor of some repute, then working at the Red Barn Theatre in Newport, Long Island, who had also purchased an option on *Cain's Book*. He didn't want to contract himself for a low budget art-house film when he knew that Knox had access to a quarter of a million pounds. Carl Esser was to try in vain to secure an extension, when, in August, his option expired.

And then, finally, Lyn and Mark had escaped from America and the family was reunited at Prestwick airport. Almost two years of separation were at an end. Things were beginning to look more optimistic. He wrote to Bertram Rota, the London bookdealer in early February, offering more notebooks and original mss for sale, and received a total of £32 ten shillings. Rota commented at the time: 'I have still to put a price on the novel you did with Logue,' (this referred to *The Lineage, The Axe, The King*, also known as *Greensleeves*, an unpublished, unfinished historical romance, almost all written by Logue) 'the Wainhouse and Lipton papers, the Cervel things, a folder of your own TS notes in goodish order and another, bulging, in rather mixed-up state, your letters from Bob (Creeley) …'

Alex anticipated receiving the film money and complained about the re-editing of a TV broadcast on which he had appeared. Next time, he said, he would insist on direct broadcast, so that his message was not sabotaged. During this period of transition, Alex had been attempting to redefine his literary objectives and his tactics. He had written in Paris that rigid, categorisations had become an inquisitorial rack to which the flesh of contemporary writing is to be twisted.' He wanted to sweep away such obstructions to clear thinking. Many new ideas had been accumulating and now he put them into an essay, titled *The Invisible Insurrection Of A Million Minds*. This was to appear in several revised editions, but the first version appeared in the *New Saltire Review* of Edinburgh in June 1962, (edited by Magnus Magnusson, who demanded some revision), although its world-wide impact was to come later with its reprinting in many countries. In a sense it represented a planting of flags and signalled the start of Trocchi's new direction, a direction he was to pursue with single-minded obsession for the next eight years. The essay itself, rather grandiose, extravagant in places, dramatic in others, hovers between manifesto and philosophical tract and Alex believed in its significance and integrity and was almost childishly pleased with it. The trouble was that this new direction led him away from the concept of novels, stories and scripts - saleable commodities which could be sold to publishers and to the general reading public, and instead led him to challenge the entire nature of literature. In a sense, this was to lead to inevitable defeat, disappointment and bitterness later. Trocchi knew at the outset that by simply sitting down at his typewriter he could churn out what was required and do it better and more stylishly than almost anyone else, but he had more in him - he was engagé - he had something of universal importance to tell the world - and he knew that it would not make him one whit better off financially. In a sense he was to sacrifice himself in a gesture of goodwill. He had a monstrous generosity, albeit benevolent, even paternalistic, towards his fellows and genuinely believed that his ideas, if adopted by 'a million minds' could create a world revolution for the betterment of mankind. He explicity rejected political solutions, but his proposals never were to be accepted by more than a handful of men and women in a handful of countries, no matter how hopeful developments were to look several years further on. But some of Trocchi's closest associates, such as William Burroughs, now suggest that the whole concept was simply a hoax – a massive grandiloquent excuse for Trocchi to avoid sitting down and writing; evidence of a massive writer's block, the brass monkey squatting on Trocchi's shoulder. Another simple truth that he willfully overlooked is that man is venal, selfish, greedy, narrow-minded and utterly unready for the utopian concepts which he espoused. It is easy to mock and to be wise after the event, but the magical lost world of the Sixties was a time of burgeoning optimism on all fronts. There was a flourishing in the ideals of a more open and experimental culture. The teenager had just been discovered and the concept of youthful rebellion was, paradoxically, well established. The old order was decaying. London was to become one of the cities in the vanguard of a new fusion between cultural experiments, popular culture and the new mass-markets for the commodities which these created. The writings of the 'beat generation' of the mid-to-late fifties in America became available in London and there was a craving for anything American. Since Alex knew many of the beat writers and had lived in Paris and America among his cultural peers, it was evident from the start that London would welcome him and that, there, he could quickly establish himself. Even if he himself was dismissive of the 'beat' tag. There was an immediate problem; Alex and Lyn had been arrested and faced prosecution. The *Glasgow Herald* ran the story on 5th July 1961: 'Glasgow Author Is Drug Addict Court Told' and Alex, whose address was read out in Bow Street Magistrates Court as Cumbernauld Road, Glasgow, told the court that in a good year he earned £1,500. He was fined £25. As a registered addict he had been receiving regular prescriptions and on this occasion had received a prescription for 100 tablets prior to travelling to the Isle of Man, where he had been unable to have it dispensed. He returned after four days, registered with a new GP and received another prescription for 168 tablets, then collected the original prescription, which he had presumably temporarily lost. 'I hadn't really done anything, but had unknowingly broken some bloody regulations pertaining to the export of poisons. With the help of my doctor ... to avoid a protracted legal affair I went along and pleaded guilty to a relatively minor offence which I didn't actually commit.' Chris Logue, who had returned from Greece, gave Alex support as a character witness (the court case was in July) and then fell foul of the law himself a couple of months later ... by taking part in a sit-down protest against 'The Bomb' and refusing to pay his fine. He spent thirty days in Wormwood Scrubs. His *Prison Diary* appeared in *The Observer*.

The Trocchi's moved permanently to London in March and rented a flat in Kilburn, in Winchester Avenue. Trocchi's continuing need for drugs - eight and twelve grains of heroin a day - was outlined in a short note found among his papers:

'I have needed drugs to abolish within myself the painful reflection of the schizophrenia of my times, to quench the impulse to get at once on to my feet and go out into the world and live out some convenient, traditional identity of cunning contriving; acting, doing, asserting myself in the world of others, desperately as men do, and competitively, against short time. The astronauts who were my heroes moved on trajectories through inner space. ... I wanted to escape out of the prison of my mind's language; to 'make it new'. The very concepts in terms of which men still ordered their lives ... these were the root and fabric of our insanity ... the dud coinage of our everyday language was the measure of our imbecility.'

If it sounded like an excuse it probably was, but a powerful statement neverthess. Trocchi was reading again and listed four works he admired, from four 'cosmonauts of inner space;' Coleridge's 'Kubla Khan', Baudelaire's 'Les Paradis Artificiels', *Maldoror* written by Isidore Ducasse, comte de Lautréamont, and Neitzche's *Thus Spake Zarathustra*. But was he looking for escape? Why were drugs continuing to play a central part in his life? After all, *Cain's Book* was behind him. Was he trying to justify inertia?

He had renewed his earlier acquaintance with Guy Debord on his most recent visit to Paris, and was thinking along Situationist lines. Debord and other Situationists had led a petition campaign to free Alex from the New York Police cells, describing him as 'an artist of the first order... pioneer of a new culture... and confirming 'the importance of the artistic innovation of which Trocchi has been to a large extent responsible.' Trocchi was the only British founder-member of the International Situationist movement, and wanted to build the movement into a powerful voice in Britain. He wanted to change the concepts of culture, literature and politics - and fuse all three into one, positive force. He wrote in his notebooks of the need for a cultural revolution; 'the solution, if there is one, lay beyond the endless tundra of nihilism ... ' He co-wrote the preface to the 1962 I.S. Anthology with Michèle Bernstein of

France, J.V. Martin of Denmark and Raoul Vaneigem of Belguim, and the *Internationale Situationiste Review*, edited in Paris by Guy Debord reprinted Trocchi's essay *The Invisible Insurrection*, which also appeared in *Anarchy* magazine in London. The essay was to be followed by others along similar lines, with more detail, and was to be highly influential in the cultural movement which Trocchi would lead, and which was, as yet, in its vestigial stages.

Allen Ginsberg was deported from Prague where he had been proclaimed 'King of the May' by 100,000 students, and returned via London to contact Trocchi. They spent some time together and Rosemary Tonks, an English poet, arranged a poetry reading in Hampstead on 25th May at which both Trocchi and Ginsberg performed.

There was bad news from America. By this time, perhaps not entirely unexpected. Don Getz, whom Richard Seaver described as 'acting and sounding like the original mysterious stranger' had apparently vanished. Seaver doubted whether he had ever intended to act in good faith. It was a sad end to the film project. There was more bad news. One of the consequences of Lyn's escape from the USA had been to incur debt of $350 to Delavan Smith, a Florida attorney, who had managed to secure her probation. Alex was responsible for paying this and hoped to offset incoming money from German editions of *Young Adam* and *Cain's Book* towards this. Seaver advised him to ask the English movie company instead for the money – 'the one place where there is really money due you.' But the deal had already fallen through. Family life with the Trocchis was far from idyllic as Alex makes clear in yet another begging letter to Girodias: 'the details of our present plight are too depressing ... Lyn left hospital early uncured, or only partially: I spent all that remained to me of the apartment money on sending her with the child to a cousin in Glasgow. On impulse, Lyn returned the next day, and so for the moment I am sleeping on the couch of a friend, Lyn in spite of her state a few miles away on another couch, and Mark at my cousin's in Glasgow ... I wanted to send Lyn abroad ... financially and emotionally that's now impossible ... I must find a small apartment where she can feel safe ... no money for rent except the royalties you promised me ... literally only five or six pounds above destitution. I am frightened that she will have to go into a mental hospital for a long time.'

Since Olympia Press was still unable to use the French mail system, Girodias employed cunning methods of sending much-needed money to Trocchi. He sent £41 carefully secreted in the covers of an architectural publication and this baffled Trocchi for a full half-hour. It was enough for him to rent a small bedsit in Hampstead, at 32 Heath Street. And it was there that he received the good news of his invitation to represent Scotland in the International Writers' Conference at the Edinburgh festival. This was to be a three-day affair in the McEwan Hall with all expenses paid and a handsome fee.

'It makes me feel quite sentimental, as a Roman general must have felt when he was called home to Rome for a personal triumph! And as I was recently called 'the hope of Scotland' and 'the grey eminence of literature' in articles in *Scotland* (the Scottish Council Magazine) and as I expect to have an exhibition of my sculpture in the I.C.A. Gallery here in London soon, the old drug fiend can hardly complain he is being victimised...'

Chapter 15: Spiking the Scots; Edinburgh Festival 1962

In the third week of August, Alex took a plane to Edinburgh and met William Burroughs, also on his way to the Conference. It was their first meeting and they got on well together. The list of famous writers attending this event is truly impressive; possibly not before or since has such a galaxy of illuminata been assembled in one place and time. The list of those who had been invited included Bertrand Russell, Muriel Spark, Steven Spender, Angus Wilson, James Baldwin, Truman Capote, Erich Freid, William Golding, LP Hartley, Rayner Heppenstall, Aldous Huxley, Mary McCarthy, Colin McInnes, Norman Mailer, Henry Miller, Naomi Mitchison, Alberto Moravia, Alain Robbe-Grillet, Rex Warner, Theotokis, Fionn MacColla, Hugh MacDiarmid, Robin Jenkins, Edwin Morgan, Neil Paterson, Douglas Young, Alex Reid. There was to be a separate theme for each of the five days.

Alex attended the first session, the subject of which was 'Contrasts of Approach', but it was Day 2 on 21st August - which caused the literary world to sit up and listen. The theme was 'Scottish Writing Today'. There are almost as many different versions of what happened that day as there were participants. Transcripts of some of the debates exist but these are riddled with misinterpretations and misheard or transposed statements. Magnus Magnusson, writing in the *Scotsman* the next day headed his large article 'Scottish Writers Stage Their Civil War' - Nationalism V. Internationalism. Other papers directly opposed Trocchi and MacDiarmid in a verbal tussle. The truth was less dramatic, but no less significant. Trocchi, who had spent much of the time in the company of William Burroughs, and making the acquaintance of other, mainly non-Scottish, writers, such as Henry Miller, whom he had long hoped to meet, felt that MacDiarmid and some of his acolytes were less than serious about modern writing. MacDiarmid in fact denounced *all* modern fiction. The novel was 'an inferior artform.' Having spent little of the last ten years in Scotland, Trocchi may have found the prevalent nationalist attitude of the Scottish writers, most of whom were unknown to him, rather irritating but he retained his decorum and waited his turn to speak. MacDiarmid, that 'old druid' as Trocchi later called him, was at the very peak of his powers and sat on top of the Scottish literary tree, a squat, uncompromising kilted genius with a claymore instead of a fairy wand. It was in-advisable to provoke him since he had many followers and by doing so, in such a dramatic fashion, Trocchi was to effectively ostracise himself from the Scottish literary scene. Only now, years after his death, is there a full acceptance that he has, or deserves, a place in the Scottish literary hagiography. This attack by Trocchi was the first time that MacDiarmid had been attacked in such a public manner.

The two had met, the previous year in the famous Edinburgh literary 'howf', Milne's Bar, when journalist Alexander Neish, who had been interviewing Trocchi for the *Guardian*, introduced him as 'the only 20th century Scottish novelist who could stand beside Lewis Grassic Gibbon'. MacDiarmid was suspicious and hostile, Neish later wrote. It was an inauspicious meeting and MacDiarmid claimed that he had not heard of Trocchi, although it was known that Trocchi and *Merlin* magazine had been subjects of conversation between MacDiarmid and Alan Riddell. Undoubtedly, MacDiarmid had been given the firm impression either intentionally or otherwise that *Merlin* had deliberately avoided offering him a platform because of the attitudes of its editor. Neish emigrated to Brazil not long afterwards but remembers the occasion as less than cordial and of course, MacDiarmid later denied such a meeting ever took place.

Professor David Daiches chaired the day's proceedings. John Calder, the London publisher, who had organised the event, noted that over seventy novelists from over twenty countries were in attendance. MacDiarmid, who had 'not read Trocchi but gathered that free sexuality and drug-taking were central to his work, launched an all-out attack on the literature that was not committed to the betterment of mankind in political terms. It could perhaps be discerned that Trocchi's greatest sin in MacDiarmid's eyes lay in his having left Scotland to become an international rather than a Scottish bohemian poet. Trocchi's counter-attack on the parochialism of Scottish writing made the Edinburgh front pages and was widely reported elsewhere. In the event, he found himself in the same camp as the best European and American novelists, whereas MacDiarmid found his support from the official delegates of communist countries.'

MacDiarmid refuted Trocchi's claim that modern Scottish writing exhibited provincial, parochial tendencies and as the discussion became an angry squabble with a number of voices raised simultaneously, Trocchi's voice was heard above the hubbub to denounce the discussion as: 'turgid, petty, provincial, stale, cold-porridge, bible-class nonsense. Of what is interesting in the last 20 years or so of Scottish writing, I myself have written it all!' He also claimed that most of the best poetry from the last century in Scotland had come from novelists such as Joyce, Henry Miller and Beckett. Then he referred to MacDiarmid in an aside as 'an old so-and-so, with a few rather old-fashioned quaintnesses that are not of my generation.'

MacDiarmid responded by claiming that he had not taken any of Trocchi's remarks personally and that he would be delighted to take up Trocchi's offer to meet some evening and discuss the identity issue. But things got a little heated when MacDiarmid returned to the question of 'lesbianism, homosexuality and matters of that kind' which he regarded as peripheral questions not worth discussing.

'I am only interested in lesbianism and sodomy,' Trocchi remarked acidly.

Dr Daiches attempted to control proceedings as Trocchi continued in full spate about human identity which was 'the only central question... it's high time we transcended nationalistic boundaries...'

This stung MacDiarmid into expostulating 'I want no uniformity!'

'I want no uniformity either,' Trocchi asserted, 'not even a kilt!'

Dr Daiches had to step in to prevent the debate degenerating and invited other speakers to makes statements but the debate ended on a humorous and even-tempered note.

Trocchi had supporters inside the hall, such as Walter Keir from Aberdeen University, who described the event as 'a wake' celebrating the demise of Scottish literature which was hopelessly provincial. Edwin Morgan also demanded that Scottish writers take an interest in the realities of the modern world, and there were others too who railed against the Scottish literary establishment represented by such as Douglas Young, Alexander Reid, and Sydney Goodsir Smith, who slept through most of the proceedings after a heavy (liquid) lunch. It was later discovered that someone had replaced the water in the decanter on the top table with a very pure malt whisky and MacDiarmid and others had been taking full advantage. Trocchi later denounced those who 'were intoxicated with their drug while denouncing mine.' He claimed also that MacDiarmid publicly referred to him, Burroughs and Ian Hamilton Finlay as 'cosmopolitan scum.' The phrase was a favourite of Stalin's. And he was to denounce Trocchi in print as 'a writer of no literary consequence whatsoever.' Extreme, even for the cantankerous MacDiarmid! In fact, the poet annoyed everyone during the next day's proceedings by his smug insistence on political commitment. The audience booed as he insisted that he was the most politically committed, and by implication, the best, writer present. Mary McCarthy and Norman Mailer were among those who responded to that implicit challenge.

Trocchi's public if relatively polite attack on MacDiarmid was to echo and re-echo around the small cultural circles of Scottish literary life and in a sense, it was a public leavetaking by Trocchi of any commitment to being a specifically 'Scottish' writer. Trocchi's idea of community was supra-national and embraced men of all nationalities. In this sense of course, it did not exist, being a community only in the metaphysical sense. Man is essentially tribal and the bonds of birthplace and cultural identity are stronger than the created bonds of affinity.

Laurence Durrell left him a scribbled note at his hotel: 'My dear Cain - call me Ishmael! It was a great pleasure to meet a great writer in the flesh - but what a pity the conference didn't offer you (and me) enough scope to carry things a bit further towards definite conclusions! But then - p'raps they don't exist.' Another short congratulatory note was left by Angus Wilson who felt that he had 'learnt from' Trocchi. In fact, Trocchi had been rather critical of Wilson's 'social pretensions' and his gentle satire of the 'English novel'. But all in all, he had reasons to feel pleased that he was now a public figure in Britain and had re-established himself among the literary movers and shakers of his time.

Chapter 16: *Cain's Book*

Heath Street, on the periphery of Hampstead Heath, the largest piece of open ground in London, is a highly desirable milieu for a writer, surrounded on three sides by trees and parkland. The *Hampstead & Highgate Observer* interviewed Trocchi on his return from the International Writers' Conference, in the tiny bedsit he shared with Lyn and three year-old Marcus. Their article was titled 'The Man With The 60 Room Dream. 'I have no literary plans. I reject the category of literature because it is highly dangerous and leads to a number of extravagances and perversions. What I want to create is an infectious ambience for the revitalisation of art, because art should be something to inform every waking moment ...'

The Edinburgh Conference had established Trocchi as the leader of a group of writers who wished to reject all stereotypes, especially those of nationally-based writing. It was the beginning of the new age of the Sixties. MacDiarmid and the Scottish Literary Renaissance had become victims of their own success, having created a strong Scottish identity which now looked beyond the borders of Scotland to express itself. Trocchi began to appear more frequently on radio and TV. Despite this popularity, he was desperately short of money for the daily essentials of living and had to beg £4 from Girodias in Edinburgh to pay the rent of the bedsit. Spurred by Trocchi's miserable financial position, Girodias had again attempted to 'pay him off':

> 'For once and for the last time, Maurice, a few facts: Never at any time did I agree to sell you a book outright. We had that argument away back in 1952 ... that was a decade ago, there's no reason why I shouldn't expect regular and dependable

royalty returns for my work. I am no longer living in this bed or that on the Left Bank...it's an impertinence to treat me as though I were...'

Alex's financial desperation - he had gone on National Assistance - was wreaked also on Richard Seaver, who had attempted to placate him by sending the money for the German *Cain* before the money was received by Grove from Kossodo. Such kindness went unnoticed and Seaver remarked: 'anything I may do on your behalf ... will only exasperate you ... I am chagrined by your petulant letter ...' From early 1963, Alex managed to obtain occasional work as a reader for Weidenfeld & Nicholson, and in late January, advised against publication of a biography of J.D. Salinger, which had already been published in the USA. He wrote a report on *A Term Of Art*, which he described as a pre-Second World War RAF Romance and 'too purple.' Extracts from his diary, taken at random, reveal a man involved in numerous projects and directions:

27th Feb: Calder's Party - *Cain's Book* launch
1st March: in 'Scotland Now' BBC Scotland, Glasgow.
7th: Canadian Interview
13th: Southampton Univ Lecture
28th: Bill Burroughs, I.C.A.
29th: meet Jack (from Sierra Leone) - Calder Lunch
2nd May: BBC interview, Luncheon TV 'Perspectives'.

He received a short, plaintive letter from his father's second wife, Caroline, still living in the house at Cumbernauld Road. His father had died while on a visit to Douglas in the Isle of Man. It was a sudden death but he was seventy-five years old. Alex joined his brother Alfred and many other members of the family at the funeral, although Jack was unable to return from Sierra Leone in time. Alfredo Trocchi was buried beside his first wife Annie in Glasgow and Caroline, his widow, disappeared into obscurity although Alf offered her an allowance. Alex himself was to greatly miss his father's style and love of music and even his ridiculous pomposity, and his regret was tinged with sadness that his father had read in the pages of his novel *Cain's Book* a satirical mockery of his mannerisms.

Lyn was having a crisis, deepened by her drug addiction and he had to escort her to the Ballamona Hospital on the Isle of Man. She was admitted on 25th February as a voluntary patient, able to roam throughout the extensive grounds of the hospital. Dr Gardner, the hospital's Scots Consultant, did not at all share Alex's viewpoint on drugs and warned him that unless he too 'kicked' the habit, there would always be temptation for Lyn. Gardner described Lyn as a model patient, and she made many friends and wrote a considerable amount of poetry and biographical prose during her stay. Four year-old Mark had been deposited in Scotland with Alex's cousin, a sister of Victor. Lyn was in a mixed ward - both men and women - and on her first morning was 'brought to heel rudely', receiving two injections of two grains each per day at midnight and at 6pm. It was a tough regime. The patients had to do light domestic work from 6.20am until breakfast, which was at 8am. There were no special facilities for drug-addicts. In 1963, there were probably fewer than several dozen heroin addicts in the UK. Treatment, of a sort, was provided in psychiatric wards.

In London, the literary scene was buzzing. John Calder held a party on 27th February to launch the Jupiter Books edition - the first UK edition - of *Cain's Book*, having taken the precaution of obtaining legal advice on the risk of the book's prosecution. Alex, who had returned from the Isle of Man that day, found himself discussing the forthcoming film of his other novel with Baroness Budeburg. The Baroness had participated in negotiations with Sam Speigel over *Young Adam* and clearly preferred the Trocchi novel to the filmscript by Mickey Knox. *Cain's Book* was 'quite a noise here in London,' he reported to Lyn. There had been leader articles in all the papers and he had appeared on TV twice within the previous fortnight, once, with Huw Wheldon on *Monitor* to discuss the appreciative reviews of the novel by the Sunday papers. One newspaper was not so appreciative. Trocchi wrote to the *Glasgow Herald* and his letter was published on 11th March: 'if the silly, prudish little review of *Cain's Book* (Scowling Scowman, 28th Feb) is the kind of treatment your Glasgow journal deals out to the only local writer who has achieved something like international recognition ... LBW's (the reviewer) triviality is symptomatic of Scotland's cultural plight ... it is not my habit to react violently to irresponsible criticism. But Glasgow is my city ... it is Glasgow, not I, who is insulted by such a crazy review. It is as a Glaswegian I protest.' The *Herald* reviewer had even managed to get the name of the central character of the novel wrong; ('Vecchi' instead of Necchi), and deplored the 'frightful, sometimes nauseating picture, in which Vecchi's sexual encounters - with both sexes - are described in lavatory wall detail and in the same language as Henry Miller ... but with none of Miller's zest and humour ...' 'Scots Wha Hae Wi' Necchi Bled!' Trocchi noted to himself in exasperation in his diary.

He appeared on six radio programmes, in one of which he was interviewed by his former lecturer, Edwin Morgan. Professor Morgan has a copy of *Cain's Book* inscribed; 'to a gentle hangman' - in grateful relief that Morgan had not pressed the drug issue unduly at that interview. Trocchi was gratified, but also rather anxious, about the high level of publicity that the book was receiving. The anxiety was well placed, as later events would prove. Walter Keir contributed a review to *Scottish Bookshelf* on the Scottish Home Service on 24th March. 'Alienation is the watchword,' he said. 'And so Necchi lives on the NY waterfront, in the very heart of Henry Miller's 'air-conditioned nightmare,' and significantly he lives on a scow or barge, that pure symbol of shiftlessness which Mr Trocchi uses in his first novel, *Young Adam*. Keir went on to dismiss those critics who had suggested that Trocchi was less holding up a mirror to nature than holding one down to ordure by quoting James Joyce: 'if it isn't fit to read, life isn't fit to live.' As in *Young Adam* there are distinct signs of Beckett's influence in *Cain's Book*. Beckett, in *Malone Dies*, had asked 'how is it the moon where Cain toils bowed beneath his burden never sheds its light on my face?' and Trocchi, in *Cain's Book*, doodling in an idle moment, begins to type: 'An old man called Molloy or Malone walked across country. When he was tired he lay down and when it rained he decided to turn

Alex, Lyn, Marcus and Nicolas, London, 1963
(Courtesy: Jack Robertson)

over and receive it on his back. The rain washed the name right out of him.' Cocteau, Beckett, Kafka, Unamuno and De Sade are quoted throughout the book to suggest the documentary nature of the 'novel'. The book is prefaced by a striking declaration from De Sade:

> 'Their corruption is so dangerous, so active, that they have no other aim in printing their monstrous works than to extend beyond their own lives the sum total of their crimes; they can commit no more, but their accursed writings will lead others to do so, and this comforting thought which they carry with them to the tomb consoles them for the obligation death imposes on them of renouncing this life.'

He liked the idea of insurrection, of contagion, of infecting or propagandising. Trocchi was a proselytiser, a man who carried his soapbox wherever he went, like a pulpit. He desperately wanted to shake society to its roots, to lock horns with hypocrisy, to *épater les bourgeois*. In another BBC radio interview in Edinburgh, he admitted that on the train to the studios he had injected himself with heroin. Later, the producer, W. Gordon Smith was taken to task for his overtly sympathetic manner and questions were even asked in parliament about the programme. Smith received the unqualified support of Hugh Greene, the Director-General over the debacle.

Despite his growing popularity with the British media, few of his American friends knew exactly what had become of him. His sudden exit had created wildly inaccurate myths and although many thought he was still living in hiding in America, his death was announced in New York. It was confidently stated that he had taken an overdose. The rumours were widely believed and continued to escalate, until, reaching the ears of Richard Seaver, a trans-Atlantic phone-call was made and Seaver - determined not to miss the funeral - heard the voice of the dead author himself! This was only the first of many curtain calls which Trocchi was credited with! Selfishly, however, Trocchi was to insist on another twenty years of life! He did not wish to be a martyr - or a myth - just yet.

While Lyn was at Ballamona, Jack and Marjorie arrived from Africa and the three made a trip to see Lyn and brother Alf in the Isle of Man. One of the rare times when the three brothers and their wives were together. Alf's business was doing well and Jack also was prospering. Marcus had five cousins; Jack's two daughters, Rosemary and Louise, Alf's two daughters, Penelope, Norma, and son, Alan, and of course, his half-sisters in New Zealand, Jacqueline and Margot.

Alex's own health began to deteriorate and was not aided by continued acrimony over foreign book deals. The Italian publisher Einaudi had failed to produce *Cain* and another, Sugar Editore, had bought a contract. A second German publisher, Rowohlt, had bought translations rights to the book. Editions Buchet/Chastel planned a new French edition for September. All this netted Alex a tiny amount of income, hardly worth the effort. But he was making plans to solve his financial plight with a much more lucrative venture: a collaboration with William Burroughs to produce an anthology about drugs. It could hardly fail. He planned to work on the book with Burroughs in Tangier and this would also be a long holiday for his family. Burroughs had stopped using heroin so Trocchi planned to 'kick' before travelling. He said so at least three times, in letters, and even in front of witnesses! They would stay in Tangier for the entire summer. It sounded too good to be true and it was to be a complete fiasco. Lyn rejoined him in London and the family stayed in various temporary addresses, including Finchley Road, Cricklewood. Alex travelled to Scotland in early May to retrieve Marcus and appear on some Scottish TV programmes. After one of which an irate GP wrote in to complain and the newspapers took up the story. Such notoriety was to ensure continual demand for his appearances and regular cheques. He was to make almost a career out of appearing on TV as 'the first prophet of permissiveness' and the media's favourite 'junkie'. He invariably gave good value, never underestimating the intelligence of his audience and always leaving them with some new thought or idea to consider. He had also started to give the first of a great many invited lectures throughout the UK, often at Universities,

Arts Festivals, or Colleges of Art. He wrote to Bob Creeley about 'sigma' - a project that had been burgeoning in his mind for several years, since publication of 'The Invisible Insurrection'.

They had planned to travel in June, but as June approached and went by and July came, the plans underwent continual revision, due to a complete lack of money. Finally, they were off. Michael Hollingshead was driving them in a small red MG sports car, hardly the most appropriate vehicle for the trip. Hollingshead managed to drive them head-on into another car only 122 km from Dieppe! Despite this mishap, in which, miraculously, no-one was injured, they continued to the Motel Raf in Estepona. There was increasing tension between Alex and Lyn and as Alex later related to Burroughs:

'I arrived in Tangier struggling in the awful ooze of someone else's determination. Tangier flashed no more real across my pathetic horizon than a Raphael Tuck postcard on a windy promenade, and I was less free during those seventy-two hours than any bus tourist ... so you and us and everything was pretty irrelevant from the beginning and after that unfortunate evening I had only one thought in mind, to get that family bit of mine back to London where I hoped to learn just what it all had to do with me anyway ... Lyn is setting herself up apart to find something or other hitherto obscured, it seems, by my shadow. And how relieved I am! To be able to give my attention to something else ... '

After seven years of marriage, it did look like their relationship was ending. Trocchi confided in Burroughs: 'it wasn't Lyn I wanted to get rid of. It was her obsession.' He enclosed a copy of his essay on the tactics of the 'Invisible Insurrection' and announced the choice of the name 'sigma' because it seemed semantically 'clean', being the symbol conventionally used in mathematics for the sum or the whole. 'Unlike most other words, it has no other traditional connotations to suggest we're quick or slow, left or right, hare-lipped or cloven-hooved.'

Alex moved into a flat in Baring Street, found for him by Abdul de Freitas, otherwise known as Abdul Malik and destined to achieve notoriety in due course as 'Michael X'. De Freitas looked like a pirate with a black beard and a ring through one ear. He was at that time a rent collector for the notorious Abdul Rachman, whose dubious methods of business led to the coining of a new word; Rachmanism. When a Labour Councillor in North Kensington began a campaign against Rachman's extortionate rents, Malik switched sides and went around his clientele assisting them to apply for rent registration from the Rent Tribunal. Some of them won dramatic reductions - rents halved or cut to a quarter. He won the respect of the black community around Notting Hill. Later, when the Fraud Squad moved in, he helped the investigations and persuaded witnesses to testify. Yet he sided with Rachman against some radical students' attempts to set up a Tenants' Association. He was a Zionist, claiming that his white father was Jewish, yet also a racist. He formed the militant Racial Action Society, whose members strutted around in hip uniforms donated by Carnaby Street retailers (from whom he got a cut). He was a curious mixture of rogue, militant Black Power leader, gambler, poet. With his trial and execution - for triple murder - in Trinidad in 1974, he entered the history books as a 'cause celebre' of the Sixties. But all that was in the future. In 1964, he soon found Alex a better place to live in St Stephen's Gardens in Westbourne Grove. De Freitas was to become an early Director of sigma and wrote of his friendship with Trocchi at some length in his autobiography; *From Michael De Freitas To Michael X*:

'One time when I had quite a bit of money, I asked Alex if he'd accept some from me and how much he needed. He said £100 would put him straight. I told him I would give him lots of £50 and with some reluctance he accepted my offer. He wanted the £100 at one time, but I had the feeling I should give it to him in two stages, so I gave him the first £50 and he was desperate or gracious enough to be very pleased. About a week later I hadn't turned up with the other half and

I received a beautiful letter from Alex asking why the hell I was keeping his money from him. I went to see him and asked what he'd done with the first sum - which was rather stupid as I'd given it to him with no strings attached and he had no reason to account to me. He got quite indignant. 'What have I done with it!' he roared. 'What have I done with it ...! I've bought flowers for a beautiful woman - that's what I've done with it!'

Lyn was living in the flat of a friend in Tennyson Road, Kilburn, and in her applications for various jobs, describes herself as 'now separated.' She was also making plans to return to the USA and wrote several letters to her attorney, Delavan Smith, asking him to investigate the position and accusing Alex of all the drugs offences. 'Alex was the one who had done the lying ...' Del Smith immediately contacted Alex to demand $250 before he took any action on his wife's behalf ... The separation of the Trocchis was to continue well into 1964.

Alex wrote to Bertram Rota offering the typescript of *La Gana*, which he had commenced translating in New York in 1957, but Rota did not wish to buy it until it was completed and pointed out that the market for the book would be dependent on Trocchi's name, not Dessouart. Alex recommended the translation, working very quickly, injecting himself in the hands with an eye-dropper almost every five minutes. Friends were astonished at his incredible skill and precision under such bizarre conditions. He could inject himself, simultaneously hold a lucid conversation while smoking cigarettes - without a break in the lines of beautiful prose he was typing. Lines so tightly-constructed that they would barely - if at all - require revision or sub-editing. This was Trocchi, the supreme master of his craft, a stylist, whose prose is never banal, never descends to *cliché* or slipshod construction. The Trocchi perhaps last glimpsed in Montparnasse.

An article on the Paris scene by Gay Taliese was published in *Esquire* and Trocchi considered taking legal action for libel because it contained a bowdlerised version of his theft of Plimpton's suits, the incident transposed from New York to Paris, and the circumstances entirely altered. The magazine refused to allow Trocchi the right to reply but eventually $5,000 compensation was paid to him. Not that Plimpton got his suits back!

The 1963 Writers' Conference at the Edinburgh Festival had not attracted much international attention. Trocchi - and MacDiarmid - were present, but the event passed off peacefully. It led to further sporadic literary skirmishing in the columns of the *New Statesman* and *Times Literary Supplement*: Alex counter-attacked in the 3rd January 1964 issue of the *TLS*:

'Mr MacDiarmid is quite correct when he denies leading the song. Sidney Goodsir Smith, taking an unofficial stroll across the stage of the McEwan Hall after the pubs had closed for the afternoon (perhaps he had heard that whisky was to be found on the speakers' table?), led the singing. Unfortunately, the song had no more satirical point than a belch, and was as irrelevant as most of what was said on the platform that afternoon ... it was simply a case of the blind drunk leading the blind. But a more serious innacuracy in Mr Levin's otherwise excellent article, and one which Mr MacDiarmid's letter pointedly fails to notice, was Mr Levin's counting Mr MacDiarmid among the rebels. For, whatever Mr MacDiarmid's views are now (and I heartily hope they have changed), in August 1962 he was indignantly denouncing such writers as Burroughs and myself as 'vermin' who should never have been invited to the conference, and in an article in *The Scottish Daily Express* on the Saturday on which the writers departed from Edinburgh he stated that the proper place for us was either an insane asylum or prison. Many of us, and no-one more than myself were astonished at the vehemence with which a man we had always supposed was a rebel denounced us as dangerous perverts. But these are the facts. At the 1962 Conference the wielder of the long moral rifle of John Knox was none other than Mr MacDiarmid.

If now, in the light of what happened in 1963, Mr MacDiarmid is presenting himself as a defender of the freedom of the conference, we are entitled to ask; freeedom for whom? Are the writings of Trocchi, Burroughs and the like - to use Mr MacDiarmid's own revealing phrase - still to be proscribed?'

17th January 1964

'Sir, Please let me assure Mr Trocchi that I have not altered the opinions I expressed in 1962 ... I do not think I can reasonably be expected to tolerate confessions, by writers I deem of no literary consequence whatever, of drug-addiction, homosexuality and the like. My altercation with Mr Trocchi arose from his claim that his own work was the only important Scottish contribution to literature in our time, and that drug-addiction, etc, were the vital issues with which contemporary literature must deal ... I objected to some of the remarks made by Mr Trocchi and others ... it was an abominable display of behaviour ...'
- Hugh MacDiarmid.

18th January 1964

'It was quite evident from Mr MacDiarmid's first speech at the 1962 conference that he had decided not to tolerate me (and my 'ilk') before I had ever reached Edinburgh. In his absurdly haughty way he dismissed as immoral rubbish all post-war fiction concerned with the problem of 'identity' and international in outlook. Then, as now, his terms of abuse were those of a rabid nationalistic moralist. Confession implies a sense of guilt. When Mr MacDiarmid threw his 'drug-fiend-and-deny-it-if-you-can-type-literary criticism' at me, I could hardly be expected to deny I used drugs. But my various statements about valid methods of extending the range of human consciousness could be construed as a 'confession' only by intellectual tadpoles already hopelessly immersed in the bitter waters of Mr MacDiarmid's moral universe.

While some ladies of Edinburgh may derive comfort from the knowledge that Mr MacDiarmid's claymore will defend them against rape at future conferences, those of us who come after Freud and Wittgenstein, alarmed by statements which take the form; "I am all for freedom ... BUT ...", will not be deceived by any of Mr MacDiarmid's assurances and denials, flat, round or square ...'

Alex moved into a room in the Devonshire House Hotel in Princes Square, a seedy area of Paddington, and it was there that a film-crew from Rediffusion TV recorded footage for a half-hour programme on Trocchi and Burroughs. The Editor, Bryan Fitzjones had to fight to have the programme shown, having been ordered to submit the script to the boss of the ITA, Lord Hill of Luton himself. The programme was eventually shown with some changes - 'we have won a very notable battle against the establishment,' Fitzjones wrote.

Tom McGrath, another Glaswegian, the founder-editor of the newspaper of the 'underground' - the *International Times* – initially designated on its masthead as 'a sigmatic newspaper' had become a close friend: 'I had gone to visit him in another room he had rented,' he recalled. 'He complained to me that he was missing Lyn, then took a noisy pee in the small sink in the corner of the room. He lay back on the bed and sighed. He was obviously bored and looking for mischief. He looked at me quizzically, "Like have you ever had any homosexual experience?" I said that I had not and that I didn't fancy taking lessons. This sent him into one of his rants at me. "Like you must be latent..." I had some hashish and I offered this as an alternative diversion. We smoked it straight from a pipe, without tobacco, and we smoked a lot of it, quickly. Within about five minutes we were in a different world, staring at each other through the weirdness of it all. Trocchi decided we should go out for a walk to see if we could find some action. We went into a cafe place on the main road where we had to share a table with another man. Trocchi didn't like the look of the man and was not into sharing. He looked across the table at the man and said, "My, but you are ugly."'

An American millionairess, Anna Grady, wished to sponsor I.T. and a large cheque was to be collected. It came into Alex' possession. He would not return it. This caused irritation that Alex casually dismissed: 'like, you've got to support the old guys behind the scenes. We're the generators of the ideas that are crucial to any enterprise. Now, Tom, I'm sure you don't grudge ... and here I have a very good idea, which I'm sure you will be interested in ...'

In early June, Alex and Lyn were reunited, and Alex handed all his financial dealings over to her to see if she could do any better; 'I just cannot seem to earn enough to live without worrying. And yet, if I add it all up I should be able to live on it. I'm in an awful mess financially and yet things are going comparatively well.' There were conflicting pressures. On the one hand, Lyn's conventional outlook; she hankered after all for the life of a conventional writers' wife, longed for Alex's success as a respected and famous writer. Her outlook was surprisingly normal and despite, or perhaps because of her experiences, she disapproved of promiscuity (what Alex called swinging) and amorality, yet she was tolerant enough, and in love with Alex enough, to accept that he was different. It was her sheer love of the man that kept them together through very difficult times and an impossible lifestyle. Alex often felt he had to conform to her ideal, and Tom McGrath in particular relates with amusement their attempts on occasion to 'make normality'. An Everyday Story Of Drug-Crazed Literary Crackpots. Tea With The Trocchis. 'Like, I want Lyn to experience the traditional British Christmas dinner, Tom, with all the trappings. Are you with me, old man?' Such events were usually strained, often disasters, though Trocchi's benevolent presence and quiet commentary could invariably soothe any crisis.

With the 1964 Edinburgh Festival looming, he had taken the precaution of writing directly to Hugh MacDiarmid in decidedly conciliatory fashion, his tongue firmly in his cheek! There was to be no official Writers' event and an unofficial event was being organised by Jim Haynes, one of the founders of the Traverse Theatre:

'Dear Mr MacDiarmid,
While there have been and will be aspects of life and art

upon which we cannot be in accord, it seems to me there must be a few vital issues upon which we can hardly fail to be in agreement, and I, for my part, am most sorry that the particular circumstances in which we first met one another were such as to bring the former into prominence and distract our attention from the latter. Amongst this latter is our common revolt against the smug philistinism of many of our countrymen. That the good folk of the Edinburgh establishment should take pride in smothering the literary side of the festival this year is for both of us, I am sure, bloody shocking evidence of their barbarism. I believe too that we are agreed that they shouldn't be allowed to get away with it, that it is a scandal and could be a dangerous precedent. I am writing to inform you that I shall be doing all in my own power to help Haynes make a success of an "unofficial conference" and to express my personal hope that you will be with us, in your rightful place at the head of our shock troops, in Edinburgh this summer. I am certain we can do much more than was ever done "officially", and at much less expense, if we can be together in this, for poetry and sanity, now. Next time I am in Scotland I hope I shall have the opportunity of meeting you privately. Really, I am not in the least anxious to continue a public sniping match with a man for whom I have always had the profoundest respect.'

The 1964 Festival became notorious because of the 'nude lady incident' in the McEwan Hall - dubbed by the press 'Lady McChatterley' - and the ritual protest burning of *Cain's Book* by publisher and author in the Grassmarket. Trocchi, RD Laing and Jeff Nuttall stayed during the festival in Jim Haynes' flat in Great King Street, described by Nuttall as 'like a Bedouin encampment,' the temporary home of actors, poets, folk-singers, dancers and artists. It was obvious that 'something' was going to happen, something wild and possibly quite subversive.

The *Glasgow Herald* noted that Alex Trocchi 'mellowed dramatically since the hectic Scottish day two years ago, popped thoughtful suggestions into the discussion from time to time, with careful tolerance drawing on impressive reserves of scholarship.' The *Times Literary Supplement's* retrospective article on the four days of the conference: 'from the opening skirmishes it was clear that the lion's share of the discussion would be taken by Hugh MacDiarmid, George MacBeth and Alexander Trocchi.' The *TLS* leader writer perceived four factions; MacDiarmid's nationalists; scientifically-minded classicists like George MacBeth, George Wightman, Martin Seymour-Smith and Jon Silkin; a 'more international but no less classical group' headed by Trocchi and the Cuban, Pablo Fernandez. They were interested in a far wider range of *kinds* of poetry. They excluded no form, or superficial lack of it ... were more open to experiment and prepared to generate 'happenings'; and, closely allied in feeling, the beats, concretes and avant-gardists like Edwin Morgan and Pete Brown.

The furore about the 'Lady McChatterley' incident angered a great many, who saw the whole thing as unworthy of notice. Among those angered by the prurient attitudes of the Edinburgh Council - who had banned the writers' event for the future because of the incident - was actor James Robertson Justice; 'Since when have we had to accept the views of an elected municipal official as gospel ... ?' Trocchi was also furious:

'There are no villains. Or so I keep telling myself. And then I come to Edinburgh during the Festival. Sodom and Gomorrah have got nothing on Edinburgh. The Pride of the City of Edinburgh is a terrible thing. It is a cancer of centuries' growth, motivated by the hateful thoughts of lost wars and departed glories. The press coverage was nothing short of a bloody scandal. Nor did one newspaper report the fact that the mood of the unofficial poetry conference was in no way tolerant of those irresponsible hysterics who sabotaged this year's conference by pretending to be shocked by a naked woman they did not see who moved like a flash across a particularly unseeable place ...'

When the discussions were concluded, the meeting took itself off to a square at the rear of the Traverse Theatre to attend a public burning of *Cain's Book* in the form of a large incendiary containing fireworks, muzzle to the sky. The reason for this was the book had been seized in a raid on a booksellers in Sheffield on the grounds that it was obscene.

Chapter 17: 'To Deprave and Corrupt'; *Cain's Book* On Trial

Cain's Book, first published in New York in 1960 and in the UK in 1963 was acclaimed by critics in superlative terms. Translated into French, it had been nominated as Book of the Month in February 1964 by the French newspaper, *L'Express*. It had been published in Catholic Spain and Italy and the publishers' publicity material claimed that 20,000 copies had been sold in the UK in 'Calders' Big Year' - alongside copies of *Tropic Of Cancer* by Henry Miller and *Dead Fingers' Talk* by William Burroughs. How then had the destruction of such a book been ordered by the courts alongside domestic refuse and the assorted detritus of the materialist society? Who was this author, Alexander Trocchi, who had written such a 'vicious and appalling document of evil...?'

The book had been among a large number of books - 2,354 copies of 906 different magazines and 95 copies of 48 novels - seized in raids on fourteen newsagents' shops in Sheffield in July 1963. The raid, conducted by senior police officers followed the obtaining of a Sheriff's warrant under the Obscene Publications Act, 1959. The confiscated stock included Arthur Miller's *Misfits* and Nabokov's *Lolita*, and it appears that while Henry Miller's *Tropic Of Cancer* was not taken, the August issue of *True Romances* was, an amusing error, and it was later returned, with its pull-out free knitting pattern intact! The confiscated material, in eleven cardboard boxes and four brown paper parcels, was displayed before the Magistrates at Sheffield Magistrates' Court on 25th February 1964, together with the newsagents and booksellers concerned. *Cain's Book* was the only hardback book. Its cover price, at twenty-five shillings, was much higher than the others, some of which were undoubtedly pornographic. The book's London publisher, Calder & Boyars, objected strongly to the charge that the book was obscene (they had commissioned a Solicitors' Report in 1962 to consider the risk of prosecution - which report had advised there *was* a 'serious risk' of prosecution) and sent a representive to appear on behalf of one of the booksellers, Mr Henry Kirk, in whose Tudor Street premises the book had been offered for sale.

The three magistrates listened to the Counsel for Sheffield Police and decided to take the unusual step of reading all the material for themselves within a period of seven weeks. The trial was arranged for 14th April.

The few observers in the public gallery who had perhaps wandered in to Sheffield Magistrates Court in hope of entertainment, on the second day of the trial, could have been forgiven for thinking that the author, Trocchi, was an American. After all, censorship was something that one thought of in connection with American paperback novels. Trocchi's book was set partly in New York. Then Trocchi himself sounded American; he spoke with a laryngeal drawl like Marlon Brando. He was tall and lean and rather resembled another American actor - Burt Lancaster - though there was also something foreign and faintly disturbing about him. Britain had had its own censorship cases; the *Memoirs of Fanny Hill* had, only a few months before, been seized and banned, Penguin Books had won their case, two years earlier for their edition of DH Lawrence's *Lady Chatterley's Lover* but Trocchi's book was different. The case against it was not primarily related to the sexual passages within it. It was manifestly not cheap pornography.

The case had attracted considerable interest; a large report appeared on the front page of the *Star* under the banner headline; SEIZED CITY BOOKS: CASE TO ANSWER; the JP's having announced on the previous day that they considered that a 'prima facie' case had been made out for the destruction of all but one of the books and magazines. Mr Bruce Douglas-Mann, Labour MP for Kensington, led the case for the defence of Cain's Book. Mr John Cotton for Sheffield Police announced that the defence must attempt to show under Section 4 of the Obscene Publications Act that the book's publication was justified as 'being for the public good on the grounds that it is in the interests of Science, literary art or learning.' Douglas-Mann called his first witness, the book's publisher, John Calder.

Calder, a dapper, balding figure, had, within 14 years, made his publishing firm into the leading avant garde publisher in Britain, primarily concerned with innovative writing, much of it from European writers. Calder was allowed to give only his own opinion of the book, and he described it as 'a very important one and very possibly one of the most important novels written by a Scottish novelist since the war. It was a book which ... had very special literary qualities and was ... the first book written by a British author with great affinities with what was known in America as the beat movement ...'

At one point during the parade of defence witnesses (which included the Sheffield City Librarian, literary critic Walter Keir, writer Kathleen Knott and broadcaster Kenneth Alsop) the prosecution intervened to ask whether Mr Trocchi was to be called. Trocchi's voice was clearly heard: 'You can call me any time!' But the next witness called was the *Scotsman's* literary reviewer, W.H.C. Wilson. Finally, Trocchi himself was called. The *Sheffield Telegraph* reported that the author was wearing cream trousers and a short cream, collarless jacket, an ensemble which rather stood out among the sober navy blues and greys of the court. His hair was cropped short and spiky.

The defence had thus far built-up a careful picture of the book's overall literary merit and played down the question of the central character's advocacy of drugs. To Trocchi this was all rather irrelevant. The book had, he informed the court, taken him seven years to write. He would not have written it if he had not thought it would have an influence. Trocchi continued in forthright style, torpedoing the careful defence case, his American drawl having a mesmeric effect upon his audience. 'I have taken every drug there is to be taken - but only those from which I know I can safely return. Drugs have an effect and if they did not I do not think I would have written the book. Coleridge was an opium addict and he wrote the greatest literary criticism of all time - *Biographia Literaria*. I do not want anyone to endure my experiences. But I am a man with something to say and the book had said it. It is worth encouraging. It is relevant to all men.'

The prosecuting solicitor referred to Trocchi's other novels as 'the most complete and utter filth.' Trocchi, he said, was a pornographer by trade. All the spurious arguments of literary merit could not conceal that his living had been made from novels of an explicitly sexual nature. There were sexual passages also in *Cain's Book* and even passages of homosexuality. Four-letter words were frequently used. Trocchi denied this: 'I used these words only when necessary. I use them scientifically and not for creating excitement.'

In summing-up for the defence, Bruce Douglas-Mann reminded the court that the book could only be banned if it was considered liable to deprave or corrupt, rather than simply shock, affront or disturb. All the witnesses, he said, had testified, without exception, that the book did not and could not deprave and corrupt. He referred to a curious twist in the proceedings whereby Mr Trocchi had been held to be personally responsible for all the actions and words of the character in his novel. 'It was suggested that it was not a novel but an autobiographical tract which he had to defend. *Cain's Book* was undeniably a novel. If a character in a novel about drinking exclaimed, "I drive better when I am drunk," it would be ridiculous to suggest that the author was advocating that people should drive when they were drunk. In the same way, Mr Trocchi should not be deemed to be advocating the use of drugs because of something he put into the mouth of a character in his novel. The book must be taken as a whole and in the context of the novel. Its effect as a whole was to discourage the use of drugs.'

The magistrates withdrew to consider their verdict. Forty-five minutes later, they returned to announce that *Cain's Book* was indeed obscene and ordered that copies should be forfeited and destroyed under Section 1 of the Act. Douglas-Mann immediately gave notice of an appeal; there was provision under the Act for a stay of destruction until the result of an appeal. Outside the Magistrates' Court, John Calder said; 'Sheffield is the only place in the world where the book has been found obscene. We shall make every effort to re-establish it here.'

The appeal was heard at the High Court in the Strand, London on 10th December 1964. The publishers claimed that there was no precedent in English or American law for the definition of obscenity to include drug-taking but the appeal was dismissed with costs and they were refused permission to petition the House of Lords.

The book was ordered to be destroyed and, according to one source, was taken to the Sheffield Corporation Municipal Incinerator, a large, undistinguished brick building, which stood on a patch of wasteground rutted with the oily wheelmarks of heavy lorries. All the city's rubbish was brought to this final destination in Penistone Road in the Hillsborough district. Apart from the smoke which emanated from the 200 foot high chimney into the skyline, and large quantities of ash, nothing would remain of its enormous repasts. The temperature of this great eating machine varied around 800 degrees Fahrenheit. On a Monday towards the latter end of December 1964, workers pulled down the tail-gate of a Sheffield Corporation Cleansing Department truck and pulled out several large cardboard boxes. One man swung his box against the metal shutter of the trap door. From a distance, the spilled contents resembled a heap of rags, but, on closer inspection, one could see that they were books. A steel-tipped boot trod on one and it slid away from the pile and lay on an oily puddle formed from a subsidence in the tarmac. The title could be seen; *Cain's Book* by Alexander Trocchi, before it too was consigned to the flames.

Cain's Book is an exceptional work, which although fixed very clearly in its various locations, has only a vague sense of time; Trocchi's concern is with the texture of significant moments and he makes little attempt to sustain narrative over more than two or three pages at a time. There are sections based in Glasgow, some in Paris, significant events in the past life of Necchi are revealed, mainly to justify the viewpoint of its narrator. And, to satisfy Trocchi's qualms about succumbing to 'literature' by writing a wholly conventional novel, his hero/narrator, Necchi, is himself writing a book - *Cain's*

Book - from which excerpts are taken. The reader is tantalised with the prospect that something is being kept back, and of course Trocchi can satisfy himself that his book is beyond definition, has no precise beginning and no conclusion, exists independently, neither novel nor manifesto. The real *Cain's Book* is unrevealed, its extent undefined; it is the work of Necchi, not Trocchi. In a wholly expert way, philosophical thoughts on the human predicament are expressed with clarity and simplicity and at the same time related closely to everyday objects, solid, tactile, in such a way that the reader is not lost in mere abstract musings. Necchi's father, in Glasgow, is the principal tool of an ironic comparison between the son, the wanderer, Cain, who obeys none of society's rules - who will not work in the slaughterhouses - and the father living a life of complaisant obedience and meaningless self-constriction, performing his ritual ceremonies and upholding traditions; a life lacking spontaneity, a living death. Trocchi employs to the full the humour of exaggeration, disproportion, even giantism. Mountains appear where molehills had been sighted. 'I kept that bathroom spotless, my father said rather gloomily ... ' 'At nine he shaved. Not before. The number of such necessary enterprises was very meagre. He had to spread them thinly over the day, as he spread the margarine over his bread, to prevent the collapse of his world.'

The burning of books and what that implies is the greatest transgression that a civilised society can enact. The conscious decision to suppress, to eliminate, to deny the existence of ideas and the originators of those ideas is a fundamental of terrorism and totalitarianism. Another source suggests that the boxes of *Cain's Book* were merely left to rot in a cellar in some municipal building. Whatever, the truth, the Sheffield Corporation Municipal Incinerator at Penistone Road no longer exists, nor are books burned nowadays by order of Magistrates and Judges. In a sense it was the decision of the judges which was 'against history' and *Cain's Book* has ultimately triumphed.

Chapter 18: Tactical Evasions; The Sigma Project

There are a vast number of tactical notes, mostly unfinished, about the progress (or lack of it) of the sigma project. Trocchi devoted an inordinate amount of time to the simple, clerical tasks of editing, duplicating and mailing the portfolio which began to emerge in 1964, from the three-roomed flat in St Stephen's Gardens - in the seedy no-man's land between Paddington and Notting Hill. The *Los Angeles Free Press* had described Trocchi's first essay as 'a revolutionary proposal ... a detailed plan for a coup de monde which must be in the broad sense cultural - to grab control of history and to promote a new order of things.'

Trocchi had written to Guy Debord; 'I am ready at any time to show my sigmatic tactics are thoroughly in the situationist tradition.' Trocchi's importance in the Situationist International; he was a member of the Central Council (the only UK member) and the Editorial Collective, is underlined by his length of membership. The S.I. was highly volatile, expulsions and internecine warfare were common, but Trocchi remained a member from its inception to its collapse and contributed to its manifestos and public statements. Unfortunately, while Trocchi wished to enlist everyone in his 'coup de monde', Debord was, like Lenin, an absolutist, constantly kicking people out until he was the only one left. 'And exclusions were total. It meant ostracism, cutting people. Ultimately, it leads to shooting people - that's where it would have led, if Guy had ever taken over. And I couldn't shoot anyone.' Eventually, even Trocchi had to go. 'Your name stinks in the minds of decent men,' Debord wrote, after Trocchi's resignation from the SI in autumn 1964. His crime was his association with 'mystical cretins' like Ginsberg, Colin Wilson, Leary and Laing.

So what *was* sigma? 'Sigma does not exist, it is merely a word, a tactical symbol, a dialectical instrument, which we, an ever-increasing number of thoughtful individuals all over the world, have found useful in the strategic game we have elected to play on an international scale...' On one level it was like a continuation of *lettrisme*, whose adherents wrote to each other and eschewed the principle of commercial publication. The sigma portfolio was typed by electric typewriter onto duplicator skins and duplicated onto coloured sheets of foolscap, stapled, and sent to several hundred persons, often themselves contributing poets, artists, writers, throughout the world, chiefly in America, Britain, France and Holland. The portfolio extended eventually to almost forty items, including an important essay on pyschotherapy by RD Laing, (which he had delivered to the 6th World Conference on Psychotherapy), poems by Michael McClure, Pablo Fernandez, Robert Creeley, a lengthy correspondence between Trocchi and Stan Brakhage, the 'Underground' filmmaker, reports by Kenneth White, Marcus Field, Ken Hollawell, Colin Wilson and Joan Littlewood. The portfolio earned itself a high reputation. It also detailed progress towards the physical manifestation of the movement - if there was a movement. There were a large number of plans over the years to establish a London base for meetings, a headquarters and office for organising events, a venue for selling publications and artworks produced from within the organisation. For sigma was also to be a publisher and a clearing house for artists to sell their wares, cutting out the agents and the middlemen. The International Collection was another project. Sculptors and artists would donate works to be sold on behalf of sigma. Although artists of the reknown of Salvador Dali, Pablo Picasso and Feliks Topolski were mentioned, the collection received few artefacts apart from Trocchi's own driftwood feelies, now dubbed futiques.

There were other practical proposals; *The Moving Times*, founded by Jeff Nuttall, a poet and musician, who was a leading sigma activist. His memories of the decade are chronicled in his book, *Bomb Culture* (Paladin, 1968), where Trocchi has more index references than anyone, with the exception of Allen Ginsberg and William

Burroughs. *Moving Times* contained poetry and propaganda designed to stir up 'insurrection' and to be provocative. Nuttall, and Beba Lavrin, (who had assisted Arnold Wesker's Centre 42 project – in some sense a rival to sigma, and undoubtedly one of the targets of the *Invisible Insurrection* essay) – attempted, with some persistence, to have it displayed on poster sites in the London Underground system – but the powers-that-be managed to prevent this. Under Alex's guidance, it then became an A2-sized handout – the size of a double page of *The Times*, printed by Villiers Publications, who were later to complain of massive unpaid bills. In turn, Alex was to be furious with them for breaking down the typeset so soon after the first printing that subsequent editions were impossible. He accused them of entirely misunderstanding the project. It was not the kind of venture that would be instantly commercial from the very beginning, and small editions initially would increase. 'A certain subtlety of subversion will be essential ... The conventional media contain the seeds of their own ineffectiveness. Our approach has to be an outflanking.' Storm the bridges and viaducts, Trotsky had ordered. Trocchi said: Seize the grids of expression! The first *Moving Times* appeared in November 1964.

In an article entitled 'Wanted: A Million New Minds', in *Leisure* magazine, there is a description of Alex wearing a tasselled skull-cap over his long hair, bright red socks, green slippers, and an ear-to-ear grin. Some unkind persons noted his resemblance to 'Mr Punch.'

On a lengthy television interview conducted by Dan Farson on Thames TV Trocchi appeared with William Burroughs and outlined his ideas:

'We need to be breaking down the division between the various arts, and considering every man just an expressive being – who use language as well as other things, but the tremendous specialisation that grew up over the centuries in Western art had to be overthrown, and I think it has been in the 20th century and I think we'll gradually go away from the idea of Burroughs as a writer, Trocchi as a writer – we mustn't consider ourselves as professional writers any longer, because that means to write novels, say, a novel as a fixed form, and it's become an economic form - it's got to be so long ... a certain kind of thing - and the publisher requires another of the same, and that's how you make your living, so you tend to do it: In the same way there are chairs of literature, and there's a Shakespeare industry, well this ... must now be rejected and in general expressive, creative men, whether they're artists or scientists must get together - beyond our old established fictions - like government and international policy and realise that we are in a world - human beings, and lots of these old forms prevent new communications coming into existence ... there are millions of individual centres of sensitive men and women all over the world who, if they could only become aware of their identity, and the fact that there were a million such identities who, acting together could create a new world, so long as they didn't take on one of these reactionary identities like the Communist Party or something like that - and it will deliver us from all kinds of past prejudices ...'

The summer of 1964 was long and hot; many hours were spent on the balcony of the Trocchi's flat, dreaming dreams and making plans – and avoiding doing any writing. While Alex declared that 'nothing money could buy would gratify me more than the realisation of our aims,' Lyn dreamed of him finding commercial success as a writer. Marcus Field, a young Australian, and his wife Sally, a dancer, lived in the flat downstairs. Often, they would while away a sunny afternoon together, drinking and smoking, with Marcus Trocchi, now a bright six year old playing at their feet. Lyn, with her miniskirts, and black leather, her hair bobbed short, was, Jeff Nuttal said, 'like a young Susan Hayward', now that she was off drugs. Alex's soft purring voice made gentle conversation like an artform in itself. It must have seemed on those occasions as if all their troubles were behind them, as if the future would be bright. St Stephen's Gardens had already become the headquarters for sigma and the movement for which sigma was the vanguard. Timothy Leary was to describe it as 'Alex's London nerve-pulse heart chamber' in his book *Politics of Ecstasy*. American poets Jack Micheline, Gregory Corso and Bob Creeley dropped in at various times. 'Normal' family life had to take second place, was difficult if not impossible. It took a special kind of inner strength to put up with the numerous comings and goings, the tension of never having a private moment. Alex rigged up his living room as a kind of office, for sigma was Alex and Alex was sigma.

Better Books' basement in Charing Cross Road, WC2 had rapidly become a centre for happenings and exhibitions and there was the Indica Gallery in Mason's Yard, SW1. Wesker's Centre 42 operated in an old railway shed in Chalk Farm, later renamed the Roundhouse. Cedric Price's Fun Palace was planned for a site at Lea River, E15 after a pilot scheme, four years earlier at Camden Town. There were a lot of new ideas in the wind. On August Bank Holiday 1964, two tribal youth cultures clashed at Margate. Teenagers were making the news. This was the dawning of the era of amphetamines and the contraceptive pill, Soho coffee bars, skiffle almost becoming merged with rythmn 'n' blues. The Rolling Stones, the Pretty Things, the Kinks and the Who were just about to follow the Beatles' lead in distracting a generation. Writers and artists who had, in a sense, created this rebellious underground ethos, remained unaware of the monster - 'Popular culture' - almost a contradiction in terms, which was just about to leap out into the headlines.

Alex was frenetically busy; he had meetings with Anthony Burgess, corresponded with Bertrand Russell, Tom Pickard, George McBeth, Colin Wilson (c/o Hugh MacDairmid), Rayner Heppenstall, Ferlinghetti, Mailer ('Alex - you old Bolshevik!'), lunched with Wesker, enthusiastically endorsed the first issues of *Playboy* and *Penthouse* (though these were, at the time, clearly intended to be more imaginative and creatively-inspiring than they are now!). Both magazines were associated with the 'underground' and the publisher of *Playboy*, Victor Lownes, was interested in publishing full-length work by Trocchi. His name apppeared on the cover of the first *Penthouse* - occasioning a letter from a clergyman who had known him at University, saying that he was shocked to see him sponsoring 'this kind of thing'. Alex had not actually agreed that his name be used but did not wish to attract attention by stirring things up. Joseph Strick, the movie director, who wished him to write the screenplay for his projected film of James Joyce's Ulysses, invited him to dinner. They met at the Grosvenor House Hotel. They had not seen each other since a cocktail party in New York in the late fifties. 'It was a most pleasant meal. When we parted, he shook my hand warmly and said; "No, I am convinced Alex. If I make *Ulysses* you will be my scriptwriter."' But it never happened. Strick made the film in 1967 and co-wrote the screenplay himself with Fred Haines.

Alex was invited to become a peripatetic lecturer in the sculpture department of St Martin's School of Art in Tottenham Court Road. St Martin's was, at the time, the foremost School of sculpture in the UK, as a glance at the staff-list reveals: Anthony Caro, Edouardo Palozzi, Robert Clatworthy, Elisabeth Frink, Philip King and William Tucker. Frank Martin, head of the department, a former Marines Sergeant Major, had transformed a small and unknown sculpture department into an international force in avant-garde sculpture and was later elevated to the Fellowship of the Royal Society of British Sculptors. Alex's contract began in October 1964 and he held his classes on Fridays between 10am and 1pm and 2pm to 4.30pm. His methods of teaching were unorthodox to say the least; he believed in exposing the students to as wide and disparate a range of influences as possible. He used his position to spread the sigma message throughout the college, inviting leading poets such as Creeley and Charles Olson to read to his classes and encouraged multi-cultural events. He planned to stage an exhibition of his own sculptures and wrote letters to those who owned various of his works, including Robert Silver, the editor of *Harpers*, seeking the loan of such pieces as 'The Accuser', 'Lear' and 'The Three Kings', driftwood pieces brilliantly painted in mesmeric lines.

He was involved in a large number of projects: he wrote to the Postmaster General suggesting a series of stamps featuring the work of British sculptors, which he considered would improve the 'aesthetic impact' of the stamps. He had rediscovered his boyhood interest in stamps when Marcus began to take an interest. He began to build up a collection, and later attended stamp auctions and traded in rare stamps, although at times of financial crisis, he often had to sell many of his favourite collections. He devised an idea for an 'alternative' late night chat show 'Night People', to help the ailing pirate radio station Radio Caroline, and he produced a list of luminaries whom he could persuade to appear. He gave a performance in Better Books in October to launch *Naked Lunch* - performing both his own material and standing in for Burroughs, who was now, immutably, in Tangier. At home, he worked on his 'De-Sade box'. This was an old wooden dresser painted black inside and out, reconstructed so that each little drawer, when opened, would be found to contain items designed to corrupt or awaken new levels of consciousness. There was something annoyingly quaint, rather than subversive about it however, and it was soon discarded. He wrote bitterly to the Managing Director of W.H. Smith's protesting at their continuing blacklisting of his books. He appeared on *Tomorrows' World*; received £200 as an inducement to accept a film proposal for *Young Adam* from Brian Hutton, planned to make a trip to Cuba and instead spent a few days in Holland with Simon Vinkenoog, one of the leading Dutch 'sigmaticians'.

It would be useless to pretend other than that he was leading a highly erratic and frankly chaotic life. There were the large number of guests and visitors at his flat, both serious and frivolous, and of course, he was taking a large amount of legally prescribed heroin. It was a miracle that any serious writing got done at all. Nevertheless, it was under these circumstances that the translations of *The Centenarian, Countess Dracula* and *The Girl On The Motorcycle* were completed for John Calder. The first two of these were a collaboration with Beba Lavrin - who made a rough draft which Trocchi rewrote. There was a central contradiction in his life, between the philantropic, utopian ideals of sigma and his desperate need for daily funds to feed his wife and children and to pay for his drug prescriptions.

He claimed from the end of 1964 and for years thereafter, to be working on *The Long Book*, and perhaps he was, though this was never to emerge, (despite Calder announcing it for publication in November 1966), except in a small number of excerpts and never achieved cohesion as a unitary piece of writing. The small excerpts that have been published are of derisory quality, almost embarrassing – as if Trocchi no longer really cared - and the work seemed to encompass almost all the 'casual' writing that he worked on from 1963 onwards. It never gained any momentum of its own and mainly incorporated lengthy diatribes against 'literature' and publishers - especially John Calder - whom he was expecting to publish the book. The title was itself the result of a misunderstanding between author and publisher; asked what he was working on, Trocchi replied 'a long book,' and didn't bother to correct the assumption that this was the title. It was intended to move beyond the self-absorption of *Cain's Book* - beyond 'identity' - the third person narrator is 'anyone' and 'everyone'. As in Beckett (perhaps self-consciously), it is a move beyond personal identity, and parallel's Burroughs' SF fantasies with a subsidary interest in 'global paranoia'. He had abandoned the first person narrative tense which he had used so well in his best books - rather as if Necchi/Trocchi had nothing further to say ... But instead of writing the new novel, he took to the soul-destroying task of copying out *Cain's Book* and *Young Adam* in long-hand in ledgers for Dr Schwartz, an agent for Texas University Library (known affectionately by Trocchi and Burroughs as 'Jake The Dentist') who paid him £35 for each. Schwartz had earlier bought his correspondence with Burroughs.

The publication of Burroughs' *Naked Lunch* according to January's 'Peace News' had re-opened the debate on censorship. The magazine referred to the 'almost casual' banning of *Fanny Hill* and *Cain's Book* in the raid on the Sheffield Bookshops, the ensuing court case at Sheffield Magistrates Court, and the appeal pending in the High Court. It seemed that the forces of darkness, led by the gross and hypocritical Grannie Grundy herself were in the ascendancy. Trocchi girded his loins for battle and counter-attacked in the columns of *New Society*. In one of several articles, a review of Ludwig Marcuse's *Obscene* (MacGibbon & Kee), in

May 1965, titled 'Lady Chatterley's Charade' he concluded: 'in the hands of serious writers today, obscenity is a form of purity; what Professor Marcuse calls 'the old indignation' is an anachronism, a collective insanity; it is a matter for psychiatry, rather than lawyers. Enough said.'

In April, his eldest brother Alfred died, having come to Guy's Hospital in London for specialist treatment. He had nearly died of rheumatic fever as a child and the operation for heart valve replacement was hopeless from the start. He died on 22nd April 1965. Alex was later to write that Alf had been to all intents and purposes his father ' ... it was he who started me reading, who sent me to the university, who confirmed me in my decision to go away to France.' There was 'a subtle link between himself and myself which derived from our almost nightly discussions about politics, religion, art, economics ... talk, talk ... that almost drove poor Marion up the pole ... a kind of common ground, which, because poor Jack at that critical period of his growing up was rotting away in a Japanese prison camp ... we were never at any time ever to share with Jack.'

Here then, is Alex, in the very midst of tragedy, commanding his troops at the front. On his return from the Isle of Man, he jokingly reprimanded Lawrence Ferlinghetti for not visiting him during his trip to London. He had also missed Timothy Leary's latest visit but Leary was arrested shortly after his return to America for possession of half an ounce of cannabis, for which he received a thirty year jail sentence and a $30,000 dollar fine! A worldwide defence fund was set up and the issue became a cause celebre, in which Trocchi was again heavily involved. He was prepared to do anything rather than write!

Chapter 19: Royal Albert Hall, 11 June 1965

With the profusion of poets and cultural figures arriving in the metropolis, it was inevitable that an event of international importance would occur. And it did. Friday 11th June, 1965 was destined to be one of the high points of the Sixties' Generation. The fullest account of what occurred that night in the Royal Albert Hall is provided in the 'Afterwords' section of Michael Horovitz's *Poetry of The Underground In Britain* (Penguin, 1969): '... instead of programme notes, ten of us - John Esam, Harry Fainlight, Ferlinghetti, Fernandez, Ginsberg, Paolo Lionni, Dan Richter, Alex Trocchi, Simon Vinkenoog and I - got our heads together the night before and improvised an Invocation, prefaced by six lines from 'Jerusalem' ... ' Handbills were circulated advertising 'A Historical gathering of many of the world's great contemporary poets'. An unprecedently large audience of over seven thousand attended, and paid 5/- or 10/- to hear poems by Adrian Mitchell, Michael Horovitz, Pete Brown, Chris Logue, George MacBeth, Tom McGrath, Harry Fainlight, Anselm Hollo, Gregory Corso and of course, Ginsberg. A Press Conference was held, on the steps of the Albert Memorial, in which Trocchi assumed the role of leading spokesman. A film, *Wholly Communion* was made of the event and a commemorative booklet was subsequently issued. The *Sunday Telegraph* of June 13th described Trocchi's role; 'Here, at the Albert Hall, he emerged as a model chairman, introducing the speakers without fuss and exercising a kindly but implacable 'guillotine' on the time allowed for each poet at the mike. Like the president of some sacrificial rite, he would unyoke one speaker from the instrument strung around his neck and quickly yoke up the next. Each poet got a very fair crack of Mr Trocchi's whip,

Alex with Ginsberg, Horovitz, Fainlight, etc, on Albert Memorial before
Poetry Festival, Albert Hall, 11th June 1965.
Photo: 'Daily Telegraph'.

so to speak.' The *New Statesman* noted that Alex 'compered the proceedings with schoolmasterly firmness.'

The event was a great success and the *TLS* declared that 'literary history' had been made by 'a combination of flair, courage and seized opportunities.' A sour note was provided by the manager of the Royal Albert Hall, Christopher Hopper, who was widely quoted after the event; 'I don't want that sort of filth here ... would you send your teenage daughter to hear that kind of thing?' The squabbling over the profits provided an even sourer sequel. In an article entitled 'Poet's Albert Hall Profits Fade', Trocchi, described as 'artistic chairman' was quoted; 'I tried to discuss the finances of the co-operative with the organisers. I am sure they are sincere people, but I'm afraid the accounts were disorganised.' The article detailed the sad facts: The hire of the Albert Hall had cost New Zealand poet John Esam £600; £200 had been spent on drinks and stationery and £100 paid to Gregory Corso (the paper took the opportunity to note that Corso was a former inmate of Sing-Sing). The BBC had paid Esam £100 for filming rights, thus some £2,000 had been received in total and assuming that the hall rental and other costs had actually been paid, the profits were expected to be upwards of £1,000. Mr Esam was, however, uncontactable. After some discussion, the BBC Copyright Department made payments direct to the poets and sent the bill to Mr Esam. This was returned marked 'address unknown, return to sender', and it was reputed that he was holidaying in Greece. The other main organiser, Dan Richter, whose wife Jill had put up front money, was ill in a nursing home. This may have meant that the sum that had gone astray was the entire £2,000. While some poets consulted a solicitor and Horovitz wrote angrily to the *TLS*, Trocchi merely deplored the entire episode; it was only the first of many disappointments that were to shake his faith in the sigma 'cadre'.

Shortly after the event, a man called Bill Harpe who was organising the Commonwealth Arts Festival in Cardiff contacted Trocchi. Would he help to organise a two-day poetry event in September? Trocchi took on the task and began contacting poets and writers. It was like *Merlin* all over again ... and dovetailed easily with sigma's continuing expansion. Ginsberg, Beckett, Ferlinghetti, Spender, Bunting, Stevie Smith and MacDiarmid sent good wishes but would be unable to attend, and eventually the list - spread over 20 countries - included mostly the younger British poets, such as Pete Brown, Tom McGrath, Mike Horovitz, Melvin Bragg and Brian Patten. Trocchi again chaired the proceedings, in the Reardon Smith lecture Theatre, with the Nigerian, Wole Soyinka, as his deputy, and himself read passages from Henry Treece - regarded as a highlight of the event by the *Western Mail* reporter. Unfortunately, following so closely upon the newsworthy Albert Hall event, the Festival was a ripe target for the well-ground axes of the media. SCREAMING PIG BARRED FROM POETS' HAPPENING (an anti-Vietnam protest - the pig was removed by officials) - and GIRLS OFFER TO DANCE IN THE NUDE (gratuitous piece of editorial prompting) were two headline stories which revealed how poetry had already become inextricably associated with stunts. Trocchi the showman, the 'architect of happenings' showed his other face when he attempted to quell the disorder, and restore sanity. 'We're not out to shock for shocking's sake,' he assured the Press. Later, he also ordered Horovitz off the stage because Horovitz' chanting was spoiling a good double-bass line. He had no hesitation in using his authority in reactionary, even despotic ways, if he felt he had cause.

The ending of the event, like its predecessor, was unseemly. He had incurred considerable expense but was never paid in full his agreed fee of £125. Harpe had resigned. There was nothing Trocchi could do. Worse, he was pursued for settlement for damage to a hotel room. The damage - two wet bedsheets - had been caused by a 22 year-old called Nicola, who had got drunk and wet the bed on which she had been deposited to keep her out of harm's way during the performances.

Upon returning to London, Trocchi decided that his consumption levels of twenty grains of heroin and seven grains of cocaine per day had reached danger point. Thus, he travelled alone to Herne Bay in Kent, on 9th October, to 'establish a beachhead'. He did not wish to stop his use of opiates, merely to regain power over his addiction which he felt was raging out of control. He took with him only enough heroin and cocaine for twenty-four hours, along with a large quantity of other drugs, including methadone and hallucinogens such as apomorphine, fantazine and LSD. He installed himself in a boarding house, whereupon he proceeded to don a blue silk mandarin's cloak 'to give an air of formality to these desperate proceedings ... ' and propped himself high in his bed, overlooking the grey sea ... to await deliverance. He had brought a large purple ledger to take notes - the 'diary of a cure' - but he refused to consider that he needed to be cured, which suggests illness. One might wonder what other name he would give to his addiction? but in the next twenty hours, melodramatic and hilarious to an onlooker, but considerably less than hilarious to Trocchi himself, he chronicled his diminishing chemical supply. He commenced in grandiloquent style, setting the scene for his 'experiment', discussing the context of his heroin use, but then the notes became less reflective, less grandiose, rather more concerned with the precise number of pills remaining: '12.46am. 21. How can I use 21 pills to bring myself down from 100? 12pm. 11 pills left. We shall take a cup of Horlicks, and then to begin with, 150 micrograms of LSD - perhaps then I shall get things in a clearer perspective ... I can't say I am not worried ... 4.30pm. There is one grain of heroin left - has been these last 4 hours. I feel if I can keep that grain there ... 6.10pm. Last fix taken. It no longer beckons from over there. I feel wonderful ... ' Readers will have deduced the inevitable end of the story; the hasty packing away of the mandarin's robe, the desperation, the panic-stricken search for a chemist, the argument over the prescription, the negation of pain in some public toilet, followed by the return to London and the realisation of defeat.

Back in the city, he was plunged into a maelstrom of meetings with solicitors, businessmen, financiers, in an attempt to get sigma off the ground as a limited company. The pressure was such that he complained to his GP: 'I just cannot manage on twelve of heroin and six of cocaine, I need an average of fifteen of heroin and nine of cocaine ... per day.' A letter published in the Guardian in 22nd

January makes clear there were approximately 342 registered heroin users in Britain at this time. In his letter, he rails against the draconian attitudes to this 'tiny minority', a most convenient target, he feels, for the self-righteous indignation of the citizens. He felt that the hysterical attitudes prevalent in the USA were becoming adopted in the UK. Critics might say that Trocchi now wished to defend his rights to use heroin having failed to curb his own usage of it. What had become a problem for him was to be freedom for others.

New Year's Day, 1966, found him wandering the city in the early hours in search of a few grains of cocaine, as he wrote to his new GP, the eccentric but well-respected Scotswoman, Lady Frankau, in a note dated 2am. In the note he speaks of his gladness that she will accept him as a patient, of the ambigious nature of his 'problem' and the facets of his personality. 'Without heroin,' he declared, 'I would not have transcended that terrible and profound anger that was in me as a young man at the cruel waste and stupidity of the world.' What had been a battlecry or a manifesto now sounded painfully like an excuse.

Despite this bravado, Alex had resolved yet again to quit drug-taking: 'I will ... be able to get rid of this terrible compulsion. I must get rid of it, for I can't go on this way much longer.' Four days later, however, he wrote to Lady Frankau again asking for a supplement ... 'I have a rather tough weekend ahead.' He blamed it in that instance, on an eleventh hour delay in advance royalties which just might have cost him the new flat and then a last minute success in other negotiations, causing the sudden arrival of Brian Hutton, the producer who had an option on *Young Adam*, and the fact that he would be at St Martins all day. All this pressure, real or imagined, provoked more letters to Lady Frankau. He had a public appearance 'in some town hall or other' which he had forgotten and which had been recalled only by a short article in a newspaper informing him that he was appearing. Therefore, could she supply ...

The Trocchis secured a lease on a luxurious penthouse flat in Observatory Gardens, Kensington. The annual rent was £245, the lease at £1,000, payable over six months, was, according to Alex, 'a gift'. By which he meant perhaps that he hoped it would be.

He petitioned his brother Jack for a loan to help pay the lease. Meanwhile, Louis Diamond, the 'swinging young lawyer' involved with sigma, who had secured their lease, took up Alex's claim that he had been defamed by a letter in the 13th March edition of the *Sunday Times*. The letter, titled 'Male Novelist's Retreat' by Eva Figes, contained the bizarre assertion that he had retreated from heterosexuality altogether, frightened by dominant females and found compensation in drugs. Louis Diamond wrote to the paper claiming evidence of people taking seriously the implication of the letter that Trocchi was no longer heterosexual and informing them he had been instructed to issue proceedings on behalf of the Trocchis. Trocchi himself wrote to the Editor on 10th April, 'I am tired of being represented in an uncomplimentary way in the various fleetsheets of the city ... this letter you published is ... the last straw ... upset my wife most seriously ... placed my young son in a very embarrassing position (7 years old and you know how cruel kids can be) ... your paper is widely read amongst a wide group of my influential friends in the United States ... some have unconscious prejudices against homosexuality ... this will have very serious consequences on our fund-raising activity ... I am famous, even notorious, for my heterosexual extravaganzas.' He ends by claiming he has been advised to sue 'brakes off.' A settlement out of court was demanded, and £500 named as the sum (moderate according to Alex's publisher, Mr Dwye-Evans at Heinemann), but Diamond needed proof that Alex was being 'oozed' out of his position at St Martins because of the 'awful disclosure' in the *Sunday Times* and such evidence would be very difficult, even impossible to obtain. There had been some complaints from parents of students and despite receiving no official dismissal, Alex was, *ipso facto* no longer teaching there on a regular basis. But was that enough evidence? A reply from the *Sunday Times*' legal adviser contained an offer 'in no way prejudicial to their complete denial of liability, to write to all those persons who had formed a misapprehension of Alex after reading the article' - if Alex supplied a list of such persons! After further legal skirmishing, the matter seems to have drifted to no more satisfactory solution.

Sigma matters were consuming all of his time: He was involved in correspondence with Bob Herschorn of Montreal and Leonard Cohen who wrote that a millionaire had offered the use - rentfree - of a tower block in the centre of Montreal for sigma - and he had a new financial backer; Nigel Samuel, son of a property millionaire, who also put money into various projects of Michael X's.

Lyn was unwell and he was forced, finally, to send her at considerable expense for a month's holiday in Mallorca. Alex himself was bedridden and was yet again attempting to 'kick' heroin, once again he failed though he did reduce his daily intake. Lyn and Mark settled into their hotel in Calvo Sotelo, Mallorca. On the 21st, in the evening, Alex received a phone call from a distraught Lyn; three days into their holiday, Mark had fallen out of a second-storey window and broken both arms. The cost of medical bills and a room with bath and meals in the hospital for five days was to come to an exorbitant £125. As Lyn explained in a letter - 'at the time of the accident, with Mark screaming in agony and carrying one broken arm in the other broken arm, I didn't stop to enquire about fees. The fractures were bad, especially the one at the elbow and he's now encased in plaster from the waist to the neck with one arm jutting out and supported by a steel rod.' It hadn't occurred to either of them to take out medical insurance.

Sigma adopted Alex's throw-away assertion that 'as artists we situate ourselves at the level of man-at-crap.' This was the era of the 'mind-expanding toilet roll texts'. The idea was, that seated alone in a cubicle, a man was at his most vulnerable to cultural impregnation. Feliks Topolski and Seymour Krim were among many who collaborated with Trocchi in concocting suitably mind-expanding verses or slogans for printing on the toilet rolls. Some were long dialectic poems, others in the form of postcards to 'The Occupant, The Chambers, East West, North, South.' Some were the work of 'Chamber Productions' - 'You wipe mine, I'll wipe yours,/ Eyes, bum, mouth, nose./We live alone, in silence.' Some were in the form of spoof detective fiction and others were merely long pieces of prose. Most were mildly interesting and in 1966, the idea was quite new and caused a minor stir. Eventually commercial companies took up the idea and within a few years, every Student Union in the country would be using 'mind-expanding toilet-rolls' of some sort and it became a *cliché*. As we have already seen, Trocchi was well aware throughout his life of the rebellious potential of a well-placed toilet-roll - whether thrown from a school window, dropped onto military barracks or placed at eye-level in toilet cubicles.

Sigma held meetings with a property company about taking over St Paul's Churchyard and Ed Dorn, editor of *Kulchur* and Visiting Fullbright Professor of American Literature at Essex University was added to the board of sigma. Even members of the Government, such as Jennie Lee, Labour's new Minister for the Arts, were now taking an interest. Since the Albert Hall event, the 'Underground' had become a very public and visible continuous event happening spontaneously all over London. Groups like sigma were already in danger of being outflanked. The Beatles had initiated the psychedelic era with *Revolver*. Pink Floyd were appearing in pubs and halls. The Underground's considered, careful, philosophical stance, previously known and espoused only by an in-group, became adopted and dispersed thinly among the millions, diverted, drained. What had been a coherent, subversive doctrine for the few was now drowned by the incoherent babble of the many. The two tribal youth cultures became fused into one; the stage was set for the world-wide psychedelic revolution of Hendrix, The Grateful Dead, Frank Zappa, Ken Kesey and his Merry Pranksters, the Diggers, the Hippies and Yippies, flower power and acid culture. In an effort to keep control of the insurrection, Alex was constantly open to new mergers with other groups and had, for some time, wanted to arrange a meeting between sigma and some radical psychiatrists, grouped around Joe Berke and RD Laing, and known as 'The Philadelphia Foundation'. The group had been formed to oppose the concept of hospitalisation, to formulate a community of doctors and patients, and break down the categorisations of mental illness - in which many of them did not believe. Laing, the author of numerous books, including *The Divided Self* and *Self and Others*, was a Glaswegian from a similar background, of similar age, and at their first meeting, they discovered that they had attended Glasgow University at the same time. There was an apparently strong rapport between the two men, and undeniably, although Trocchi would not admit to such sentimentality, this was due to the 'Glasgow connection'. 'Like, Ronnie and I are swinging,' Trocchi would say, and they would be seen squatting together on the floor, foreheads touching, or, high on mescalin, fencing with kids in the street. Their closeness was undeniable, but in reality, they had little in common. The entirely-boorish (my opinion) Laing did not read any of Trocchi's material, nor did Trocchi read any of Laing's (so-called) writing. It was their image of each other that was important in the relationship. Laing claimed to me, in a hostile and unfriendly interview, several weeks before his death, that Trocchi had seen the possibility of forging a link between art (sigma) and science (Philadelphia Association), but denounced him as an 'ultra-conservative counter-revolutionary, a romantic utopian.'

Alex had reasoned that if these two groups could collaborate, create perhaps a joint community in the country, the intellectual high-ground could still be maintained. Jeff Nuttall went ahead and booked Braziers' Park in Oxfordshire for a weekend conference in the first weekend in July 1964, which both groups would attend. At Trocchi's insistence, everyone would bring their wives, a curiously priggish request.

Various published accounts of this weekend exist: Jeff Nuttall's version appeared in *Bomb Culture* (1968) and Tom McGrath's *The Innocent*, appeared in part in the *Edinburgh Review* (1985). The setting for surely one of the most bizarre confrontations of the Sixties was a large country house owned by a Quaker community. Alex prepared his inaugural address on tape-recorder. He was using tape-recorders extensively at this period, and a large number of reel-to-reel tapes survive, largely uncatalogued. He admitted right at the start that 'no-one has been very articulate on the subject of what precisely we are about in congregating here this weekend.' He then went on to speak of 'seizing the grids of expression' - of 'ecletic lightbulbs which can be turned on in mutual recognition by means of various tactical sigmals ... click ... click ... click ... ' He quoted Kropotkin's remark that the future is in the hands of free associations not of centralised governments. The conference began ... and soon degenerated. There was considerable unease, friction - which Trocchi tried to dispell. Laing and others began drinking, others got high. Spray paint covered one of the walls. The avant-garde artist John Latham had destroyed a book as the centrepiece of an angry protest on the wall. The Quakers were brought out of their bedrooms in the middle of the night by the disturbing sounds of anarchy.

Trocchi overdosed on cocaine and had to get Tom McGrath to help him next morning with a heroin injection to calm him down. Then he reappeared in the lecture room, puffing affably on a pipe and quelled the growing disorder. He read a letter of support from Bob Creeley and began outlining the next stage in the campaign.

Alex was involved from the earliest stages with the London Free University project. In January 1966 he attended meetings in Queensway and Powis Terrace, in the company of such diverse figures as Brian Epstein and Michael De Freitas. He published an article on the movement in the sigma portfolio. Dr Joe Berke, one of psychiatrists of the Philadelphia Association, published an article in *Peace News* calling for a Free University of London similar to the Free University of New York. In the article he specifically related the idea to sigma; a brotherhood of intellectuals lecturing for no fee to anyone who cared to listen. The project did not take off until two years later, when, as the London Anti-University it had influential support of all the alternative cultural figures plus political radicals like C.L.R. James. At that time, it had acquired a campus, at Rivington Street in Shoreditch, and put out a catalogue of staff and classes, of a bewildering variety. Yoko Ono's 'Connection', for example, offered 'to connect people to their own reality by means of brain session and ritual.' Some classes were even more esoteric, but it is easy to deride from the distance of history. Unfortunately, the 'anti-university' became more and more like a real university and failed to live up to Trocchi's aspirations. He discontinued his services as an 'anti-lecturer'. But that was in the future.

Beris Sullivan was assisting him with his correspondence. The first task to which Beris applied herself was the question of the

Frank Harris reprint in *The Olympia Reader*. Letters were sent to Grove and to Girodias, pointing out that the entire extract from *Life and Loves of Frank Harris* was by Alex and not Frank Harris. Girodias replied that he was surprised to hear that Grove had paid him nothing for the Frank Harris extract. 'They presumably paid that to Frank Harris' estate; an amusing confusion. And yet they were perfectly aware of your being the author.' He enclosed a contract for a reprint of the fifth volume of the Harris Memoirs. Good news arrived from America - Seaver; 'I owe you an apology. Indeed in the *Olympia Reader*, the good hunk of the Harris material is in fact yours.' However, Alex had already been paid, in the sense of having been previously over-paid! He wrote again, urgently, to Insel Verlag in Frankfurt, trying to hasten their negotiations with Grove. Insel had written, but only to confirm the 'difficulty' with Grove. 'God knows,' Alex wrote, in exasperation, 'the present conglomeration of circumstances is almost unbelievable.' To make matters worse, Alex had now spotted a mistake in the contract - 'my wife, being American, typed dollars for pounds.' The $500 advance is far too low, compared to that for the NEL edition which had netted him an advance of £750. Since the mistake is partly his, he offers a compromise, and this was duly accepted.

The Trocchi family enlarged by one on 28th December 1966. A second son, Nicolas Adam Trocchi was born in Westminster Hospital. But it was a bad time to arrive in the Trocchi household. Lyn and Alex were at loggerheads, her post-natal depression leading to pointless bickering and Alex was beset with worries caused by the attempt to convert Project Sigma, an unsuccessful Limited Company, into a registered charity.

Chapter 20: Uncle Hamlet, searching 'for a plausible end'

By 1968, it had finally become obvious that Alex Trocchi was unlikely to produce another masterpiece. The impetus to write was dissipated. He was a writer in abeyance, for while his books were in print in several languages and continuously reprinted in the Seventies, only two new books emerged and both had been written long before. There were to be a great many proposals, suggestions and schemes but most never progressed beyond a brief profile or a sample chapter or two. This would be enough for him to get an advance. Then began a long correspondence during which deadlines were revised, ignored, rescheduled. The project would end in squalid arguments over the advance money - long since spent - and demands for its return. Publishers were more interested in him than they had ever been. Corgi was clamouring to print the Lengel novels and Cape wanted him on their lists. But with commercial success now within his grasp, he found that the will to accommodate it had entirely gone. There were a large number of film proposals and directors have considered most of his books, but none became films until David MacKenzie's *Young Adam* in 2003. Bad luck, a malignant fate, now stalked him and he was unable to escape its machinations. All that was left was to eke out his notoriety, become a living legend, and die with as much dignity as he could assume. He put it rather nicely himself in his diary:

'All those words. Ideas, unfinished thoughts, so many reams of the stuff ...into which, if I reach for a page, I am ... sometimes ... relentlessly drawn. After all, they *are* my own notes, and from time to time I can remember the circumstances in which they came into being. Ah yes, that was the time ... and suddenly the bright impulse which took me back is thwarted, extinct. Yesterday's bearings. But they are not the less true, I suppose, although sometimes the very sight of them makes me want to throw up ... and no wonder, all those titles! All those plausible beginnings! What I am looking for, I told myself over the years, is a plausible end. Like the overdose with which I have been accredited how many times since I fled from New York? My God! I thought you were dead! Yes, indeed, the plausible happening, the plausible end ... or even the implausible one, so long as I could write *fin* at some point or other, and the gesture be in some profound sense fitting. But of course it was not to be. Plausible or implausible I had no end in sight, nor would have before dying, and then someone else would have to write it. Meanwhile, I was and am as usual knee deep in the disordered thoughts of more than a decade. Uncle Hamlet, quite gone into middle age, and still undecided.'

So what had gone wrong? The late Sixties should have represented the very apogee of his fame. Many of the movements that he had spearheaded had been validated on an international basis. He should have been a cult hero of international status. Up there, with his peers: Lennon, Leonard Cohen, Norman Mailer, Jim Morrison, Ken Kesey, Burroughs, Ginsberg ... He had been in the vanguard of the Sixties which had stormed the ramparts of 1950s moral stagnation - yet was a forgotten hero. To those insiders, of course, he remained the genius he had always been, a 'writers' writer', intimate with all the movers and shakers. But times had moved on. And of course everything went sour in 1968. Americans rioted in Watts, or marched in Berkeley, burned their draft cards, sat-in, fought with police to the soundtrack of Hendrix's mangled, apparently ironic, rendition of *The Star Spangled Banner*. In Paris, Situationists joined the student riots and battled the gendarmerie. Sweet reason had given way to violence. It was not Trocchi's way. And books were appearing every week which of his friends, to the new London generations, which, attracted by his notoriety, and his drugs' connection, clustered around him and made him their high priest, their sage. One never knew who of that wide pantheon of his friends and fellow sages might phone or call round unexpectedly. No-one was turned away. And here he would regale his audience with the story of how he had been conned out of writing the famous screenplay, of how his influence on Ken Kesey and Alan Sillitoe had never been acknowledged, of how the notorious Candy was a 'rip-off' of his own work.

His flat was sometimes like Grand Central Station, and there, in the gloom of his booklined study, ankle deep in bills, paint tubes, syringes, driftwood sculptures ... sat Trocchi, often gowned in a long embroidered purple, green and blue burlap dressing gown and tasselled smoking cap, benevolently dispensing wisdom and imbibing opium from a beautiful brass 'bong' - or hookah pipe. Lyn, the woman who lived with him longer than any other, said: 'Alex, who is a great man, but no bargain, says "I will not tolerate a world that rejects me." He thinks he is God, he really does.' A great man, but no bargain. To many he *was* a kind of ironic God. Leonard Cohen had described him as 'the contemporary Christ'. His childhood dreams of deification in the backgreen cellar in Bank Street had been in part fulfilled. He had followers, worshippers, acolytes.

And over all the detritus of the flat prowled the beautiful Burmese and Siamese cats, supremely indifferent heirs to the magnificent hauteur of their owner. Occasionally they would sniff critically at the thickening dust visible on the lid of the electric typewriter.

Trocchi was highly considerate towards all those young persons who came to him seeking salvation, money, sponsorship, drugs. He was perhaps too generous for his own good. The police were convinced that he was at the centre of a large drug-dealing cartel and his flat was often raided. Once, the police found a quantity of jewellery in his study, £2,000 worth, stolen from a room in the Hilton Hotel. A young house guest was responsible but in the raid, the 'bong' and a small quantity of opium was discovered - which were more obscene than anything he had ever written. Obscene on a far less literary, less subtle, less worthwhile, level. The rebellion became adopted by the masses, the sigma project was swamped by less imaginative - but more easily understood schemes - and lost in the mass incoherence and persistent clamour of the second-rate. His books were reprinted continuously, such that almost every few months there was an advance on one or more of the titles, but, of course, it was Maurice Girodias who was overseeing much of the reprinting and Girodias doled out royalties in very small, irregular sums and persistently tried to get Trocchi to sign away his royalty rights, hoping that perhaps one day, when Trocchi was desperate enough, he would. Meanwhile, whether Girodias knew - and he may have conspired in it - the novels themselves were widely pirated. An entire book could be written about the sharp methods of one in particular - Hollywood publishers Brandon House - and how they cheated Alex out of, at a conservative estimate, quarter of a million dollars on six best-selling novels. There were at least three other major pirates, and a host of minor ones, exploiting his works in America; Greenleaf Classics, Collector's Publications and Shorewood, who never paid him one red cent. Even when Trocchi saw a contract, there were extremely shady deals, with the mafia reputedly involved in at least one of these deals. Thus, the amount of money he did receive was miniscule, and he was never far from poverty. Several times he was evicted from his flat and taken to court for rent and rates arrears and pursued for services bills. In 1970 he attended Kensington Magistrates' Court to appeal against debt actions for rent and rates arrears totalling over £300.

In his top-floor penthouse in Observatory Gardens, a leafy, tree-lined Kensington street, he gradually settled into the comfortable ooze of obscurity and middle age, making only occasional forays out into the limelight. He talked of numerous projects - indeed he talked of little else - and had the knack of making them appear urgent, immediate, vital, as if they would take off at any moment. These projects' aims and stages of development varied from day to day. Talking about them saved him having to sit down and write them. He sent out hopeful signals to all his visitors, to the wide circle were confiscated and Alex was charged. They did not discover his laudanum, which, being a dark liquid, was kept in a bottle labelled 'Stephen's Ink'. Trocchi's outspoken views on drugs were guaranteed to attract police attention, but he took great pains to avoid the possibility of being charged with 'intent to supply', claiming that he gave free drug counselling, actually talking young people out of using drugs. The police wished to prove to the world that the leading drug radical was no more than a degraded junkie wallowing in squalor and irresponsibility. Despite this, the clarity and originality of his views on the Brain Report and drug legislation have been given wide exposure in serious medical and academic journals and, in 1968, he was invited onto the panel at the Law Society Conference in Brighton, to appear alongside spokesmen for the Home Office, psychiatrists and Senior Drugs' Squad policemen. It was an unbelievable opportunity to take his views and criticisms into the midst of the enemy camp, unfortunately he was ill, unable to attend and the opportunity was lost.

Illnesses of one kind or another were beginning to play a significant part in his life, and the worst forms of illness from which he suffered were the fictitious variety. He began to avoid invitations he previously would have relished. He did have some real illnesses of course; he slipped a disc and it pained him now and then, he had numerous ailments associated with his long-term drug habit. But the illnesses were more often than not a convenient way of avoiding his obligations, his deadlines.

Trocchi resumed his friendship with Scottish publisher William McLellan, who visited him several times and told him of the Scottish nationalist landslide in the municipal elections of 1968. McLellan related it to the theories of the *Invisible Insurrection*. There was a need, he felt, for 'international leadership for this vast inchoate revolt.' Trocchi, and McLellan (like MacDairmid and many others) was intensely interested in the Social Credit proposals of Major Douglas, whom he described as 'a Scot who saw clearly.' McLellan tried, but failed, to get the SNP to adopt the proposals as policy and Trocchi's interest lapsed when he saw how overtly political - with little cultural content - were the policies of the SNP.

He had been considering a volume of reminiscences of Paris based around *Merlin*, using most of the original published material from the magazine, with introductory passages and anecdotal links. He was full of the project for some time, and sure that it could be completed in a matter of months. It was barely even started. Then there was the collection of essays which would include his previously published work on Orwell and Max Frisch; the novel *American Nights* sold to Johnathan Cape for one of the largest advances he ever received - £750 - which never progressed beyond a couple of short sketches and the title. Correspondence about *The Pornographer* novel, which he had been contracted to write for Lancer Books in New York continued for several years. He spent their $2,500 advance money and wrote only two sample chapters. He had discovered an ease and glibness with the language of the publisher and he traded his good name and his enviable sales reputation for advances. All he had to do was write a simple plot outline, a couple of short sketches, conjure up a title and obtain the money - or a third of it, since the rest of the money was payable on publication - and that would remain beyond his reach. Even if he finished the book, the fatalist inside him knew that he would be unlikely to get what he was owed, or the royalties would not exceed the advance or the publishers would decide to cut him out of the deal and pay nothing at all. 'So really old man, you see I have no incentive whatsoever to finish the book. Now, I have a better idea, and your help is crucial...'

True, his financial circumstances were miserable, liable to become so suddenly desperate that he had - simply had - to get money immediately, now matter how, or from where. True, Lyn was increasingly unstable and from 1968 to 1969, they lived apart, then she needed to be incarcerated in an asylum for several periods for her addiction. The children's needs must be met ... And he was still a junkie, indeed probably the longest-surviving and best-known junkie in the world, with all a junkie's needs. Specifically, he needed a large cocktail of heroin and cocaine at regular intervals just to keep insanity at bay. These circumstances conspired against the stability to sit down and work. He had more than enough good excuses to avoid having to confront a typewriter in the cold light of day. And even when he did find himself in that unaccustomed posture with fingers poised above the cold keys, more often than not he would discover a pressing need to write a letter to ... whoever - upon some urgent sigma matter - to Bertrand Russell perhaps, or Colin Wilson - or John Lennon. Now that the sigma project had faded from view and removed one good and long-running excuse for prevarication, he became a man of causes: Michael X must not hang! The Brain Committee must think again! And perhaps just one more letter of sweet reason to Brandon House may soften the demonic Milton Luros's hard heart ...

Michael X, in early 1973, was in prison in Port of Spain, Trinidad for triple murder. The correspondence between Trocchi and Malik is extensive. Of all who had known Michael in the UK, Trocchi was the most committed and persistent in working for his release. He wrote numerous letters to all who might have influence and originated a telegram to Dr Eric Williams, the Prime Minister of Trinidad, calling for clemency and appended on that document the signatures of many of his closest friends and associates including Marion Boyars, William Burroughs, John Calder, Eric Clapton, Leonard Cohen, Marianne Faithfull, Jim Haynes, Marcus Klein, Kit Lambert, John Lennon, Bill Levy, John Mitchell, Yoko Ono, The Hon Alice Ormsby-Gore, Cedric Price, the Hon Michael Portman, Dan Richter, Nigel Samuel, Feliks Topolski, Simon Vinkenoog and Jamie Wadhawan. He launched a furious onslaught on VS Naipaul in the *Sunday Times* for his 'utterly pitiless and analloyed condemnation' of Malik. All to no avail.

The sigma organisation, if it could ever be called such, had faded away and the portfolio and all its associated publications took up considerable space in Trocchi's flat. Gradually, it all disappeared and became disordered. Lists of subscribers and interested persons, over which he had so laboriously worked, became hidden under dusty piles of new papers. Only in the Netherlands was the idea still alive (the Sigma Centrum in Amsterdam, Government funded, was a major cultural centre well into the Seventies) and Trocchi made numerous trips to Holland to participate in cultural events. He was regarded with veneration there, due to continued demand for his novels, and due also to his friend, Simon Vinkenoog, who constantly mentioned Trocchi's work as an influence on his own. Sigma in London failed in its attempt to become a Registered Charity and remained a Limited Company. The directors - Burroughs, Topolski, Choules, Hatcher, Diamond, Dorn, resigned one by one until Trocchi was the only one left. Money dwindled to nothing, donations dried up and press interest fizzled out. In the end, the project had been too utopian, too wide ranging with not enough tangible proof of its existence. If they had, like the Dutch, acquired an actual headquarters, then perhaps the project would have gained momentum. It didn't take Trocchi long to invent a new project, which he announced in the *International Times* on 26th February 1970 as 'a new exercise in sigmal tactics'. It would be a secret underground tabloid and include contributions from Burroughs, Ginsberg, Lennon, John Mitchell and Trocchi. 'My Own Business' (M.O.B.), a piece of prose by Burroughs became its first editorial. It apeared as an enormous poster-sized sheet, lavishly illustrated by Feliks Topolski, with poetry, fiction and articles - its price? One 'sigmark'. Scripts began to pour through the mail from writers wishing to get involved, but the sheer mechanics of organising such ventures were now past him, even with the valuable assistance of such as Jeff Nuttall and Richard Lee, and a second issue was not produced. 1970 was a year of exceptionally heavy debt for him, and he was delighted to be awarded a Writers' Grant of £500 from the Arts Council. This was immediately attacked in the press. The *Daily Mail* of 16th March headlined a large article THEY'RE GIVING AWAY YOUR MONEY TO SPOONFEED HIPPY 'ART'.

'The Arts Council is making some astonishing decisions about the way it shares out its £9m a year budget ... some of the money has gone to a patron of the underworld - an anarchist and member of the drugs world ... Alexander Trocchi aged 44, a former pornographer and self-confessed heroin addict.'

Alex was quoted in the article: 'It got me out of a hell of a predicament. I was very hard-up. What am I doing now? A couple of books ... I'm an underground cultural entrepreneur.' A spokesman from the Arts Council felt brave enough to comment: 'We think he is a good writer.'

For years, Trocchi had been attempting to complete *the* definitive non-fiction book on drugs. Several publishers had been interested and several large advances had been obtained - and spent by its initial collaborators: Trocchi, Henry Charles Hatcher and William Burroughs. Later, R.D. Laing was mentioned as another collaborator and George Andrews (author of *The Book of Grass*) and John Michel (author of *View Over Atlantis*) and Trocchi spent many hours getting high and making tape recordings of long, stoned conversations. So many tape recordings were made and so much material outlined that several typists had to be hired, at the publishers' expense, to annotate and edit them. Despite the mass of material, very little of real interest was being unearthed, very little certainly that could be used in the book. The recordings continued until they became an end in themselves, and the book was forgotten. It was a wonderful excuse to get high for days on end and pretend that work was being done. The work was to include an essay Trocchi had published in *Books And Bookmen*. But not the alarming misprint which that journal had seen fit to bestow upon it. The substitution of 'prescribed' for 'proscribed' infuriated him when he discovered it. 'It makes nonsense of the statement,' he angrily complained to the Editor. Bad luck dogged his every footstep. Unable to make progress, the publishers employed a ghostwriter Sandra Shulman, and in the end, removed Trocchi from the project entirely, although he had to agree to his name being used on the cover. His name was valuable on a project. Girodias had already deduced this. Girodias had been desperate ever since the publication of new editions of *Helen And Desire* to obtain a new Lengel book - preferably under Trocchi's real name. He wrote to Trocchi in glowing terms, outlining vistas of hitherto undreamt of wealth for both of them if only they could between them produce a new Lengel. But he was forced finally to concede that a new Lengel was unlikely ever to appear. He changed tack and offered a deal. If he could find a competent writer to work 'in the style' would Trocchi agree to his name being on the cover? Trocchi furiously rejected this. There was only one Lengel and one Trocchi and it was he! Girodias had to content himself with reprinting *Thongs*, which he produced in October 1969, at a cover price of £1.95. It sold 17,000 copies in the UK within one year, having built-up an advance order of 2,000 prior to publication, yet did not, according to Girodias, cover its $2,000 advance!

The republication by Tandem Books of *Angela - The Story of a Strange Woman* by 'Jean Blanche' triggered another lengthy correspondence war. The novel had first appeared in 1959 under the imprint of Castle Books, a subsidiary of Book Sales Inc. Despite being merely an inferior rewrite of *Helen and Desire*, it was a Trocchi rewrite of a Trocchi novel, and as such valuable property. Tandem Books were a subsidiary of Universal Publishing, and therefore in the same company as Book Sales Inc., with whom Girodias was dealing over the rights to *Sappho*. The issue became hopelessly complex. The legal tangles that now ensued between the author, Tandem Books and Girodias, and between all these parties and Castle Books were increased, since their original contract was 'irregular'. In the end, Tandem simply went ahead and printed 250,000 copies and, taking advantage of the confusion, paid Trocchi nothing. As with the *Sappho book*, he received no payment for *any* of the editions.

But Trocchi was a master of conceits with a prevarication for every occasion. His collection of poetry, mostly written in the 1950s, had been promised to Calder & Boyars. Although these poems needed only minor revision, the work was delayed and further delayed from the original deadline of 1st March 1968, and finally appeared in both paperback and hardback editions in 1972. It was given thoughtful reviews by literary critics and carries a foreword by William Burroughs. The poetry is of two genres; the older poems, written in the 1950s, betray clear influences of the metaphysical poets, particularly John Donne and are archaic in style, whereas the material added in the 1960s and 70s suffers from some of the gimmicks of Sixties poetry, verbal trickery and crudity. It was an unsatisfactory collection. Burroughs remembers Trocchi's defensiveness about his poetry, and in his foreword tactfully avoided giving any opinion on their merit - or otherwise. There are some interesting and well-wrought poems in the collection, mostly from the Cap d'Ail period: 'A Little Geography Lesson For My Sons And Daughters', 'Myrtle With The Light Blue Hair', 'Winds From The Bosphorus', 'Portrait'. The cover blurb hyperbolically described the book's publication as 'an event of great significance ... undoubtedly a notable addition to the published work of one of Scotland's finest writers.' While there was little doubt that any new book by Trocchi would be an interesting event, this volume fell considerably short of what the reading public expected from him. The public wanted something as good as *Cain's Book*. When it became finally apparent that this was a forlorn hope, they gradually lost interest in him.

Chapter 21: Underground Man

But it would be a mistake to think that Trocchi was completely dormant. Such was his desperation for money that he was forced into completing a series of translations for Calder & Boyars and these were in a literary sense, highly successful. First of these had been the outrageous and picaresque *I, Jan Cremer* in 1965, from the original Dutch, then Andre Pieyre de Mandiargues' *La Motocyclette* in 1966. Due to the long-running quarrel between Calder and Grove, Trocchi's translations of both appeared only in the UK. The American edition had been produced with Jan Cremer practically living in the Grove office breathing down the translator's neck. Then he had taken his large advance (and the pneumatic Jayne Mansfield) to South America, leaving Grove to deal with the disastrous sales' figures. The UK edition fared much better. Calder's edition, *The Girl On The Motorcycle* featured the young Marianne Faithfull on the cover, long hair hanging down, clad in black leather astride a powerful motorbike. As this picture might suggest, the book is an erotic fiction employing a simple structure and even simpler plot: a young woman leaves her sleeping husband to ride through the countryside of northern France to Switzerland to meet her lover. As she rides, episodes of her experiences with both men recur to her. The novel is successful in that it manages, in its sustained sensuality to hold the tension until the sudden, shocking end. The translation was published to coincide with the film, starring Faithfull and Alain Delon.

In 1970, Trocchi's translations of *The Centenarian* by Rene de Obaldia and *The Bloody Countess* by Valentine Penrose appeared. *The Bloody Countess* was filmed by Hammer Films as *Countess Dracula* starring Ingrid Pitt, Nigel Green, Maurice Denham, Sandor Eles and Lesley Anne-Down. For some unknown reason, Trocchi received no screen credit for it. He had completed the translation of the book (by Valentine, the wife of his friend Sir Roland Penrose) in 1965, with the assistance of Beba Lavrin. It was the tale of 'Erzsebet Bathory, La Comtesse Sanglante', a Hungarian Countess who recaptured her youth and beauty by bathing in the blood of murdered virgins. Beba Lavrin also collaborated with Trocchi on *The Centenarian*, the rambling monologue of an octogenarian Count, whose recollections include his many wives, his childhood, his rival - gored by a bull - his numerous conquests and adventures. Alex had read the book in Paris in 1959 but wrote that it had bored him after the first 40 pages. 'Sexual fantasy and practice, recited in cold, clinical prose, are rarely off the author's stage. But he also writes lyrically and with great beauty,' wrote the *Sunday Telegraph* critic. 'Tremendously exhilarating'; the *Sunday Times*. Playwright John McGrath had done an earlier translation of the book but Trocchi had derided this: 'Frankly, it is so bad, he probably does not have any French worth mentioning.'

Trocchi's brilliance as a translator was widely recognised. He could make a book burst into new life in its new language. In most cases, it is considered that his translations improved the original. In 1974, Granada brought out an edition of *La Gana* by Jean Douassot whose translation Trocchi had begun in New York in 1958. Jill Neville reviewed the book in the *Observer*; '*La Gana* has an almost too powerful stench of one kind of truth and is marvellously translated by Alexander Trocchi. Written in a direct, stabbing style, it positively groans with life ... the book pullulates with slang, which must have given Mr Trocchi some translation headaches ... '

Meanwhile, *Cain's Book* continued - and continues today - to be anthologised and reprinted. Sections appeared in *Oyster, Evergreen Review Reader, The Book of Grass, The Addict* anthology, *Out of Our Minds* (Penguin), *Drugs From A - Z* (McGraw-Hill) and *Man's Magazine*, and there were editions printed in Germany, Netherlands (from two publishers), Argentina/Spain, two editions in Italy from separate publishers, a Danish edition and in the UK the Quartet edition appeared in 1973. Grove reprinted the novel in 1979. New English Library reprinted *Young Adam*, the third British edition, in 1966 (and *My Life And Loves*) and there was an Italian edition of *Young Adam*, a Danish *Thongs*, a Dutch edition of all six Paris novels (indeed, *Carnal Days* was published similtaneously by two separate publishers in the Netherlands in 1969), a Dutch edition also of *School For Wives*. There were German editions of *Thongs* and *My Life and Loves* and a collector's limited edition by Girodias of *Life and Loves* and *Helen and Desire*. Tandem, the British subsidiary of Universal Publishing & Distributing Corporation, brought out *Sappho of Lesbos* in 1971, since then reprinted several times including, in 1986, by Star Books. Girodias, aware of the goldmine potential of the Paris novels, to which he never surrendered his 'publishing rights', kept the novels continuously in print. The average sales of an edition of each of the best-selling novels; *Helen* and *Desire*, the *Carnal Days* and *Life and Loves* was 300,000 (according to a letter from Girodias) and these sales figures seemed undiminished by the number of editions. Even when Brandon House put out mass paperback - pirate - editions of the novels in 1967 in America, Girodias' sales were unaffected. Indeed, he sold *Helen* and the Harris Memoirs, now retitled (since their inauthenticity had become accepted) *What Frank Harris Did Not Say* to a company he himself owned - Beeline Books, an imprint of Kable News. When these books appeared, he firstly refused to pay the £1,000 advance on either, pretending he had no connection with the company, and later, when no royalties were forthcoming, cooly advised Trocchi to write to Beeline and declare himself as the author!

Girodias did not take the incursion of Brandon House into his territory lying down. If there is one thing a rogue hates it is a worse rogue than himself! The 'Frog Prince' hired lawyers and began to sue everyone within reach. He successfully sued Marvin Miller of Collector's Publications of California - who subsequently went out of business - and Greenleaf Classics and then began the long battle with Milton Luros of Brandon House.

The story of the Brandon House editions of Trocchi's novels would, as has already been said, fill an entire book on its own. Brandon House were first mentioned in early February 1967 in a short letter to Alex from Jack Hirschman, who had known him in Venice West, mentioning Brian Kirby, an editor at Brandon House as a personal friend. Kirby professed to be an admirer, but admitted that his boss, Luros, was 'difficult'. 'He doesn't trust writers,' Kirby explained. Trocchi was, nevertheless, initially pleased to hear of their publishing plans for *Helen and Desire, Carnal Days, White Thighs, School For Wives* and *Thongs*. Kirby explained that there was some urgency and Trocchi dutifully wrote short introductions to most of the novels. Robert Creeley wrote the introduction to *Thongs* and Hirschman himself wrote postscripts to *Helen* and *Carnal Days*. Trocchi was promised advances on royalties of $750 per book with $250 for the introductions; one thousand dollars per book, a total of $5,000 advance money - but clearly based on a royalty of 4% of the cover price of each. There was a peculiar delay in the arrival of contracts - a flurry of transatlantic telegrams - and they arrived unsigned. Trocchi signed his copies and returned them. He never received the completed signed contracts. By this time, of course, he had sent Brandon all the introductions. He received no money, no contracts. After long letters throughout the Autumn and costly transatlantic phone calls, he was reassured that Luros himself would be flying to London and would settle all outstanding matters. In the meantime, he had heard that *White Thighs* the first Brandon novel to appear had sold 50,000 copies in the *first week* and was reprinted in March, in May and in July. At a conservative estimate that added up to *at least* 300,000 copies printed during the first five months! And, according to Kirby, all of the five titles were in the same best-seller bracket.

While Alex waited for Luros to arrive he slipped a disc and was thus prostrate when:

'Beaming Mr Luros turned up finally at the end of October, at which time he came to see me and spoke of villas with swimming pools in Los Angeles, and wouldn't I like to go over there etc ... an offer which over the past two decades has been thrust at me by many publishers and whatnots, but always in the context out of which I might justly expect not descriptions of castles in Spain, which I don't wish anyway, but dollars and cents owed at once by contract. However, I had no wish to alienate Mr Luros who was becoming sweeter than any meringue by the minute, and whose fundamental honesty anyway I even now hesitate to finally doubt, and I therefore agreed with him that he should go home to his hotel and his wife (his better half) to consider the facts expressed by me, that he could now see my point very clearly, and that he tended to agree with me...'

"But of course I cannot take that sort of decision without referring to the little woman. Tell you what, I have to go off to Bremen tomorrow, but as soon as I get finished there I'll be back and you will be the first on the agenda. That should be around Friday morning." 'Needless to say my heart jumped a little at the thought of his once again taking off into the blue, particularly as in my crippled state I was in no position to follow him, and so I extracted a vow as intense as that offered by Moses in connection with his firstborn. The very thought of his hanging me up, and not coming to some satisfactory agreement with me before his return to the States was too much for Milton's fine feelings.' "Alexander! So help me! If only you knew my little lady! I ask you to take it from me that I will not step aboard an aircraft without first discussing matters again with you personally."

Injun Big Trust: "If Injun can count on this truly Mr Luros then he can relax in ..."
Milt: "You can trust me Alexander, as I trust my little woman."

'Well, Milton gets back from Bremen some time on the Saturday I think. I catch the little woman on the telephone and try in a few words to impress upon her the importance for all concerned of Milton getting in touch with me and some satisfactory agreements being reached. She is very reassuring, and Milton will 'phone me as soon as he gets back to the hotel. As it reached midnight I decided, damn it, I'd ring him first thing in the morning. Well, he has rung Steve (novels by 'Steve' - John Stevenson and Iris Owens were also pirated by Brandon in the same manner) and has given him to understand that on replacing the receiver he will be getting in touch with me. An hour later, he and Mrs Luros leave by limousine for London airport (I feel Steve might have given it quarter of an hour or so and then checked whether or not I had received the call). However ... when I have found out that the bird has flew I phone Steve and he says: "Well, it might not be so bad because Luros has left a number of books for me and evidently a cheque for you. He also promised to be in touch..."

'Can you imagine,' Trocchi wrote, 'how I, still flat on my back and scarcely even able to move, was affected by the sight of a cheque for $1,000? Had it been for $10,000 I might have withheld judgement, but still I should have expected a telephone call from Mr Luros as soon as he returned to Brandon House.'

While Trocchi fumed in London, he became aware of Girodias' duplicity in the matter. Initially, it seems that Girodias had been prepared to licence the pirates in some way, giving them some kind of authority to use the novels while pretending to Alex that he knew nothing whatever about it. Probably because of this ambivalence, Luros felt he was safe in defrauding the author. Later, of course, when Girodias realised the success of the Brandon editions – unlike the other minor pirates he had undeniably already done deals with, whose editions tended to be amateurish, and no threat to his own – he began all-out attack. The correspondence, much of which survives, between Alex's agents, Girodias, Brian Kirby and Brandon's lawyers reveals the true nature of what Girodias himself (certainly somewhat of an expert!) called 'one of the most extraordinary and repulsive tales of deception and treachery ever,' yet, paradoxically, it was at this point in time that Girodias offered Alex $500 to sell all his rights in the retitled Harris book, arguing that it was really a new property entirely! Notwithstanding that it had been Girodias who had purchased the eighty or so typed pages of Harris' manuscript in 1954 and handed them to Trocchi, and notwithstanding that this had ended up as a 220 page book, Girodias now attempted to claim that less than one quarter of the book was Trocchi's own work – which contradicts his own letters and his previous claims! Alex's agents at this time were Victor Briggs & Co, and they were also considering a separate action against Brandon. Girodias wanted a collective action by Trocchi, Stevenson and Owens for breach of contract and was convinced this would lead to an out-of-court settlement. Alex's agents advised him to avoid any of Girodias' schemes, and expressed incredulity at the methods of the 'Frog Prince'. Girodias was a splendid charlatan, a man of some style; Trocchi described him as 'a 19th century shark.'

A study of the correspondence makes it quite clear that Girodias had had a meeting with Brandon before consulting either Trocchi or Stevenson. Brandon hired Stanley Fleishman, a Beverly Hills lawyer, to defend them, and the legal fencing began. The matter was never resolved and Alex received no further money. In 1977, a new editor, Harold Straubing, (and Brandon House were now located in Chatsworth, California) wrote to inform Alex of motion picture negotiations for *Helen and Desire* and *The Carnal Days of Helen Seferis* and offered the author 'shares on an equal basis. This is our standard agreement with authors.' It was a sick joke. Trocchi wrote a cautious letter, drawing attention to the previous pirating of his novels, but assuring them that if they now wished to provide an accounting of total sales of the novels and deal fairly with him in the future, he would recommend that they proceed with negotiations on the films. Strangely, or perhaps unsurprisingly, there was at first no reply to this letter then a brief letter arrived to say that as yet no firm film offer had been received, though Straubing now mentioned an inquiry from another major studio about *Thongs*. He assured Alex that, if films were made of either of the three books, they would wish to reprint them. It sounded like a threat, nor did he make any apology for their previous treatment of Trocchi. The offer for *Thongs* came through on 5th May. The Producer was Bunny Oliver, of Dancer Fitzgerald Sample Inc. of New York. Demands by Alex's new agent, Anthony Shiel, that Brandon produce an accounting and sales figures for the five pirated novels drew a reply from Fleishman. His investigations revealed 'that in 1967 Mr Trocchi sold all rights in five novels to Brandon for flat payment of $1,000 each. We are certain that Mr Trocchi will remember these transactions with Mr Luros in London in 1967.' This was rubbish of course. Why would a publisher who already possessed 'all rights' send the author contracts subsequent to such dealings - which would *reduce* the rights they had already paid for? At a cover price of 95 cents for each of the five novels and an estimated sales total of 3 *million* copies, Brandon had cheated him out of an estimated quarter of a million dollars. They now cheekily informed Trocchi that his letter authorising Brandon to go ahead with film negotiation supported their complete rights to his books. Alex was advised to construct an affidavit which was circulated to the film company, to Brandon and to Fleishman. They claimed they did not receive it. Then they claimed that their reply had been lost in the post (it later arrived, with, it must be said, a much later postmark). Then they claimed that it was Alex who had not returned signed contracts to Brandon in the first place. This was palpable nonsense and the correspondence ended there. From then on, all negotiations about the film ignored Brandon House and proceeded between Alex, his agents, Bunny Oliver and her agents.

The project had started badly but soon Oliver and Trocchi were confident of success. Rather unwisely, Trocchi agreed to write the screenplay himself and Oliver flew to London for intensive script meetings. There were arguments over his finished script and further changes were required. Oliver demanded all the Glasgow location be removed. Trocchi found the task of writing the screenplay rather boring and added embellishments. Oliver flew to Greece in despair for a long holiday. They both had entirely different conceptions of the project. Trocchi had worked extremely hard on the screenplay and felt, not unnaturally, somewhat aggrieved. Oliver then hired a new screen writer, Michael O'Donoghue, but the film was never made.

There were many abortive film deals. Arthur A. Seidelman, a leading American producer who had worked with top American actors, and had an enviable record of production success, took a movie option on *Cain's Book*. Seidelman's approach, Alex agreed, was certainly in line with his own attitude. The film was to be made in England. Trocchi requested that a young friend, Jamie Wadhawan, be incorporated into the production side of the film if possible. Seidelman agreed, and wrote to Wadhawan. Seidelman began to arrange the finance.

Subsequently another option was taken for *Cain's Book*, this time by Joko Films, an offshoot of the Beatles' empire, to be directed by Dan Richter. John Lennon was keen on promoting the project. A ninety page outline was sent by Richter and Trocchi made some emendations. Shooting was to begin in mid February 1973. Donald Pleasance, cast as the father, wrote to say that he was 'now familiar with your book and admire(d) it very much. I have now read the film script and if all goes well and the date works out, I would be delighted to be in it.' Donald Sutherland was initially cast as the Necchi/Trocchi character, then Keith Baxter's name superseded his. Eric Clapton and Keith Brown were to provide a sound track and shooting was to begin in August.

Dan Richter wrote from the Chelsea Hotel to confirm another twelve months option on film rights, but it is clear that he was taking increasing liberties with Trocchi's material, for Trocchi wrote complaining that film rights and options needed to be licenced and licences cost money. Richter's reply was that Jacques Sterne, producer of *Junkie* and *The Sorrow And The Pity*, had taken a six-month option. Richter believed there was a real possibility of the film coming into being for Sterne was married to a Rothschild and presumably had the funds ...

Jamie Wadhawan, a young film student had first visited Observatory Gardens in 1968, to make a twenty-six minute documentary film *Cain's Film* amidst the chaos of the Trocchi's preparations to spend some weeks in Paris. The film, Wadhawan's 'graduate piece' for which each student had been given £150, was premiered at the London Polytechnic in Regents' Street. The documentary features an interview with Alex and comments from Burroughs, Topolski, Jim Haynes and R.D. Laing. Wadhawan later made two more short films; *Man With A Hat* about Alex's old friend from Paris, the Greek sculptor, Kosta Alexopolous and *Marihuana Marihuana* on the Amsterdam drug scene, in 1973. Trocchi was given screen credits on both and features in the second. These two films were given a preview with a reception, in the Rank Preview Suite at 127 Wardour Street on 11th December 1973 (which Trocchi failed to attend) and shown in the NFT later in the month. Meanwhile *Cain's Film* was scheduled for British TV.

Alex's need for an alternative source of income had led him to take a second-hand books stall in the Red Lion Arcade in Portobello Road Market in Notting Hill. He soon diverged into antiquarian and rare books and moved his stall to various other locations. For about six years the stall was in the Kensington Hyper-Market in Kensington Road, then, in 1983, moved to Antiquarius in Chelsea's King's Road. He became somewhat of an expert in valuing books, rare manuscripts, antiques and paintings. Here again was an excellent excuse for not writing. The stall came to be managed by Marcus Klein, an American he had known since his days in Paris, but Trocchi felt it necessary to personally attend sales at Sotheby's and Christies and acquired some expensive and extremely rare stock. His reputation in the rare books trade was merited by his knowledge of the subject. Of course, the business did not make his tax position any easier to understand and there were furious arguments every year after his tax demand was presented; he had a running battle with the Inland Revenue, who were convinced that the business was making profit in excess of £6,000 by 1979. His overheads, including paying Klein and a travelling salesman cost £3,000 and rent was £2,500. He estimated he was making a profit of between £3,000 and £4,000 after all costs were taken into account.

He often enjoyed his notoriety, and revelled in the title of 'one of the first prophets of permisiveness in this country' which had been bestowed upon him by Brian Magee in April 1972, when he appeared on the Thames TV programme *Something To Say*. He was on fine form and almost the first suggestion he made was to Katherine Whitehorn, Magee's other guest; that he and 'Kathy' should make love ... 'but first of all I would have to ... I suppose make myself delightful enough to Katherine, and I doubt whether we could manage it tonight, but that would be the great triumph, and that's how I would like it to end...' In the hour of the programme, Trocchi dominated in a heated debate on the state of modern marriage and monogamy. To justify his opposition to conventional monogamy, Trocchi told the story of a friend who had just been released from prison after three years and arrived at their door, unloved and depressed. He had told Lyn to 'take him upstairs' and informed the audience that his wife and himself had other partners and exhibited no jealousy towards each other. How much of the story was true and how much sheer bravado can only be guessed, although, of course, one remembers that he had put his wife onto the street in America years earlier and this was not much different, except perhaps now he was boasting of it as liberation, whereas before it had been borne of desperation. Questioned closely on where he would draw the line on this sexual freedom, Trocchi revealed that he would not allow his son, then thirteen, to have affairs with other men. At first, when asked what he would do if he found that an Italian man had been seducing his son (who was on holiday, on his own, in Italy), Trocchi replied flippantly that 'an Italian man is just as good as an English man,' but, pressed to answer properly, he was forced to agree that he would not be happy about it and accepted that no juvenile should be 'interfered with' ... 'we must draw the line.' As Whitehorn said 'Well, that's something ... goodness, we've found something we agree on...' Later, he agreed that it was a concession but stated that his idea of sexual freedom was only for consenting adults. In his passionate attack on what he called old-fashioned morality - he contradicted himself several times, and really, it is hard to accept that he believed all that he was saying. He considered himself not committed to monogamy, and although he had had several short affairs during both his marriages, he had lived a fairly monogamous life. 'Definitely monogamous enough so that the kids get the point.' He felt however that no one should set out to be monogamous, and would need to find their own way.

A few weeks after this programme's transmission, an event occurred which showed that the forces of reaction were still on the alert. In June 1972, Scotland Yard police officers raided the warehouses of Universal-Tandem and seized 130,000 books, thirty-three separate titles, including *Thongs*. A trial on the grounds of contravention of the Obscene Publications Act, 1959 was arranged for 13th October in Magistrates' Court, Stratford. It was a reprise of that day in Sheffield Magistrates' Court, when *Cain's Book* had been on trial. He attended as a witness for his own book on the second day, amongst other witnesses such as Edna O'Brien, John Trevelyan, John Calder, Grahame Green and William Hambling MP. The defence counsel was again Bruce Douglas Mann, Labour

MP for North Kensington and the decision to ban the book was upheld. The police were continually raiding the London offices of the Olympia Press at the time. *Helen and Desire* being among the books confiscated in the numerous raids. Douglas-Mann, also Girodias' lawyer, was quoted in the *Evening Standard* under a headline: THREAT TO SUE YARD OVER BOOKS; 'The actions of the police in this matter appears to constitute a wholly unwarranted interference with the conduct of our client's business.'

After the case was over, Trocchi and Burroughs travelled to Ecclesdon Common near Worthing for the Sci-Fi Convention at Phun City - a three day festival of music and outrageous behaviour. He and Burroughs lounged in the large marquee, heavily stoned, watching bemusedly, indulgently, the antics of the younger generation, like sages of the tribe. Creeley and Mick Jagger were also there and Marianne Faithfull - who was part of Trocchi's scene in West London. Burroughs taped some of the 'tribal dances' while a Hell's Angels group physically removed a TV crew because they hadn't paid for film rights. At this time too, he was in contact with John and Yoko Lennon regarding the cost of Michael X's trial in Trinidad. He was at pains to assure them he was 'not trying to twist your arms.' In September he participated in Anglia TV's *Drugs by Satellite* programme. And then, just when everything seemed to be getting better - a devastating blow:

Lyn contracted hepatitis and Alex sent her to see a Harley Street specialist. Various friends helped to look after Mark and Nicky and the bookstall while Alex spent much of his time with her. She had been admitted to St James' Hospital in June where she had fiber-oesophagoscopy, then was transferred to Guy's Hospital, where, on 9th November 1972, she died. She was thirty-five. The death certificate, signed by Dr D.J. Nutt, Registrar, gives four causes of death; liver failure, chronic active hepatitis, serum hepatitis and septic arthritis of the right foot. She was cremated at Honor Oak Crematorium, Brockley Way, SE4 on 14th November. Trocchi's luck was running out. His son Marc, the golden boy whose school career had been excellent, was outgoing, extrovert, good as expressing himself and creative. He too was to be struck down. I am grateful to Paul Ahearne, a former school friend now living in

Australia who shared his memories of Marc. They had been friends since primary school and had then gone to Holland Park School together. Paul said: "We trained in Tae Kwon do at a time when the whole world wanted to study martial arts, and spent many hours chatting as young adolescents about the world ahead of us. We were keen cyclists. While I managed to cobble together sufficient funds to buy a second hand Claude Butler bicycle, Marc was given a purpose built *Tour de France* type bike by his dad's good friend, Eric Clapton. Marc and I had first girlfriends together (the girls were school-friends too) and we used to listen to *Layla* on Marc's stereo and dream of our girls. Marc first became sick while working on his dad's book stall on Portobello Road. What started as a back strain was later diagnosed to be very serious cancer, which young Marc, at 15, couldn't beat. He wouldn't see any of his friends while he was sick."

Marc spent months as an in-patient at the Royal Marsden Hospital for Sick Children. He suffered for three years from cancer of the throat and then he too died, on 21st May 1977, less than six years after his mother. The cause of death was given as carcinoma of the nasoprarynx. He was cremated at Mortlake Crematorium.

On 30th May, the day of Mark's funeral, the funeral Director, Mr B.G. Albin, wrote to say that Lyn's ashes had been moved from Honor Oak to Mortlake. He referred also to the breakdown of a car during the funeral and commented; 'how proud I was to see such courage in yourself and your younger son - this is something I shall always remember ...'

Alex wrote to Lyn's parents:

'Until Mark died ... I take it you do know of his death ... my emotions were so tautly sprung I found myself quite unable to be involved seriously in things. And during the last few months with hs condition deteriorating ... towards the end so fast, so utterly ... for me everything else was in abeyance. He was taken to hospital for the last time and I was in and out of his little room all the time. As the days went by it became so regular I began to take it for granted he would be there in the morning. And the suddenly he had gone in

Marcus and Nicolas Trocchi, c.1976
(Courtesy: Sally Child)

his sleep ... so they told me on the telephone. I howled like a dog. How much I had wanted to be there beside him holding his hand: They said it would have made no difference. It did to me ...'

There was something of a reconciliation, through grief, with Betty and Morris Hicks, Lyn's parents, and Alex sent Nicolas over for an extended holiday with them in Indiana. He later wrote to thank them for giving Nicolas such a wonderful time: 'He hasn't stopped talking of the wonderful grandparents ... and other relations too ... "although I just met her I really love Betty and Morris just like I loved Lyn!" He wants to go every summer. Christmas too maybe ... there'll be no stopping him now. He's found the rest of his family and he won't let go. I can't tell you how happy it makes me. In a way it brings me close to Lyn again ... If I haven't talked much about Mark, it is because he took half my heart with him when he went ... Betty ... you will understand how I, who watched over him day by day for 18 years have wept for him, and still weep at moments when I am alone ... And then, near the end, when his nose was bleeding and it wouldn't stop, he cried out "Oh God, Alex, I don't know what I'd do if I hadn't got you!" I took his poor thin little body in my arms ... What can one say? Until he was fifteen he was mentally and physically beautiful. During the three years he took to die ... his heroism was wonderful ... I can't talk about him any more ... I shall have the ashes of Mark and Lyn together now. Soon I shall bury them and plant a rose tree on the grave.'

Both Trocchi's daughters visited England in 1973 but only Margot spent time with him, feeling instantly at home with him, but Jacqueline and Alex did not meet, neither apparently prepared to make the first move, even although she had her children with her, Trocchi's grandchildren, whom he would dearly loved to have seen. She was in England to try the equestrian circuit with her three horses and she returned to England in 1984. Both the daughters were very fond of Lyn. Margot offered to look after Nicolas in New Zealand. Now eleven years old, having suffered the loss of his mother, and his older brother, Nicolas seemed relatively unaffected by the double tragedy. He was described by Mr Durden, the

Headmaster of Fox Primary School in Holland Park as 'a charming, dreamy boy with a gentle manner and a delightful sense of humour. Intelligent and thoughtful. Very popular with his classmates.'

To try to introduce some normality into their family life and to help with the domestic chores, Alex was introduced by Robert Creeley's wife, Penny, to a young New Zealand girl, who for six years was to be a second mother to Nick. In the same week that Marc died, Sally Child, a beautiful twenty-four year old, took to the task of lightening the gloom that had decended upon the flat. Gradually, over a period of several months, a closeness developed between the author and the nanny. After several months they became lovers. Sally admits that she fell in love with the author and set out to seduce him. Alex was sufficiently surprised and serious about it to write to her parents in New Zealand, on 1st December 1977:

'For some time now I have felt that I should write to you. To tell the truth, I find it difficult to know what to say. We don't know one another and you are so very far away. The point is, I feel I must try and set your mind at rest about Sally.

As you know, she lives with me. I don't know whether you know, or have guessed, that we have become lovers. I'd like you to know that this didn't happen casually, nor did it happen quickly. We had lived in the same house for two months before it happened. I believe you know I am fifty-two years of age and a long-time heroin addict. Frankly, at the beginning, it never occurred to me that we should become involved. Now that we have, and now that we both seem to be sure we want to continue to live together, I am most anxious to reassure you about the fact that Sally will be safe with me. Please put your mind at rest Sally will not be using heroin. I promise you I shall look after her as though she were my own daughter, that through me she will come to no harm.

For the rest, I think I should rather leave it to Sally to tell you about me. She is a dear, wonderful intelligent girl, and I am most fortunate to have her with me.'

Jane Lougee contacted Alex in 1979 and they arranged to meet in Paris and make a trip together to Majorca by car for old time's sake. Jane had inherited part-ownership of a house in Deya. He eagerly looked forward to it, but in the end it was a nightmare. He could not travel without his drugs, turned up at the rendezvous four days late, Jane had her poodle with her, Alex insisted on driving, there was an accident (he hit a mailbox), confusion, and arguments. In the end, he demanded to be let out at the next town and next day it took her all morning to find him. He handed her a small silver box, they said goodbye, he returned to London, she continued alone to Majorca. It was a sad end to their great romance. He also greatly anticipated his first wife Betty's visit to London in 1981. She found him greatly changed, reminding her of the rabbit in *Alice In Wonderland* - 'I'm late, I'm late ...' with only occasional flashes of the old Alex. She was surprised to see how like his father he had become, almost pompous, grandiose. Alex for his part confided in Sally how old he thought Betty had looked.

The picture of Trocchi now is autumnal. He was a man shadowed by deep grief. Trocchi mourned the deaths of his second wife and first son and separation from his first wife and two daughters, and the grandchildren he would never see. His mind was turning more and more to the past, to the idea, specifically of an autobiography; but how to begin it? He would need tremendous energy for the task, and felt that he had little stamina for it. His career had lapsed, projects arose and were ignored, opportunities came and went. His day would start late with a visit to his bookstall in his Mini. He was not an expert driver, tending to be rather incautious, especially at junctions. Then he would repair to the house for some lunch. His appetite, albeit his heroin addiction, was hearty. He had always had a gourmet's eye for the best of foods and wines, and his fridge often contained literally dozens of different cheeses. His study was a depressing place in daylight, with its ravaged filing cabinets, overflowing onto the floor, the unsorted detritus of the years, and he would spend many hours avoiding it in the afternoon in the *Elephant & Castle* or the *Catherine Wheel* in Holland Street, over a vodka and coke, or would perhaps linger over a capucchino in the

Alex and Sally, c.1978.
(Courtesy: Sally Child)

Cherry Pie on Kensington Church Street, usually reading, wearing a small pair of steel framed half-moon spectacles and his bulky leather jacket. He was well known in the area, and had a great many friends, one of the closest being Eric Clapton who bought Nicolas an expensive bicycle on a birthday as he had for Marc some years earlier. When the pubs closed at 2.30pm, he would transfer to the Lindsay Club in Church Street, frequented by TV actors, writers such as Scot Gordon Williams and Ian Cochrane from Northern Ireland and attractive young women with someone you could half-recognise. It was a gloomy cavern of a place in the basement, small, but with an ambience which Alex liked. He liked to talk and many (including this writer) enjoyed listening to that soft purring voice with its verbal tics; 'D'accord, old man…' and the sense of inclusion which it casually conferred. There were a couple of pool tables and a large overhead colour TV. It was a place where you could hide out and Alex had a part share in the club. Afternoon would slip into evening and he would invariably find himself in a small party driving to a restaurant in Chelsea or South Kensington for a meal and some wine and then back to Observatory Gardens for some opium or advocaat or cocaine or simply a smoke of hashish. In this way, he had avoided the issue for another day. In a small way, I tried to persuade him to take up various literary projects, wrote a biographical essay on him which he corrected and suggested a collection of short stories might easily be possible to collate. I also passed on, with his permission, several stories for publication and tried to interest BBC Scotland in a biographical programme – to no avail. I remember that he invited me (and my friend Neil Davidson) to join him and Sally at the launch of a play 'Mayler' at a small church-cum-theatre in South London. The play had been written by someone who had just been released from a significant stretch in prison. It was a grim drama, full of violence and many apparently criminal associates turned up for the launch. Neil and I were amused with Trocchi's sartorial choice for his attendance at the event - garbed in almost floor-length black overcoat and two-tone shoes. We never asked him if he was in disguise as a mafia don but the adulation he received at the launch was unexpected.

Sally, taken by Nicolas Trocchi, 1982.
(Courtesy of Sally Child)

He had several recurrences of his back problem and was in traction for some weeks. Meanwhile, Sally completed her course at the London School of fashion and began to run a stall in Covent Garden market, designing, and selling, her own dresses. Alex was proud, and wrote to Jack, now in Limassol:

'as you can see, I am able to write once again, and had been hoping in the not too distant future to be coming down to Limassol to discuss our Mediterranean future together ... I seem to have transcended my writing block, *und Gott* be thankit! The book business goes on pretty successfully, but of course, apart from the bread and butter aspect, it is no longer my principal concern ...'

Then Alex went to his doctor one day and discovered that he had a malignant tumour in the lower lobe of his left lung. There was a 90% chance of a successful operation, the Doctor told him. He went into hospital, and a portion of his left lung was successfully removed. He recovered slowly and was more or less confined to his home for a long period of recuperation while his broken ribs healed. But soon after, a bad cold developed into lobal pneumonia and within two days, on 15th April 1984, he was dead. I got a phone call from George Rodney – I hadn't seen Alex for about six months – telling me of his death. It was a shock. He was only 59. None of us had expected him to die so soon.

Alex Trocchi's funeral, held on Wednesday 25th April at Mortlake Crematorium was sparsely attended; twenty persons, or less, mostly relations including Jack who had flown over from Singapore. Christopher Logue read Marvell's 'Definition of Love' and a personal tribute. It was a non-religious ceremony - no-one else said anything - and at its undefined conclusion (or disintegration), Miles Davis' jaunty, irreverent theme from *Sketches of Spain* blared from hidden speakers as Trocchi's coffin slid towards the flames. Twenty years on, the author was following his book into the purgatorial flames. Outside the sun shone down on the glorious greenery as the small group dispersed. I walked back to central London in my shirt sleeves, declining, for some reason, a lift with

George, Sally and the others who were going on to John Calder's for a wake. As Christopher Logue recalled, 'it was dismal... too downbeat. Somehow I wanted something more...'

A few months later, Sally collected the ashes from the undertaker and placed them on the mantlepiece alongside the jars containing the ashes of Lyn, Marcus, and the Burmese and Siamese cats; a collection of five containers in a row. One day, Sally and Nick noticed that Alex' jar was not there ... They never did discover what happened to it. Alex Trocchi's final resting place is unknown. There was a mysterious fire in the flat, for which no cause was ever found and many of Alex's belongings and papers were destroyed in the blaze. Those papers that survive have blackened edges.

And the story has one terrible final twist. Barely six months later, just after his eighteenth birthday, Nicolas went missing on the day when he and Sally moved back to Observatory Gardens to live in the flat directly beneath their own, which was too badly fire-damaged to live in. It was later established that he had gone back up to the soot-blackened penthouse and jumped off the roof, a truly appalling tragedy.

But there are survivors and hundreds of friends and colleagues throughout the world who remember Trocchi with affection, wry amusement, sheer indignation or outright anger. He lives on, in a literary sense at least transcending death. Perhaps his story is a potent warning. A monster? The title is ironic, but he could be construed variously as a genial, selfish, neurotic, generous, pretentious, benevolent, manipulative and fantastic creature of myth, composed of incongruous and contradictory elements; a surprisingly cautious leader of extreme cultural revolutionaries, a strong man with a terminal weakness, an outrageous literary hoaxer who was a writer of great skill and perception; a shy outspoken genius in the motley of a hustler.

Alex with his cousin Sylvia at Louise's wedding reception.
(Courtesy: Jack Robertson)

Chronology

1925 Alexander Whitelaw Robertson Trocchi born in Glasgow, 30 July. Family moved from 29 Smith Street to 15 Abbotsford Place, then 26 Bank Street.

1930 Alexander attends Hillhead Primary School in Cecil Street. His brothers Alfred, and Jack and his cousin Victor are already there.

1937 Hillhead High School, Oakfield Avenue. Alex plays rugby, tennis and cricket.

1939 Evacuated on 1 September, to Cally House School at Gatehouse of Fleet. Meets Betty Nan Whyte, his future wife.

1940 Death of his mother, Annie Robertson, 4 January, funeral in Glasgow.

1942 Leaves Cally in disgrace on final day after dormitories incident. Attends Glasgow University. Jack is missing presumed drowned.

1943 Aged 18, registers for service with Fleet Air Arm on 5 February, pilot training in Canada. Discharged for toilet roll incident and transfers to navy, service on HMS Campbeltown on Arctic Convoys to Murmansk, promoted to Acting Leading Seaman. Jack is POW in Osaka.

1946 Released on 16 November in Class A, declines Commission and attends Glasgow University to study for MA in English & Philosophy.

1947 Against advice, marries Betty Whyte at Blythswood Registry Office on 15 January and they move to cottage at Balfron to be pig breeders.

1948 A daughter Jacqueline Anne born, 15 January.

1950 Graduates MA with Second Class Honours after falling asleep in finals. Awarded the Kemsley Travelling Scholarship and travels with Betty and Jacqueline in Italy, Greece, Turkey and Yugoslavia before establishing himself in Paris where his first long work, the poem 'How At Thebes Tiresias The Prophet Told' is accepted by Princess Caetani, editor of *Botteghe Oscura* in Rome.

1951 Second daughter Margot Francoise born, 30 May.

1952 Living in hotel in Rue De La Huchette and working on early issues of *Merlin*. Moves to Jane Lougee's apartment in Auteil and rewrites earlier ms of *Young Adam* novel. Separates from Betty.

1953 The first of the Olympic Press novels, *Helen and Desire* is completed, in eight days and published under nom-de-plume of 'Frances Lengel'. Collections Merlin publishes Beckett's first novel in English, *Watt*.

1954 *Young Adam* novel appears as 'Lengel' novel by Olympia Press, followed by *The Carnal Days of Helen Seferis*. Living in Montparnasse, decree of divorce 3 June. Jane Lougee returns to America, 10 August.

1955 Olympia publish *School For Sin* and a spoof Vol 5 of the Frank Harris biography *My Life & Loves*, also *White Thighs* but Trocchi, increasingly addicted to heroin, leaves Paris and briefly returns to London.

1956 Enters US on 10 December and acquires job on river barges. Working slowly on *Cain's Book*. Travels widely in US and Mexico. Betty emigrates to New Zealand in February, taking his daughters with her. Meets Marilyn Rose Hicks.

1957 13 August 1957, marries Lyn Hicks in Tijuana, mainly residing in Brooks Avenue, Venice West, Los Angeles (where lodger Allen Ginsberg is writing *Kaddish*).

1958 Travel to Las Vegas in April for two months. 3 October, son, Marcus Alexander, born in New York.

1959 *Cain's Book* is completed and enters publication process, March. On 22 July, in Wellington, New Zealand, Betty raises action for desertion which is served on him at 159 Newark Street, Hoboken.

1960 Raises furore on NBC news broadcast when he injects himself in front of cameras. A prescription in his name is found in possession of a 16-year-old girl. He is arrested but bailed with the assistance of George Plimpton. Followed by police, he is observed injecting himself on a station platform. Lyn is arrested but Trocchi escapes on train and hides out in Greenwich Village.

1961 April, facing charges of supplying drugs to a minor, he is bailed and smuggled over the Canadian border with a false passport, assisted by Leonard Cohen in Montreal. Escapes to Aberdeen. In New York, *Cain's Book* is published by Grove and an edition of *Sappho of Lesbos* by Castle Books.

1961 Living in Heath Street, Hampstead. *Young Adam* appears in new version, published by Heineman. *Cain's Book* re-appears in Black Cat edition from Grove and Castle Books publish *The Outsider* which he edited (with Richard Seaver and Terry Southern). 5 June, is arrested and appears at Bow Street Magistrates Court charged with possession of heroin, receives £25 fine.

1962 Is leading participant at Edinburgh Festival Writers' day, clashes with Hugh MacDiarmid. French edition of *Cain's Book* is nominated as Book of the Month by *L'Express*, Paris. Lyn and Marcus arrive in England.

1963 *Cain's Book* published in UK by Calder, 27 February. Copies seized in raid on bookshop in Sheffield. Publisher and author are charged under 1959 Obscene Publications Act. *Young Adam* goes into second UK edition from Pan Books. *Writers In Revolt* (which Trocchi co-edited with Terry Southern) published by Frederick Fell, New York. Trocchi edits *The Moving Times* and sets up the sigma project. Appears frequently on TV and radio and is appointed visiting lecturer at St Martin's Schoolof Art.

1964 15 April, Sheffield Magistrates Court declares *Cain's Book* is declared obscene and corrupting. Stocks are to be burnt at Sheffield Municipal Incinerator. Edinburgh Festival – ritual burning of the book in Grassmarket as protest. 'Invisible Insurrection of a Million Minds and Sigma: A Tactical Blueprint' is published in City Lights Journal number 2. Trocchi family moves to 6 St Stephens' Gardens, W2.

1965 Publication of four stories in *New Writers 3* by Calder, the translation of *I, Jan Cremer*. 11 June, chairs the Royal Albert Hall 'happening' attended by 7,000, which is filmed as 'Wholly Communion' by Peter Whitehead. Attends his brother Alf's funeral in Isle of Man.

1966 Publication of translation of *Girl on the Motorcycle* by Calder. *Young Adam* – NEL reprint. Reads at Empire Festival, Cardiff. Working with RD Laing and Burroughs on book on drugs and the creative impulse. Calder announces new Trocchi novel, *The Long Book* (never completed). Nicolas Adam Trocchi born, 28 December.

1967 Brandon House of California reprint five of the erotic Paris novels, some with postscripts supplied by Trocchi – dispute over fees and royalties. New editions of *Girl on the Motorcycle* by Four Square and by NEL.

1968 *I, Jan Cremer* new Panther edition, and three reprintings of *Girl on the Motorcycle* by NEL as tie-in to film starring Marianne Faithfull.

1969 *Thongs* reprinted by Olympia Press, Paris. *I, Jan Cremer* Panther new edition. 1 October, in West London Petty Court to dispute rates debt.

1970 Awarded £500 Arts Council grant; widely attacked in tabloid papers. The Centenarian published by Calder, two new editions of *I, Jan Cremer* and Olympia Press publish new edition of *Thongs*.

1971 UK edition of *Sappho of Lesbos* by Universal-Tandem

1972 *Man At Leisure* poetry collection published by Calder, plans for Apple films production of *Cain's Book* shelved. June, copies of *Thongs* seized in Stratford, attends Magistrates Court, Stratford, 13 October but book remains banned in Stratford. 9 November, Lyn dies of liver failure and chronic hepatitis.

1973 *Cain's Book*, Quartet edition. *Man At Leisure* selected by Sunday Times as one of the dozen best poetry books of year. Trocchi leads world-wide campaign to release Michael X from Trinidadian jail.

1974 Calder publishes Trocchi's translation of *La Gana*

1977 Marcus dies of throat cancer, 21 May. Robert Creeley's wife recommends Sally Child as au-pair for Nicolas.

1979 Attends Cally House re-union. Grove Outrider edition of *Cain's Book*. Re-union with Jane Lougee over several days holiday in Majorca.

1981 Brief re-union meeting with first wife Betty in London. Attends Kit Lambert's memorial service in Covent Garden, 11 May.

1983 *Young Adam* reprinted by Calder.

1984 15 April, dies of lobar pneumonia, funeral at Mortlake Crematorium, 25 April, Nicolas commits suicide by jumping from the roof of the apartment at Observatory Gardens.

Terry Southern with Andrew Murray Scott, at East Canaan, Conn., June 1989
(Courtesy Gail Gerber)

William S. Burroughs with Andrew Murray Scott, at Lawrence, Kansas,
July 1989.
(Courtesy: Jon Blumb)

Further Reading

Campbell, Allan, and Tim Niel, (editors) *A Life In Pieces: Reflections on Alexander Trocchi*, Rebel Inc/Canongate, 1997

Campbell, James, *Paris Interzone*, Secker & Warburg, 1994

Campbell, James, 'Alexander Trocchi', London Magazine, April-May, 1992.

De St Jorre, John, *The Good Ship Venus: The Erotic Voyages of the Olympia Press*, Pimlico (1994) 1995

Kravitz, Peter, (editor) *Edinburgh Review*, 70, 1985, contains essays and reminiscences by Christopher Logue, Edwin Morgan, John Calder and Tom McGrath.

Nuttall, Jeff, *Bomb Culture*, MacGibbon and Kee, (1968) 1970.

Scott, Andrew Murray, (editor) *Invisible Insurrection of a Million Minds: A Trocchi Reader*, Polygon, (1991), 1995.

Scott, Andrew Murray, 'Mr MacDiarmid and Mr Trocchi: Where Extremists Meet', *Chapman* magazine, Edinburgh, 83, 1996.

Scott, Andrew Murray, 'Portrait of Cain', *Cencrastus* magazine, Edinburgh, 11, 1983

Scott, Andrew Murray, 'Snapshots of Trocchi', *Cencrastus* magazine, 38, 1991

Southern, Nile, and Josh Alan Friedman (editors), *Now Dig This: The Unspeakable Writings of Terry Southern 1950-1995*, Methuen, 2002.

*Professor Edwin Morgan, Sally Child and Tom McGrath at the launch
of the first edition of The Making of the Monster, John Smith University
Bookshop Glasgow University, 1990
(Courtesy: Marion Sinclair)*

Trocchi Bibliography

Novels:

Helen and Desire, Olympia Press, Paris, 1953, under pseudonym of 'Frances Lengel'. Reprinted variously, and in French, Italian, Spanish, German, Dutch, Japanese, once as *Desire and Helen*, and by Castle Books, New York, 1959, as *Angela* under pseudonym of 'Jean Blanche'. Printed under Trocchi's own name by Brandon House, California, 1967, Olympia Press, London, 1971 and Tandem Books, London, 1972. Also a Collectors' Limited Edition by Olympia, date unknown. Rebel Inc / Canongate Books, Edinburgh, 1997.

The Carnal Days of Helen Seferis, Olympia Press, Paris, 1954, under pseud. of 'Frances Lengel'. Reprinted variously, and in Dutch, German and Italian, also in unauthorised edition as *The Return Of Angela* by Castle Books, New York, 1959, under pseud. of 'Jean Blanche'. Reprinted under Trocchi's own name by Brandon House, California, 1967.

Young Adam, Olympia Press, Paris, 1954, under pseud. of 'Frances Lengel'. Reprinted with 4 stories as *The Outsider*, Castle Books, New York, 1960. First UK edition by Heinemann, London, 1961. Reprinted by Pan Books, London, 1963, New English Library, London, 1966, John Calder, London and New York, 1983. Also appeared in numerous unauthorised editions, by Keimeisha of Japan, in 1955 and once retitled as *Seeds of Desire* from Castle Books, New York, 1959. Reprinted 1994 by Calder Publications and 1996 by Canongate, Edinburgh.

School For Sin, Olympia Press, Paris, 1954, under pseud. of 'Frances Lengel'. German, Dutch, Italian, French editions, Japanese edition by Keimeisha, 1955. Reprinted under Trocchi's own name as *School For Wives* by Brandon House, California, 1967.

Frank Harris - My Life and Loves: Volume 5; An Irreverent Treatment, Olympia Press, Paris, 1954. Reprinted variously, and in Dutch, German, Italian, French editions. Reprinted as *What Frank Harris Did Not Say* by

Olympia Press,(Travellers Companion Series) New York, 1966 under Trocchi's own name, by New English Library, London, 1966, and by Brandon House, California, 1967. Also a Collector's Limited Edition by Olympia, date unknown.

Thongs, Olympia Press, Paris, 1955, under pseud. of 'Carmencita de las Lunas'. Editions in German, Danish, French, Italian. Reprinted by Brandon House, California, 1967 under Trocchi's own name, and by Olympia Press, London, 1971. Blast Books, New York, 1994.

White Thighs, Olympia Press, Paris, 1955, under pseud. of 'Frances Lengel', and by Keimeisha, Tokyo, 1955. Reprinted under Trocchi's own name by Brandon House, California, 1967. Blast Books, New York, 1994.

Sappho Of Lesbos, Castle Books, New York, 1960. First UK edition by Tandem Books, London, 1971. Reprinted by Star Books, London, 1986.

Angela, (see *Helen and Desire*); Castle Books, New York, 1959 under pseud. of 'Jean Blanche'. This was a different version of the other *Angela*, completely rewritten by Trocchi himself.

Cain's Book, Grove Press, New York, 1960 (two editions). First UK edition by John Calder, London, 1963. Editions in Germany, France, Netherlands, Argentina, Spain, Italy, Denmark, often from several different publishers Reprinted by Quartet Books, London, 1973. Third US edition by Grove Press, 1979. Third UK edition by Calder, London, 1983. Grove Weidenfeld, New York, 1992.

Translations:

Eleven Thousand Virgins; Memoirs of a debauched Hospodar by Guillaume Apollinaire, (from French) Olympia Press, Paris, 1953 under pseud. of 'Oscar Mole'. May have been reprinted under title of *The 11th Hour of Whips*. (No copy seen).

I, Jan Cremer (with RE Wyngaard, from Dutch), Calder & Boyars, London, 1965. Reprinted by Panther Books, London, 1968, 1969, 1970 (twice).

The Girl On The Motorcycle by Andre Pieyre de Mandiargues,(from French) John Calder, London, 1966. Reprinted by Four Square, London, October 1967, and New English Library, London, November 1967, 1968 (three times).

The Bloody Countess by Valentine Penrose,(from French) Calder & Boyars, London, 1970, reprinted shortly afterwards, to tie-in with the film as *Countess Dracula.*

The Centenarian by Rene de Obaldia, (from French), Calder & Boyars, London, 1970.

1789 The French Revolution Year One, by Sophie Lemasson and Jean-Claude Penchenat, (from French), *Gambit* vol 5, no 20, Calder & Boyars, London, 1971.

La Gana by Jean Douassot, (from French), Calder & Boyars, London, 1974.

Poetry:

Man At Leisure, Calder & Boyars, London, 1972, hardback and paperback editions.

Editorial:

Writers' Revolt (with Terry Southern and Richard Seaver), New American Library, New York, 1960.

Collected Merlin Magazine (1952-5) reprinted in hardcover volume by Kraus Reprint, Nendeln, Liechtenstein, 1970.

The Sigma Portfolio (duplicated) items 1 - 39, London, 1964-67.

My Own Business, London, 1970, poster-broadsheet

Short Stories:

New Writers' 3, Calder & Boyars, London, 1965 contains 'A Being Of Distances', 'The Holy Man', 'Peter Pierce' and 'A Meeting', which had appeared in 'The Outsider' (see 'Young Adam')

Contributions to Periodicals:

Scots Review, Edinburgh, Nov 1950 - April 1951, monthly articles under the byeline; 'Paris Letter'.

Botteghe Oscura, Rome, 1951, long poem 'How At Thebes Tiresias The Prophet Told'. 1952, 'A Being Of Distances' short story.

Nimbus, London, 1952, poetry

Tomorrow, London, 1953, short story reprinted

Points, Paris, 1953, the short story 'Peter Pierce'.

Paris Review, New York, 1958, a section of *Cain's Book* titled 'The Citadel'.

Evergreen Review, New York, 1958, 'A Note On George Orwell'. 1963,
    reprinted both *The* 'Invisible Insurrection Of A Million Minds and
    'Sigma: A Tactical Blueprint' essays.

New Saltire Review, Edinburgh, 1962, 'The Invisible Insurrection Of A Million
    Minds' essay.

International Situationist Review, Paris, 1962 (and various other editions, and
    of the I.S. anthology) co-authorship of editorial. Reprint of 'Invisible
    Insurrection' essay.

Anarchy, London, 1962, reprinted 'Invisible Insurrection' essay

Scotsman, Edinburgh, 1963, 'Don't Ask Your Grannie' essay.

Los Angeles Free Press, LA, 1963, reprinted 'Invisible Insurrection' essay

New Society, London, May 1965, 'Lady Chatterley's Charade' (review); 'Drugs
    Of Mind', 1970.

Ink, London, 26 June 1970, 'The Junkie: Menace or Scapegoat':

International Times, London, June 1969, 'Watch That Gnome', essay.

The Olympia Reader, New York, 1966, extract from *Frank Harris Memoirs Vol 5*

Sections of *Cain's Book* appeared in numerous American periodicals at various
    times, *including Oyster, The Book Of Grass, The Addict* anthology, *Out Of
    Our Minds* (Penguin), *Man's Magazine Drugs From A-Z*

Screen Credits:

Man With A Hat Director; Wadhawan, London, 1973. 40 mins, Producer,
    David Scheuer

Marihuana, Marihuana Director; Wadhawan, London, 1973. 40 mins, Producer, David Scheuer.

Cain's Film Director; Wadhawan, London 1968.

Young Adam Director; David Mackenzie, London, 2003

All queries regarding The Alexander Trocchi Estate and reprinting requests should be addressed to: Sally Child, 13 Hornsey Lane Gardens, London, N6 5NX.

Index

C

Caetani, Princess Marguerite Chapin 28, 29, 224
Cafe Bonaparte 37, 55, 99
Cain's Book v, vi, xi, xvi, 3, 69, 86, 90- 92, 94, 100, 113, 118, 120, 127-129, 132-134, 137, 138, 145-148, 159, 161-163, 165-167, 175, 199, 201, 207, 208, 210, 224-226, 232, 234
Cain's Film 208, 235
Calder, John vi, vii, viii, ix, 141, 146, 147, 162, 164, 165, 174, 175, 195, 200, 210, 221, 225, 226, 229, 231, 232
Calder & Boyars 73, 163, 195, 198, 200, 232, 233
Cally House xiii, 9, 10, 11, 223, 226
Cameron, Ian viii, 12
Camus, Albert 36, 73, 74, 128
Candy 54, 55, 191
Canet-Plage 47
Canetti , Elias 92
Cap D'Ail 199
Capote, Truman 140
Carmencita de las Lunas 76, 84, 85, 232
Carnal Days of Helen Seferis 76, 80, 115, 206, 224, 231
Caro, Anthony 173
Cassady, Neal xvi, 105, 106
Castle Books 113, 115, 116, 198, 225, 231, 232
Centre 42 Project 170, 172
Chaplin, Sidney 64
Chatham 15, 16
Chester, Alfred 42, 44
Child, Sally ii, vi-viii, 215-221, 226, 230, 235
Clapton, Eric v, 195, 208, 212, 218
Clatworthy, Robert 173
Cohen, Leonard xvi, 124, 125, 184, 190, 191, 195, 225

Collection Merlin 49, 52, 55, 64, 73, 75
Collins, Sir Godfrey 33, 35
Commonwealth Arts Festival 179
Corneille 53, 65
Corso, Gregory 105, 172, 177, 179
Cortends, Ray 92
Countess Dracula 174, 200, 233
Creeley, Robert viii, xvi, 49, 62, 63, 134, 152, 169, 172, 173, 187, 203, 211, 215, 226
Creevey, Elizabeth (see Whyte, Elizabeth Nan)
Cumming, Don viii, 126

D

Daiches, Dr David 141-143
Daily Mail 196
Dali, Salvador 169
Davidson, Neil 218
De Freitas, Abdul (Malik) see Michael X
de Obaldia, Rene 200, 233
De Sade, Donatien Alphonse 43, 49, 82, 150
De Wet, Louis 47
Dead Fingers' Talk 162
Debord, Guy 89, 99, 137, 138, 168
Delon, Alain 200
Deutsch, Andre 109, 132
Deya 63, 216
Diamond, Louis 183, 196
Donleavy J.P. 55, 75
Dorn, Ed viii, 185, 196
Douassot, Jean 113, 201, 233
Douglas-Mann, Bruce, MP 163-165, 211
Dow, Mary Mackenzie 1
Down, Lesley-Anne 200
Durrell, Laurence 86, 144

Riddell, Alan 38, 41, 42, 141
Rillie, Jack viii, 19
Robbe-Grillet, Alain 140
Robertson, Alf 3, 6, 12, 13, 22, 27, 29, 35, 88, 127, 146, 151, 176, 223, 225
Robertson, Annie (see Trocchi, Annie)
Robertson, Jack viii, ix, 3, 6, 17, 27, 35, 92, 101, 146, 151, 176, 183, 220, 223
Rodney, Hon George v, 220
Rosenthal, Irving 106, 107
Ross, Peter 11, 31
Rossett, Barney 120
rue Campagne Premiere 69, 71, 90
rue de la Huchette 43, 46, 60
rue du Sabot 50, 51
Russell, Bertrand 31, 74, 140, 172, 195

S

Sabre, Mel 96, 99, 100
Samuel, Nigel ix, 51, 52, 73, 77, 109, 118, 128, 184, 195
Sansom, William 48
Sappho of Lesbos 114, 115, 198, 202, 225, 226, 232
Sartre, Jean Paul 31, 36, 48, 58, 64, 73
School For Wives 66, 71, 86, 202, 203, 231
Schwartz, Dr Jake 175
Scott, Paul Henderson iii, iv, v, vii, xiv, 227, 228, 229
Scott-Miller, Melissa v
Seaver, Richard W viii, 43, 51, 53, 74, 121, 146, 150
Seed of Desire 115
Seidelman, Arthur O 207
Shaw, Irwin 55
Sheeper 106
Sheffield Magistrates' Court 162, 210
Shinkichi, Tajiri 62
sigma project 152, 153, 168, 169, 170,

172, 173, 174, 179, 180, 181, 183, 184, 185, 186, 187, 192, 195, 225
Silkin, Jon 160
Sillitoe, Alan 46, 191
Silver, Robert 71, 107, 173
Simenon, George 128
Sinclair, Charlie xiv, 92, 99, 230
Smith, Delavan 138, 154
Smith, Frank viii
Smith, Martin Seymour viii, 63, 160
Smith, Mary 53, 66
Smith, Patti xvii
Smith, Roy viii, 11, 14
Smith, Sir Matthew 92
Smith, Stevie 180
Smith, Sydney Goodsir 143, 155
Smith, W. Gordon 150
Snyder, Gary 105
Social Credit 193
Southend 17
Southern, Terry viii, xiv, xvi, 43, 44, 52, 54, 56, 60, 92, 99, 100, 108, 109, 116, 225, 227, 229, 233
Soyinka, Wole 180
Spark, Muriel 140
Speigel, Sam 147
Spender, Stephen 74, 140, 180
St Martin's College of Art 7
Steele, Max 64
Sterne, Jacques 208
Stevenson, John 44, 204, 206
Strachan, Cecil xiii, 6, 20, 22, 23, 131
Straubing, Harold 206
Stravinsky, Igor 55
Strick, Joseph 173
Sully, Russell 31
Sunday Times 183, 195, 201, 226
Sutherland, Donald 208
Svevo, Italo 49

Lightning Source UK Ltd.
Milton Keynes UK
UKOW02f0844010816

279668UK00001B/25/P